LC

The Theater Dictionary

BY THE SAME AUTHOR

A Dictionary of Forces' Slang: 1939–1945
(WITH ERIC PARTRIDGE & FRANK ROBERTS.)

Sea Slang of the Twentieth Century

Glossary to Wavy Navy

THE THEATER DICTIONARY

*British and American Terms in the
Drama, Opera, and Ballet*

BY

WILFRED GRANVILLE

PHILOSOPHICAL LIBRARY

New York

Upsala College
Library
East Orange, N. J.

COPYRIGHT, 1952, BY
THE PHILOSOPHICAL LIBRARY, INC.
15 EAST 40TH STREET, NEW YORK 16, N. Y.

PRINTED IN THE UNITED STATES OF AMERICA

For
Eric Partridge
Scholar, Humanist, and Good Friend

FOREWORD

"I presume thou wilt be very inquisitive to know what antick or personate actor this is, that so insolently intrudes upon this common theatre . . . whence he is, why he doth it and what he hath to say. . . ." Thus Robert Burton in *Democritus to the Reader*, the introduction to his wise, entertaining and wholly delightful *magnum opus*, THE ANATOMY OF MELANCHOLY. So might the reader of this record of theater speech ask by what authority the writer has compiled his glossary.

The answer is that he felt, during several years of active engagement in the theater—as actor, producer, stage director, and, occasionally—acting manager—that such a book, hitherto unattempted, was urgently needed, and that a record of the technical, colloquial and slang speech of the twentieth century stage should be made before many terms and phrases used by "old Pros" died with their passing. So the "dressing-room jottings," remembered conversations—whether at the *Ivy*, theatrical gatherings, or on "train-calls" during provincial tours, and much reading, mainly *ad hoc*, have resulted in the following pages in which, I hope, a not inadequate account has been rendered of the language of the theater.

That there will be other glossaries, I have no doubt, and I am conscious of omissions of terms that may have been coined since the commencement of this work. In so vast a field complete comprehensiveness is not possible, and I ask indulgence if a searcher's pet terms and phrases are not found. But, in order that such terms (provided they are not merely *nonce* words) may not be lost to the language, I would be grateful for notes, or lists, of words or phrases worthy of preservation and of value to the glossary. Cockney rhyming slang, though extensively used in vaudeville theaters is not strictly eligible since it has been adopted from Cockneydom and is not endemic to the theater. I have, however, included a limited number of the common rhyming terms, as I have also included a number of *Parlyaree* phrases or words (e.g. *scarper*,

FOREWORD

letty, dinarly, etc.), although the use of this odd speech is far less common than in the Victorian era. Most of these words and phrases (see **Parlyaree** in the glossary) come from the circus or fairgrounds, booth theaters, or *fit ups.*

I have thought fit to record a few "critics" words and a number of technical terms used in the science of elocution and phonetics, since these terms may be met in theater literature, or reviews in the journals and newspapers.

An apprenticeship with a famous Shakespearean Company; membership of the last company to tour the "celebrated Compton Comedy Company"; engagements in provincial touring companies; in resident repertory, in opera and in the West End of London provided inside knowledge of the theater without which this dictionary could not have been compiled. And I am indebted to the following for most valuable and unselfish assistance in my work: the dedicatee, Eric Partridge, for allowing me to graze in the theatrical pastures of his *Dictionary of Slang* (3rd ed. 1949), and *Name into Word* (1949); Sir St. Vincent Troubridge, Bart., who gave me access to his scholarly notes on theater speech, and permitted me to consult the relevant passages in his valuable contributions to the periodical NOTES & QUERIES, entitled *Notes on the Oxford English Dictionary;* Christopher Fry for helpful communications; Cyril Chamberlain, London stage and film artist, and friend of my theater days, for a useful and pellucidly annotated list of stage managerial and other terms. I am particularly grateful to the directors of the Strand Electric and Engineering Company Ltd., who generously allowed me to quote material from their excellent little glossary of *Technical Theatrical Terms* edited by A. O. Gibbons, with collaborators.

To my American publishers, The Philosophical Library Inc., New York, I am indebted for matter contained in their *Encyclopaedia of the Arts,* edited by Doctor Dagobert D. Runes & Harry G. Schrickel (New York, 1945), and to Dr. Joseph T. Shipley, who kindly gave me *carte blanche* to use terms in his scholarly work *A Dictionary of Word Origins,* also published by the Philosophical Library.

Of the theater friends who have helped me in various ways I would particularise Miss Marjorie Ames who, in addition to making sound suggestions, supplied a list of musical comedy terms, and Miss Elizabeth Keen who lent me material, and whose amusing conversation brought several half-forgotten terms to mind.

In treating of etymologies my debts to Skeat, Wyld, Weekly, and the *Oxford English Dictionary* are obvious. Words derived from the Greek have been transliterated for the convenience of the reader.

If I have seemed to "spread myself" over biographical notes it is because the people named have done valuable service to the theater and are deserving of more than casual mention. And, if objection is made that I have given hospitality to seemingly undeserving terms and phrases my excuse is that such terms, however fatuous or ephemeral they may appear at first glance, have gained currency in the theater and are, therefore, eligible for inclusion in the glossary. My choice in this matter is probably arbitrary but I ask the indulgence of my critics.

Full acknowledgment has been given in the text to authors whose works I have consulted. My apology is given to any I may have omitted.

A special word of thanks is due Craig Timberlake, who has been kind enough to review this work for its prospective American public. His amplification of terms essentially American and his frequent comments on theatrical usage in the United States will delight the general reader and prove of value to students and craftsmen alike.

WILFRED GRANVILLE

The Theater Dictionary

A

Abbey, the. The Abbey Theatre, Dublin, the first Irish national theater which was founded by the late Miss A. C. F. Horniman in 1904. Under the vigorous direction of the poet W. B. Yeats (born 1865, Senator of the Irish Free State from 1922 to 1928, and a Nobel Prize winner) and Lady Gregory, the Abbey Theatre became the focal point of the Irish literary movement. The early works of J. M. Synge, Lord Dunsany and others were first produced here. The theater was destroyed by fire in 1951.

above and below. (stage furniture) The direction "cross above settee" is used in preference to cross *behind* settee, likewise an actor crosses below rather than *in front* of furniture. This usage was determined by the UP and DOWN STAGE direction.

acoustics. The properties of hearing in a theater. The phenomena of sound. Special materials which deaden the transmission of noise are used in the building of modern theaters, especially Opera Houses. The word derives from the Greek *akouein,* to hear.

act. To portray a character in a play or perform upon the stage as singer or variety artist. 2. A vaudeville "turn." 3. One of the periods into which the action of a play is divided.

act-change. See CHANGE AN ACT.

act-wait. The interval (American *intermission*) between the acts of a play. The ENTR'ACTE.

act well. (Of a play) Easy to produce or perform. Having all the attributes of dramatic art; good lines and plenty of scope for histrionics. "What's the new play like?" "It ought to run, it *acts well* in rehearsal, but you never can tell how these turn out on production." Often a play has shown promise at rehearsals and fallen flat "on the night." In U. S., *plays well.*

actable. (Of parts) Offering opportunities for the exercise of dramatic art, as distinct from the "CUP AND SAUCER" role in which a player sits on the stage uttering epigrams.

acting area. That section of the stage set for the performance. The area round the furniture and within the LIGHTING AREA.

acting area lantern. A circular floodlight suspended on a batten immediately above the ACTING AREA.

acting lady. (Brit.) An inferior actress; one who hopes that her appearance and dignity will compensate for her lack of histrionic ability. The term, now obsolete, dates from the time of Mrs. Langtry's social-cum-theatrical success in 1882 which set up a spirit of emulation among society women who tried their luck on the stage, often with lamentable results. The term connoted incompetence and was even used by dramatic critics and journalists. J. Redding Ware, in *Passing English of the Victorian Era,* quotes from *Entr'acte,* 1883: "Acting ladies, in my opinion, should be severely left alone. There is no pleasing them or their friends." (Lily Langtry—1852–1929—was known as "The Jersey Lily" and appeared under her own management in London and New York where she was very successful and popular.)

acting manager. The business manager "in front of the house" who *acts* in the interests of the theater management, and has complete control of everything on the auditorium side of the curtain, as well as being responsible for the well being of the company acting in the theater. He pays the artists and staff, supervises the affairs of the "box office," acts as host to the guests and patrons of the house. If with a touring company he works in liaison with the resident manager of the visited theater. He also makes the travelling arrangements from town to town, and organises the advance publicity, and program matter. He is known colloquially as the FRONT-OF-HOUSE-MANAGER. In U. S., The *company manager.*

acting play. One providing plenty of scope for dramatics. The reverse of a LITERARY PLAY, which depends upon the effective delivery of lines for its success.

acting time. See RUNNING TIME.

action of a play. The speeches, movements, and stage business. Cf. THE BUSINESS OF THE STAGE.

actor. A performer on the stage. The term has its origin in the Latin verb, *agere,* to do, act, and is strictly applicable to players on the LEGITIMATE STAGE rather than to those in music halls (Brit.) who are usually called artists.

actor laddy. (Brit.) An actor of the Victorian school of melodrama. He used to wear flamboyant clothes and address his fellows as "laddy."

actor manager. A leading player who rents a theater and runs his own company. Also one who tours a repertoire of plays under his own management, playing the leading roles himself.

actor proof. A part so written, and with such brilliant lines, or business, that any player would succeed in its portrayal.

actor's bible. See early 5 STAGE.

actor's church. The church of St. Paul, Covent Garden, London. The present vicar is a former actor. In New York City, Actors' Temple, St. Malachy's Church and Church of the Transfiguration (Little Church Around The Corner).

A.C.U. (Brit.) The Actor's Church Union.

actors died with Irving! (Brit.) A catchphrase directed against a "cocky" beginner by an old actor. Now obsolescent, if not obsolete. (Sir Henry Irving—1838–1905, was the first actor to be knighted and so freed the profession from the "rogues and vagabonds" stigma.)

actor's preparation. The studying of his part in relation to the play as a whole. His plan of portrayal and general "feel" of the character.

actress. A "female actor." In Shakespeare's day there were no women players, all female parts being acted by young men or boys, and it was not until the Restoration period that women began to appear in the theater, though there is a record of the Italian Isabella Andreini (1562–1604) as professional actress, and on the French stage women had made their appearance. In England, however, it was in 1660 that the first actress made her debut in the part of Desdemona in Othello.

actresses will happen in the best regulated families! (Brit.) The philosophical catch-phrase used when a scion of the nobility falls in love with an actress. A parody on *accidents will happen in the best regulated families!* The phrase was coined at the time when Gaiety girls were marrying into the peerage.

adagio. Slow movements in stage dancing. The *grand adagio* is "the emotional climax of the traditional classic repertory in a ballet performed by soloists as a stylised love-duet, ornamented by brilliant turns, held poses, lifts, and foot work, in which the cavalier effaces himself to display the grace and technique of his lady." (Lincoln Kirstein, General Director, New York City Ballet.)

adaptation. A play that has been taken from a novel or one that has been adapted to suit a different audience from that to which it has played during its metropolitan run. 2. A foreign play translated and adapted for English consumption.

additive lighting. The primary colours of light are the monochromatic red, green, and blue. By suitable mixing of these hues any colour can be produced on the stage. Thus: red plus green plus blue will produce *white* light, red plus green produces *yellow*, blue and green = *peacock-blue*, red plus ½-green = *orange*, blue plus ½-red = *cerise*, and so on. There is an excellent chapter on colour mixing in *The Technique of Stage Lighting* by R. Gillespie Williams. (Pitman, London.)

Adelphi drama. (Brit.) Plays acted in the tradition associated with the old Adelphi Theatre, London. This house was noted for the "meatyness" of its fare, and the amplitude of the actors' performances. Hence any acting technique savouring of melodrama is dubbed "Adelphi," though the term is seldom heard to-day. The Adelphi's motto was "good plays and fine acting" and the audiences certainly had their money's worth. Among the many dramas that toured the provinces for years were: *The Colleen Bawn, The Octoroon, The Worst Woman in London,* and that great play *The Harbour Lights,* which starred William Terriss, son-in-law of the late Sir Seymour Hicks, and the "heart-throb" of the period. Terriss was a firm favourite with playgoers, rivalling Lewis Waller—who inspired the K.O.W. (Keen on Waller) Club—, and all London was shocked when Terriss was murdered at the stage-door of the Adelphi Theatre by a jealous and megalomaniac "super" who had borne him an unjustified grudge. The ghost of "Bill" Terriss (as he was affectionately known by his fellow players) is said to haunt the narrow passage between the Strand and Maiden Lane where the stage-door of the theater was situated. The Adelphi was re-designed some years ago.

ad lib. To continue to "gag" or improvise and so "fill in" when an actor has missed an entrance cue and there is a STAGE WAIT. Cf. PONG.

advance. The number of seats booked in advance of a performance, or the money matured at the box-office. "What's the advance like?" Cf. SHEET.

advance manager. An official who travels ahead of a touring company arranging the local publicity, etc. Cf. BILL INSPECTOR. In U. S., also *advance man*.

advance notice. The posters, newspaper publicity, lantern slides, etc. that precede a play's visit to the local theater.

agent. A theatrical agent who places plays, librettos, songs, sketches, etc., and obtains engagements for artists.

agents, do the. To go the rounds in the agency district, searching for work. In U. S., *make the rounds*.

agent's ten percent. The amount payable by one for whom an agent has obtained the engagement. *Ten per-cent* of his salary is paid in commission. In U. S., agent's percentage varies according to his services, as prescribed by Equity.

air. To broadcast a play, or excerpts from one. "We are being *aired* on Wednesday, so there will be a run through for 'cuts' on Tuesday morning."

air man chair. (Brit.) a jocular transposition of CHAIRMAN (music hall term now obsolete).

aisle. A gangway in the auditorium. From the French *aile,* a wing (of a church). The present-day spelling was, according to Ernest Weekley, the common form in France during the 16th-century.

aisles, I had 'em in the. A comedian's boast that his gags so reduced the audience to helplessness through laughter that the people at the end seats fell into the aisles. Cf. NOT A DRY SEAT IN THE HOUSE.

Aldwych farces. (Brit.) The immensely successful farcical comedies by Ben Travers which starred that unsurpassed team,

Ralph Lynn, Tom Walls, and Robertson Hare. The plays: *It Pays to Advertise*; *Tons of Money*; *The Cuckoo in the Nest*, and *Thark* packed the Aldwych Theatre during the 1920s.

al fresco. An entertainment in the open air. An Open Air Shakespearean Theater like that in London's Regent's Park, or in Scarborough's Peasholme Lake where *al fresco* opera is presented. Al fresco Concert Parties are very popular in seaside towns or City parks during the summer months. Italian *al fresco*, in the fresh (air). In U. S., *summer operetta, stadium concerts* and the like.

A little less off and a little more on! A sarcastic injunction addressed to a "dressing room star" who is full of facetiousness and arrogance, but has no marked talent to justify his attitude.

all Broadway cast. This means as much, or as little, as FULL WEST END CAST. q.v.

all in. (Brit.) The full-board tariff in theatrical lodgings. "Are you catering for yourself or do you want 'all in' terms?" (Theatrical landladies). Cf. CATER FOR ONESELF.

allongé. An elongated line in an arabesque. q.v. (ballet).

all round actor. A versatile artist who can be trusted with any type of "responsible" part.

all star cast. The (frequently mendacious) billing by a touring management of a metropolitan success. Occasionally such a cast does tour the principal cities but it is either a preliminary run to Town production, or a short tour following the play's withdrawal from the theater where it has had a long run.

alphabet. It is an old theatrical saying that any actor worthy of the title could earn a "round" (of applause) by reciting the alphabet.

also rans. The tail in the cast of a play. From the sporting papers' reports on race meetings: "Also ran, So and So, etc." See TAIL. In U. S., also *bit players, walk-ons*.

alto. The lowest voice in boys and women (contralto); men who sing alto to-day do so with a trained head voice (falsetto). The compass of the true alto lies within two octaves—from the lowest A of the treble stave to the E or F.

altogether please! (Brit.) An invitation to the audience to "join in the chorus" of a music hall song. There is at least one *all together please!* in a Xmas pantomime, or seaside Concert Party.

amphitheater. The upper circle or lower gallery. Originally the Roman theater used for gladiator fights and the like. Greek *amphi*, around. Seats set round an arena.

anachronism. A chronological error. The representing as co-existent something that could not possibly be. Out-of-character scenery or stage decoration. The use of modern idioms of speech in a period play. A *locus classicus* is in Julius Caesar, Act II, scene I, where Cassius announces that: "The clock has stricken three." Of course, there were no clocks in Caesar's time. The inadvertent wearing of a wrist-watch in, say, Goldsmith's *She Stoops to Conquer* would provide an anachronism, as would the expression "You're telling me!" in a Victorian play. The word is compounded of the Greek *ana*, backwards and *kronos*, time. Cf. PROCHRONISM and PARACHRONISM.

angel. To finance a play, or player. "Unless somebody can be found to *angel* this show it will have to come off." Perhaps from *guardian angel*? 2. Noun. A backer, from the verb.

appear in a play. To act in one, or even stand on the stage as a supernumerary.

apprentice school. Any reputable school of acting. E.g. the Royal Academy of Dramatic Art.

apron. The much-reduced modern version of the apron on the Elizabethan stage which used to extend well into the auditorium and round which part of the audience sat, or stood. Today the apron is the space between the SETTING-LINE (q.v.) and the footlights. At the Shakespearean Festival in the Memorial Theatre, at Stratford-on-Avon, in 1951 there was a reproduction of the apron stage. Cf. BLACK.

aquashow. A seasonal entertainment that has become popular in recent years. Aquatic turns are performed in tanks on the stage or in suitable settings according to the size of the theater. Latin *aqua*, water. In U. S. *aquacade, water ballet*.

arabesque. A posture of the body on one leg with the other stretched out behind, one arm in front, the other behind. An extremely graceful pose in ballet.

architrave. The technical term for the moulding round windows, doors, etc. in stage scenery.

arena show. An open air performance in an auditorium capable of holding from 10,000 people. See AUDITORIUM. 2. In U. S. the term *arena* is now generally used in reference to *theater-in-the-round.*

argentine. Material used to give the effect of glass in stage windows. Imitation silver. From Latin *argentum,* silver.

aria. An air, or song in Grand Opera, or in an Oratorio. Pronounced *ah*ria. Italian. Cf. NUMBER.

aristocratic parts. In the days when romantic drama was at its zenith the cast resembled a page from *Debrett* or *Burke's Landed Gentry.* Dukes, Lords, Viscounts were the rule rather than the exception and stage newspaper advertisements insisted that artists should be "capable of *aristocratic parts.*"

arrange. (music) To adapt a score for incidental music or otherwise prepare it for the orchestra. "Musical interlude *arranged* by" is a frequent notation on theater programs.

Art Theatre. Where plays are produced for "art's sake" on a non-profit-making principle. In the United States the term usually applies to amateur dramatic societies.

artificial comedy. See COMEDY OF MANNERS.

artistes. (Brit.) Generic term, in contracts, for actors and actresses. "Wanted artistes, all lines, for Repertory Season, play as cast, etc." (Advertisement in professional newspapers, *passim.*)

artistic failure. A play that misses fire and is universally damned by all the dramatic critics.

ascension, make an. To forget one's lines. They *fly* out of one's head. Cf. BALLOON, DRY-UP, STICK, and PONG. In U. S., also *fluff, blow up, go up, chase a kite.*

ashcan. A compartment-type footlight unit. Cinema influence. In U. S., motion picture slang, an arc light in shape of an ash can.

aside. A *sotto voce* remark for the benefit of the audience and, supposedly, inaudible to the rest of the cast on the stage. Stage villains in old-fashioned melodrama were much given to asides.

A.S.M. The Assistant Stage Manager. A euphemism for "general stooge" and the job is usually carried out by a stage beginner who combines his minor functions with that of small-part actor. A.S.M. is a thankless task bringing little of the glory implicit in the title, but this form of stage apprenticeship has to be endured and is extremely valuable training, especially in a resident, or touring repertory company. If a youngster is keen and observant he can learn much about the elements of his profession. When in the Prompt Corner, either "holding the book" or merely "standing by," he is able to watch the principals and so learn the importance of pace, timing, the judicious pause, and other technicalities of the actor's art. Moreover, the constant changing of scenery and lighting in the productions will instruct him in stagecraft, and stage management. Most stage managers, having gone through the mill themselves, are indulgent and make allowances for beginners. To-day many A.S.M.s are women who have an instinctive sense of stage decoration (in the technical sense), and are very conscientious in their work. They are excellent prompters and far more reliable than males in this respect. In the absence of a call boy the A.S.M. calls the actors.

à terre. (Of a ballet-dancer's foot) On the ground.

athletic droll. (Brit.) See KNOCK-ABOUT COMEDIAN.

at liberty. The American version of RESTING. It sounds nicer than out of work. In U. S. the euphemism *available* is also used.

atmosphere. The pervasive influence of a play. The contributory factors of lighting, scenery, acting, etc. designed in consonance with the theme of the play.

at rise. The position of the actors *at* the *rise* of the stage curtain on any act, or scene. "At rise, Mary is seated at a desk (L.C.) writing a letter." Cf. DISCOVERED.

attitude. That adopted at the finish of a pirouette. (ballet-dancing)

attraction. An entertainment that draws the business. Hence BOX-OFFICE ATTRACTION.

audience. The "house," or patrons of the drama. Those assembled to *hear* the play.

audience proof. A play whose success is a foregone conclusion. One that is also ACTOR PROOF.

audition. A hearing of the voices of applicants for parts or chorus of a musical play, or opera. It is also applied to the legitimate stage and the reading of parts.

auditorium. The seating accommodation in a theater or concert hall. Boxes, stalls, pit-stalls (Brit.) on the ground floor (the American orchestra). Dress, and upper circles, and gallery upstairs. 2. A theater or hall with large seating capacity.

auditory. An audience; auditorium; any place allotted to *hearers*, a theater or concert hall.

Audley, John. See JOHN AUDLEY.

Auguste. A clown's assistant, or feed. From the German, *auguste*, a fool, or village idiot.

Augustus Druriolanus. (Brit.) One of the nicknames of the late Sir Augustus Harris, manager of Drury Lane Theatre. Cf. EMPEROR AUGUSTUS, and DRURIOLANUS.

autumn tour. From late September or early October to Xmas. Cf. SPRING TOUR, and SUMMER TOUR.

aviary. (Brit.) The chorus girls' dressing-room. *Bird* is the slang term for a girl. (Stage managers' colloquial)

B

back. To support (finance a production or artist).

back batten. Is also known as the sky batten and lights the back-cloth only, not the acting area on the stage. See entry at BATTEN.

back-cloth. The drop scene at the back of the setting. It may represent a garden, street scene, or merely be a plain sky-cloth. In U. S., *backdrop*.

back-cloth star. A subsidiary actor whose position on the stage is near the back-cloth but who tries to draw attention to himself by the use of by-play in an attempt to create a CAMEO.

backer. One who finances a production. Cf. ANGEL.

back of the green. Behind the scenes. J. Redding Ware, in his delightful *Passing English,* suggests the off-rhyming of *green* with scenes, and refers to the traditional green curtain. Pure rhyming slang would, one feels, reject *scenes* and rhyme *greengage* with stage; thus *back of the green* would mean "back of the stage." See GREEN.

background music. This is a survival of the days of melodrama when music was played throughout the tense scenes. The more restrained music of to-day is played during the quiet, sentimental scenes, and is more effective in screen plays.

backing. Pieces of scenery, painted in consonance with the setting, are placed behind door, window, fire, or garden spaces. A hall-backing, for instance, has a bench, or hall stand in front of it to give "verisimilitude." Window backings are often part of the general back-cloth picture of a garden. It is very important that backings are adequately lighted. 2. Financial support.

back row of the chorus, she came from the. Said of an actress who has risen the hard way, from the smallest beginnings.

backstage. Anywhere behind the curtain, though the term more

11

specifically refers to the dressing rooms where the artists receive their friends. "Come backstage after the show and have a drink." Cf. BEHIND.

backstage cover. (Brit.) An insurance "cover" provided by the British Actors' Equity, which compensates artistes for the loss of, or damage to, luggage or general effects, stage wardrobe, etc. at any place where they are performing, or in transit between such places. The advantage of this "cover" scheme is that it applies to all places where Equity members work and not only to theaters.

backstage gossip. Theatrical "shop" in dressing-rooms, or Clubs. Cf. GREEN-ROOM GOSSIP.

backstage influence. Implies nepotism or a "friend at court." "Knowing someone who knows someone, etc." Said enviously of an actor who has obtained an engagement in a West End production.

backstage staff. All workers whose duties are carried out behind the curtain. E.g. stage-carpenters, electricians, property-men, stagehands, flymen, firemen. Also dressers, and, of course, that important functionary, the STAGE DOOR KEEPER.

bad. Is used in reference to faulty technique. "I don't like that cross above the settee, it looks bad." (Producers') (In U. S. directors.)

Baddeley Cake. (Brit.) Each year at the Drury Lane Theatre a cake is cut with great ceremony on the stage and eaten by members of the company appearing there. An actor of that name, a former cook, made the cake on a certain date every year and when he died—in 1794—he left the interest on £100 to provide the Baddeley cake for his successors but he did *not* leave the recipe. This pleasing custom of eating the cake has been carried out ever since, and the ceremony is always reported in the Press with a picture of the leading player in the act of cutting the cake.

bad dress rehearsal means a good opening, a. An old proverbial phrase that is often true, though the converse holds equally good; a *good dress rehearsal* being sometimes followed by a "shakey" opening. And a good opening performance is no guarantee that the second night won't see the actors FLUFF or even

DRY-UP. Stuart Palmer uses the proverb as an epigraph in the first chapter of his detective novel *Four Lost Ladies,* 1950, and undernotes it "a Broadway Proverb."

bad join. When two flats do not cleat together closely enough they show the backing light through the *bad join,* or gap in the wooden frames. 2. The front of a wig that is not properly painted into the facial make-up.

baffle. Any suitable sheet of material used to prevent a spill of light where it is not necessary.

bag. To loop up a cloth border.

baggage man. (Brit.) He is in charge of a theatrical company's property baskets, personal trunks and whatnot, and occasionally appears on the stage in a one-line part, or as supernumerary. In a touring company he helps on the stage with the properties, or scene changes. In professional theater, U. S., property men are not permitted to double as performers.

balcony. Originally called the *belconey,* (from the Italian, *balcone,* a scaffold) is the tier of seats above the dress-circle and below the gallery. It is known as the upper-circle in some theaters; in others it is a superior term for the gallery. In legitimate theater, U. S., refers to all "upstairs" seating.

balcony front spot. A spotlight lantern mounted in a cage in front of the balcony. Used to light the curtain and downstage acting area.

ballabile. The finale in ballet when the assembled corps moves symmetrically on the stage to end in a tableau.

ballad opera. Was very much the rage in England during the 18th-century. The opera was "built" round popular airs. Gay's *The Beggar's Opera* is a perfect example of this type of opera.

ballerina. (plural ballerinas or ballerine.) A female ballet-dancer. (Italian diminutive.)

ballet. A magma of music, mime, and CHOREOGRAPHY q.v.

ballet blanc. A filmy, white ballet skirt. Cf. TUTU.

ballet master. See MAÎTRE DE BALLET.

ballet mistress. She is in charge of the *corps de ballet* and responsible for their preparedness for the stage, and general welfare.

balletomania. A term believed to have been coined by Arnold

L. Haskell, an authoritative writer on the Ballet, and founder of the Vic Wells Ballet School in London. The word means *ballet fever* and refers to those never-miss-a-performance enthusiasts known as *balletomaniacs* or *balletomanes*.

balloon. To forget one's lines. (American) Cf. ASCENSION and CORPSE.

balloon tire. A sag under an actor's eyes. In U. S., *Columbus Circle* (colloq.)

balsa wood. A very light wood used in the making of properties which have to be used as weapons so that the recipient of the blow is unhurt.

band-parts. (Brit.) A catch-phrase used when a particularly good story has been told or a witty gag has been inserted at rehearsal. "That's pretty good, I'd like to have the band-parts." Cf. TOURING RIGHTS.

band-room. The orchestra rest-room adjacent to the orchestra pit. It is situated under the stage.

bankroller. A very popular actor or actress. A BOX OFFICE ATTRACTION who brings in the banknotes. (American)

bar bells. (Brit.) Are sounded in front of the house *bars* to warn patrons that the rise of the curtain is imminent.

Bard, the. William Shakespeare, the "prince of playwrights."

Bard specialist. An authority on anything Shakespearean. (American)

Bare-stall family. (Brit.) Empty seats (stalls). A jocular, or rueful, reference to a poor "house." Cf. WOOD FAMILY, and PLUSH FAMILY.

barnacles. (Brit.) Hangers round the stage doors of music halls who hope to "get off" with chorus girls as they leave the theater. 2. Men seeking jobs as supers in big productions, or unemployed stage-workers hoping to get work.

barnstormer. A "ham" actor. One who used to perform with a touring company that rented barns and raved (stormed) therein to a rustic audience.

barrack. To deride; jeer; boo, etc. This method of showing disapproval is far less prevalent to-day than in the Victorian era when plays received severe criticism when they fell short of an audience's expectations, or were downright bad. The term, originally used on the cricket fields of Australia, derives from the New Zealand word *borak* meaning derision.

barré. The steadying rail round the walls of a ballet-dancing studio to help pupils to balance.

barrel. A tube-like batten for holding spotlight lanterns.

Basil-dress. (Brit.) The uniform worn by members of the British Entertainments National Service Association (ENSA for short) of which Sir *Basil* Dean was head. The term near-rhymes with battle-dress; the costume was not unlike that worn by soldiers. Cf. ENSATAINMENT.

baskets are in, the. A catch-phrase used when there is a "full house" in a provincial theater. At the turn of the century many touring companies were stranded through lack of local support, so that, in order to settle their account with the theater management, the property baskets had to be left behind as security. Cf. TRAVEL ON ONE'S PROPS.

bass. The lowest male singing voice which generally has a compass from low F in bass clef to F two octaves above, though some very deep basses exceed this limit.

basso-buffo. The bass who plays the comic part in opera.

basso-cantante. The singing bass who possesses a higher register than a basso-profondo.

basso profondo. The lowest register in a bass singer. Literally a deep bass. Cf. BASSO CANTANTE.

bat. A harlequin's "wand" used in the old-fashioned HARLEQUINADE.

Bath Assembly. (Brit.) A festival of music and drama held in March each year under the auspices of the Glyndebourne Society. An echo of the assemblies in this gracious city during Beau Nash's time when Bath was the center of elegance and gaiety.

bathos. An unintentional anti-climax which often occurs in sentimental or music hall songs or poorly constructed dramas. "From the sublime to the ridiculous." The first use of the word in this sense was in Alexander Pope's parody of Longinus' essay *On the Sublime*. The Greek meaning is depth.

batten. A steel or wooden bar which supports lighting equipment, cloths, borders, French flats, ceilings, etc. Cf. BARREL.

battens, No. 1, 2, 3, and 4. Are the lighting battens with their compartments containing lamps, filters for colour media and reflectors. *No. 1* is the batten nearest the proscenium opening, *Nos. 2, 3, and 4* are equi-distant, the last being used to light the back-cloth or CYCLORAMA. In U. S., also *first pipe,* etc.

batten out. To stretch canvas on battens. The stage carpenter's job on tour.

batten, spot. See SPOT BATTEN.

Bay. (Brit.) The late Henry Baynton whose Shakespearean Company was the forcing ground of talent. An Old Bensonian, "Bay" had an excellent team and his standard of production was extremely high. The yearly season at the Savoy Theatre, London was a theatrical "event," seats being sold out at every performance. Henry Baynton was a brilliant Hamlet, which part he played numerous times. He also revived Henry Irving's melodrama *The Bells,* himself playing Mathias. The atmosphere of the Baynton Company was much the same as that of Sir Frank Benson's and the two have been classed the Oxford and Cambridge of the stage, from the large sprinkling of graduates in both companies. The film stars Robert Donat and Eric Portman learnt their business with "Bay" as he was affectionately nicknamed by members of his company. **bay** (2.) A space between the stacks of flats in a scene dock. Scenery is packed between scaffolding poles.

Bayreuth. The town in Bavaria, Germany where, at the Wagner *Festspielhaus,* an opera festival is held yearly.

Bayreuth hush. The stillness following the conductor's joining his orchestra in the Wagner Opera House. This admirable custom of observing silence could be adopted with advantage in some English theaters.

beam angle. The angle of the spotlight *beam* in relation to the stage-lighting plot.

beam borders. Are used for Tudor settings to represent *oak beams.*

Beau Brummell type. A stage "exquisite." One who excels in costume comedy. Beau Brummell (1778–1840) was a friend of the

Prince Regent. He was wealthy, witty and the *arbiter elegantiarum* at the Bath assemblies. He over-spent his fortune and escaped his creditors by fleeing to France. He died in poverty.

bedroom and sitting-room. (Brit.) As opposed to the COMBINED-ROOM, these apartments connote success in the provincial theater. Cf. COMBINED-CHAT.

beef and liberty! (Brit.) The motto of the famous Beef Steak Club of Irving Street, London, W.C.2., which was started by the comedian Richard Estcourt circa 1700, when he was made the first Provider. Many front rank players, literary men, artists, and celebrated wits are members.

before the lights. In front of the *footlights* in a theater, that is, performing on the stage.

beginner's play. One written by an author in his novitiate as a playwright.

behind. Short for:—

behind the curtain. On the stage itself shielded from the gaze of the audience. Cf. BACKSTAGE.

benefit night. See:—

benefit performance. One given for the benefit of a particular artist, organization or charity.

Bensonian. (Brit.) A member of the old Bensonian Shakespearean company. See the entry at "PA."

Bensonian window. (Brit.) A window in the Shakespeare Memorial Theatre at Stratford-on-Avon, dedicated to the memory of Sir Frank R. Benson and members of his famous company who appeared at this theater which was founded by Sir Frank who produced at the early festivals.

berry. Short for RASPBERRY q.v.

bespeak performance. Sir St. Vincent Troubridge, Bart., has communicated the following definition: "A 'bespeak' was when a local nobility (peer, mayor, colonel of regiment, etc.) patronized a provincial theater by 'bespeaking' or commanding a particular play, visiting it with all his friends, etc., and also giving *the manager* a donation of from 5 to 20 guineas."

between the acts. The entr'acte. It is a theatrical expression, seldom used by laymen, to denote the ten or fifteen minutes "rest" between the acts of a play, or is the long interval in a musical comedy. "Come round and see me between the acts." "Let's go over the new lines between the acts."

biank. (Brit.) A shilling. From the Italian *bianco,* white. The term is a PARLYAREE survival of days when booth-theaters were common on fair grounds. See CAROON and compare the Cockney slang *brown,* for a penny.

big name. A star whose name guarantees good business.

biggy. A big-name. A top ranking stage or film star, or one who is TOP OF THE BILL in vaudeville. A bringer-in of money. In U. S., *headliner, drawing card.*

bijou theatre. A Little Theater where everything is done on a small scale. Plays are produced in curtains, or in symbolic settings. A theater holding about 500 people.

bilk the landlady. (Brit.) To leave without settling her account. To cheat, as in the card game *cribbage* where to *balk* (of which *bilk* is a thinning) is to spoil one's opponent's score. Cf. SCARPER.

bill. The program in a vaudeville theater.

bill board. A hoarding in the vicinity of a theater upon which the "six sheets," or larger bills are posted. Hence *bill board pass,* the free ticket issued to tradespeople who allow advertising matter to be pasted on their walls, or show small bills in their premises.

bill inspector. (Brit.) The man responsible for theater billing. He is in charge of the posters and distributes the requisite number to the bill-stickers who cover the billing districts. Daybills for display in hotels, public houses, and shop windows; "throwaways" (handbills), etc., all come within the bill inspector's orbit. Cf. PUBLICITY AGENT.

bill, on the same. In the same program at a variety theater. "Danny Kaye and I were on the same bill at the Paladium."

bill, out of the. Said of a variety artist who has suddenly left the program.

bill, top of the. A star vaudeville artist who heads the program. His name eclipses the rest. "I see Bob Hope is top of the bill at the 'Vaudeville' this week."

billy. A single block and tackle used for hoisting scenery. Adopted from the nautical *handy-billy,* and probably so named by an ex-seaman stagehand, or flyman, a job that attracts many sailors accustomed to marlinespike work with ropes and pulleys.

bio-box. (Brit.) The projector-room, at the back of the auditorium, used to house the projector which shows the advertising slides on the screen placed in the proscenium arch during an interval, or before the curtain rises. The *bio*graph, or early "magic-lantern," was the precursor of the cinematograph. In U. S., *projection booth*.

bird, the. A demonstration of disapproval from the audience. Hisses, boos, cat-calls, slow-clapping, the "raspberry" (q.v.) and other—often tangible—reminders have been known to stop the show on occasions when a performance has been rank bad. The hissing suggests geese, hence *bird*. See GOOSE, SHRIEKING OSTRICH, and LINNET.

Birmingham screw driver. (Brit.) A hammer. From the habit of lazy workmen who hammer a screw into the wood, then finish off with the last few turns of the screwdriver (stage carpenter's term).

bis! A variant of *encore!* which, be it noted, is seldom used in France. Instead *bis!* (Latin for *twice*) is the usual cry of approbation. Cf. 'CORE!

Bishop of Broadway. The veteran actor Harry Irvine who, born in England, went to America in 1915. He portrayed many ecclesiastical roles in Broadway theaters.

bit part. A very small part indeed; "two lines and a spit." What used to be known as "the carriage waits, me Lord" part.

bite cues. To cut in on a fellow actor's speech, or understress a cue-line, thus spoiling the speaker's next line which would be unintelligible to those in the audience who missed the cue-biter's SPEECH.

bits. Isolated scraps of dialogue gone over at rehearsals. "There will be a CALL (q.v.) tomorrow at eleven-thirty to go over bits."

biz. Short for BUSINESS.

black. (Brit.) The APRON in front of the stage is usually painted black. "He addressed the audience from the black." The edge of the footlights.

black and white artiste. (Brit.) A music hall entertainer specialising in swiftly executed caricature drawings in black crayon on a white board, or white on a blackboard.

blackface comedy. See NEGRO MINSTRELS.

black light. Ultra violet light. (Electrician's term.)

blackout. The cue *blackout* in a light plot means that every light on the stage is switched off. In revues a *blackout* acts as a "quick" curtain to a sketch. It often cloaks the lowering of a front cloth for the next item which may be some lively patter by the comedian while the next set is being erected behind the cloth. 2. To forget one's lines; have a mental *blackout*.

blackout curtain. See the above entry.

blacks. Black velvet borders and wings used in certain types of intimate revue.

blanking paper. Sheets of blue paper pasted over bills when a play has been withdrawn and the theater is DARK q.v.

blinders. Bright lights beside the proscenium arch which are focused on the auditorium thus *blinding* the audience so that they cannot see a quick change of scenery on the blacked-out stage. In U. S. occasionally used to mask scene changes on *al fresco* stages that do not have curtains or shielding screens.

blobby. (Brit.) An electrician's adjective to describe any uneven lighting on the stage. The term is also used by producers (in U. S., directors) thus: "Electrics! I don't like that blobbiness over the door; try another medium in the amber spot."

blood and thunder. (Brit.) Lurid melodrama as presented to the sensation-loving audiences at the drama houses south of the Thames during the reign of Queen Victoria. There was much *blood and thunder* in these productions. Hence:—

blood tub. (Brit.) A theater showing such fare.

blower. An electrically-driven fan for removing a large volume of air. It is often used for wind effects in storm scenes.

blue gags. Salacious "wisecracks"; sexual allusions, or situations. Material for the censor's *blue* pencil.

blueology. A jocular American term for the presentation of *blue* material in vaudeville, or revue. The art of rendering *risqué* lines less offensive by subtle treatment.

board. Short for the stage switchboard.

board-light. The lamp on the Stage Director's, or Electrician's board by which plots can be read during the performance.

boards, the. The stage, hence *on the boards,* in the profession. The wooden boards of the stage itself.

boards, tread the. To act a part on the stage. "No better actor trod the boards than Henry!" (An old actor's pronouncement concerning the great Sir Henry Irving.)

boat truck. A wheeled platform on which boats were built to "sail" behind a "sea" row. Used in Gilbert & Sullivan's *The Gondoliers*; the *Swan Lake* ballet, and in many stirring melodramas of the sea in the days of spectacular drama. The truck is used for a variety of purposes to-day. Cf. BOGIE.

bobby pins. Grips used by actresses to keep their hair in place. From *bobbed* hair.

bobbysoxers. Teenage fans who, armed with autograph albums, besiege stage doors and generally make a nuisance of themselves. They wear bobby socks and are the American equivalent of London's GALLERY GIRLS.

bogie. (Brit.) Another name for the boat-truck. A North Country dialect term of unknown origin, it may have entered the theater vocabulary via railway workers who refer to their hand-trucks (barrows) as bogies. Stage carpenters loading scenery at station goods-yards often borrow these bogies to lighten the labor of carrying heavy pieces of scenery and properties. This etymology-defying word is also applied to the four-wheeled under carriage of a locomotive engine. There seems little doubt, therefore, that *bogie* is a railway adoption.

bole. A golden brown pigment used by actors to achieve the deep sunburn effect in tropical plays.

bolt. A measure of canvas for scenery. A roll of canvas.

bombast. Hyperbolical language. Grander speech than situations allow.

bon bon. A spotlight lantern that concentrates light on an artist's face. In U. S. a large, round 2,000 watt spotlight.

boo. To deride a scene, or a particular artist (imitative). See BIRD.

book and lyrics. The "book" is the story and dialogue in a musical comedy or opera; the "lyrics" are the vocal numbers. See LIBRETTO.

book-flat. A pair of hinged flats that look somewhat like a book standing on its base. See FLAT, FRENCH for detailed description.

book-wing. A double flat hinged in the middle which, opening like a book, can stand by itself without bracing. It is used chiefly for masking purposes.

booking office. A theater booking agency in the city. Patrons are able to book seats through the agency which communicates with the theater concerned. Cf. SHEET. In U. S., *ticket agency*. The term *booking* refers to engagement of a person or company for performance.

booked up. All seats reserved at a performance. Cf. SOLD OUT, and HOUSE FULL. In U. S. a performer or company with a full schedule of bookings.

boom. Is short for BOOMERANG. 2. (of a play) to do good business.

boomerang. A mounting for spot, or flood lights, which can be set one above the other to illuminate a backcloth or cyclorama. Booms are also extremely useful for side lighting.

booms, portable. Self explanatory.

boot. See SLOAT.

born a gentleman; died an actor. A traditional theatrical "crack." A worse fate would be, some aver, "born an actor; died a gentleman."

born in a property basket. The boast of one who has been on the stage since childhood. Born of a theatrical family . . . almost in the dressing-room where the baskets are kept. See SKIP.

bosh lines. The violin strings used by puppet-show men for operating their marionettes. From *bosh*, a Romany term for a fiddle.

bos'un's chair. In full, a boatswain's chair. A rope suspended seat that can be hoisted to any desired height and is used by stagehands working away from the fly platform, or at any height that a ladder cannot reach. It is also known as a bos'un's stool.

bottom lighting. Footlights, ground rows, backing lights, cyclorama floodlights, etc. that are plotted to illuminate the lower part of the setting. Cf. TOP LIGHTING.

bow, take a. To take a curtain call. Acknowledge the applause by *bowing* to the audience. An old theater convention. U. S. slang: *do the bends, nod*.

bow teller. The stage manager who, able to hear the strength, or weakness, of the applause from his prompt corner, *tells* the artists when to take another call (*bow*).

Bowdlerization. An expurgated version. Doctor Thomas Bowdler (1754–1825) published an edition of the works of Shakespeare, "in which words or expressions are omitted that cannot, with propriety, be read aloud in a family." He also brought out an emasculated edition of Edward Gibbon's *The Decline and Fall of the Roman Empire* which started a fashion, during that squeamish period in English literary history, of "family" versions of the classics. In the name of "propriety" many unforgivable acts of bibliocide were committed, and it was not until fairly recently that books and plays were freed from the hands of Bowdlerizers, and franker translations of classical plays have appeared.

bowl. The amphitheater, especially an al fresco one like the Greek Theatre at Bradfield College where a play in the original Greek is given each year by the Collegians.

box office appeal. The drawing power of a leading player. It is commonly shortened to *box office*: "The new musical at the Palace is sure to have a run; Buchanan is *box office* any time." In U. S., slang expression *boff*, language of theatrical trade journal, *Variety*.

box office keeper. The official in charge of a theater pay office in front of the house.

box office manager. Is in charge of the box office in a theater. He acts in telephonic liaison with the theater ticket agencies and arranges his sheets accordingly. A clever box office manager is a valuable asset to the management.

box office plan. The seating plan of the house. There is a separate sheet for each part of the auditorium.

box scene. One made up of flats, forming the back and both sides, as opposed to an open set consisting of a backcloth and wings. In U. S., *box set*.

boys and girls. The traditional informal address of a Stage Manager. "Now, boys and girls, you'll have to pep up that scene in Act II, it is dragging and isn't going as well as it did when we opened." In the *No. 1* companies this mode of address has fallen into desuetude, and the more dignified "Ladies and Gentlemen" is used.

brail line. A length of thin cordage used to brail (haul up) something into position.

bravo! brava! bravi! Acclamations at performances of grand opera. The Italian respectively for a male, a female singer, and singers collectively.

break. The holding up of a rehearsal for, say, a homily by the director, or for luncheon. 2. In tap dancing, a slight pause in the rhythm. 3. The American colloquial sense of *fortune*: "So and So had a lucky break in that Broadway show last fall."

break into pictures. To leave the stage for the more lucrative Cinematic field.

break out of character. To address, or reprove an audience.

break-up. A piece of scenery designed to collapse at cue. E.g. in an earthquake scene in melodrama, or the collapse of a shelled or bombed building in a war play. In U. S., *breakaway*.

breeches part. A male role portrayed by a woman (obsolete).

bridge. Part of a stage that can be electrically or hydraulically raised or lowered in accordance with the plot. 2. A platform over the orchestra pit with steps leading into the auditorium for the use of the director during rehearsals. It saves his constant use of the pass door.

bridle. Two or more ropes or chains attached by a ring eye or shackle to the end of a grid-line and fitted, at intervals, with clips, to a batten or barrel and thus distributing a heavy load of lighting, or other battens, flown-flats, etc.

brief. A complimentary ticket. A free pass to the performance. From the German *brief*, a letter, or short note. In U. S., *comp, paper, Annie Oakley*.

bring in. To switch on stage lighting that has been "off" until the *cue*. A typical light plot entry: "at cue, *bring in* spots, battens and two circuits of floats." The electrician switches on whatever lighting is indicated on his plot.

bristle trap. (Brit.) Has flaps of bristle or birch twigs through which an actor may emerge slowly onto the stage.

broad comedy. Slapstick, or farcical comedy played on crude lines with all the points labored, and "comic bits" introduced for the sake of cheap laughs. A deliberate playing down to a simple audience on whom the subtler technique would be wasted.

broad (of technique). The transpontine style of acting: a tendency to rant in dramatic scenes, or to overplay, or clown in comedy.

Broadway hit. A New York success.

brodie. A failure, a flop, something that does not quite succeed. Eric Partridge (Name into Word, 1949) says: "In American 20th-Century slang 'a jump; an attempt'; and *do a brodie* is 'to faint; to die' but also 'to try.' The former occurs in, e.g., Godfrey Irwin's entertaining *American Tramp and Underworld Slang*, 1931, the latter in Jack Callahan's *Man's Grim Justice*, 1929. The origin lies in an obscure or, at least, disputed episode in the life of one Steve Brodie, who jumped—or failed to jump—from the old Brooklyn Bridge and who afterwards, such being the reward of national notoriety, became a successful saloon-keeper." A further reference to Brodie is in *Styles in Crime* by Charles E. Stills, 1938. Another sense of doing a *brodie* is "to fail after tremendous and boastful advance publicity" (letter from Sir St. Vincent Troubridge 17 May, 1951). In U. S. colorful variations include *bust, egg, turkey*; *fold, lay an egg, go west*.

brogue. The stage version of the Irish or Scotch dialect; any exaggerated form of "regional" or rural speech used by character actors. Cf. MUMMERSETSHIRE.

broken down actor. One of those pathetic figures around "Poverty Corner" in London, or the New York equivalent. Unemployed, and usually, unemployable. Many of these men have done excellent work but, for reasons best known to themselves, they have dropped out of the race, though it is simply *anno domini*.

broker's men. (Brit.) The characters for two comedians in pantomime. Usually a well-known "double-act" is engaged for the parts.

bronchial. (Brit.) A member of the audience whose constant coughing distracts the artists. "I could throttle that bronchial in the third row. He is a perfect menace."

Bronx cheer. The American version of *raspberry*.

budger. (Brit.) A comedian who can be relied upon to move (budge) a stubborn audience to responsiveness, or at least risibility (vaudeville term).

buffo (feminine buffa). The Italian for comic, burlesque, hence *Opera buffa,* comic opera. Compare the French *buffe,* echoic of a blow and suggestive of *slap*stick comedy technique.

buffoonery. Stage fooling, broad comedy business. From the French *bouffon,* a jester, ex the verb *bouffer,* to puff (the cheeks). The term is cognate with the Italian *buffone,* from *buffa,* a joke, itself from the verb *buffare,* to blow out the cheeks, as does the jester in his facial grimaces.

bug hole. A variant of the more usual FLEA PIT q.v.

bull frog. A deep-voiced melodrama actor. This original meaning has spread to any actor with such a voice. Like the croaking of a frog.

bumper house. (Brit.) A house-full performance. *Bumper* means anything large. From the brimming glass (bumper) of the roistering days when England was "merry."

bunch lights. A cluster of lights in a wing or any position needing extra illumination which cannot be provided by standard lighting.

burg. An American town, irrespective of size. (American touring actors'.)

buried in the provinces. (Brit.) Playing a part in a touring company, or in resident repertory in a provincial town. Forgotten, if ever known, by London managements.

burlesque. A stage parody. A travesty of a play, or "take-off" caricature of a celebrity, or fellow artist. Any form of bathos introduced in a revue, or vaudeville act. From the French via Italian *burlesca,* from *burla,* a jest, mockery. Cf. COD VERSION. In U. S., also theatrical entertainment consisting of *low comedy* and *leg show.*

burlesque house. A small vaudeville theatre where broad comedy is the staple fare. In U. S., home of the *strip teaser,* whose art involves the rhythmic removal of raiment.

burlesqueries. Theaters that specialise in burlesque and slapstick comedies. (American.)

burletta. A short burlesque. Italian *burla,* and the diminutive *etta.*

Doctor Joseph T. Shipley says that the term is now used in America as a legal definition of a play with enough music to evade patent restrictions.

burletterise. To turn a comedy into a burlesque by broadening the business and altering the dialogue to obtain readier laughs when the play is presented to simple audiences. (obsolete)

burnt cork artist. A "white man" in blackface. He makes up his face with burnt cork.

burnt sugar. Diluted in water, is used to represent drinks on the stage.

bus. So marked in the Prompt Copy, and an actor's "part," is short for *bus*iness, the *actions* to be carried out. It can mean anything from the casual lighting of a cigarette to the throttling of the villain.

business of the stage. Everything to do with actions carried out by the artist, as opposed to dialogue.

busk. (Brit.) To play a musical instrument, or sing, to a theater queue, or outside a public house. From the old French verb *busquer*, to seek one's fortune. It is cognate with the Italian *buscare*, to filch, prowl . . . with that end in view.

busker. (Brit.) A queue entertainer, whether as a performer on an instrument, a singer, or acrobat, conjurer, or patter-artist. See BUSK.

buskin. A high boot anciently worn by tragedians to give them height. 2. Generic for the theatrical profession, or acting generally.

butler part. Any part of a male servant: butler, footman, valet, waiter and the like.

butter and egg man. A man with no artistic pretensions who puts on "shows" for the sake of financial gain. He might as well sell groceries.

butterflies in the stomach. Symptoms of first night nerves felt by all sensitive artists—indeed, the better the artists, the more prone are they to this truly dreadful—and dreaded—sensation. From the heavings and fluttering in the stomach while waiting for the cue to go onto the stage.

buzzer. Any bell cue, e.g. the curtain warning signal.

by-play. Business between two characters in a scene, mostly carried out in dumb show, while the main action continues.

C

cab tire. Flexible wire cased in a rubber protective coat, insulated and used for temporary installations, usually out of doors. It much resembles a cab tire.

cackle. (Brit.) An old term for stage conversation, dialogue generally. Specifically, it refers to that unpunctuated flow of almost unintelligible patter from a comedian when covering a dry-up, or missed entrance cue by a fellow actor. Ware, in his record of the term quotes the Stage newspaper—the "actor's bible"—of 1885 which defines *cackle* as: "A convertable substantive or verb which carries meaning for which it would be difficult to substitute any other word nearly as effective, and there is a world of satire in its application to a human goose."

cackle thower. (Brit.) An assistant stage manager, or whoever acts as prompter. From the preceding (obsolete).

cacology. An elocution technicality for bad diction; solecistic pronunciation; indistinct articulation, or general infringement of the law of phonetics. From the Greek *kakos*, bad, and *logos*, word, or speech.

cacophony (of music). Raucous, or ill-timed execution by an orchestra, or instrumentalist. *kakos*, bad, plus *phone*, sound.

cage girl. A box office ticket seller in an American theater. She works behind a wire-fronted guichet. Also *ducat hustler*.

call. In theater parlance any *notice* is termed a call, the notice board being the *Call Board*. Thus are rehearsals "called," not ordered: "Don't forget there is a call for Act III tomorrow morning at 10.30 sharp"; "What time is the *band call* (orchestra rehearsal) on Monday?" 2. A *curtain* call, when the star or full company make their bows to the audience at the end of an act. In vaudeville when an act has gone exceptionally well and the audience clamours for a repetition, the performers *play a call* (Brit.) (tantamount to an encore) which can be either a

28

repeated performance of the act, or a different item. "You can play a call tonight if they ask for it, but make it short." The term *call* is peculiar to the theater and may have been adopted from the nautical system of issuing orders by bos'un's call, or "pipe," but it is more likely that it is merely a *calling* together of the company.

call board. A theater notice board, bulletin board.

call book. See entry at CALL BOY.

call boy. A lad who calls the acts, and individual actors, during the running of the play. He stations himself beside the stage manager in the Prompt Corner and acts under his orders. His first call is half-an-hour before the Overture, when he calls: "Half-an-hour please!" Fifteen minutes later he calls "Quarter-of-an-hour please!" These warnings have the effect of hurrying the laggards, and discourage dressing-room gossip, as the precious minutes are flying. As soon as the orchestra leaves the band-room under the stage the boy calls "Overture and Beginners, please!" which brings the actors who "open" the play onto the stage to take up positions in which they will be "discovered" at the rise of the curtain. Once the curtain is up the boy calls "Curtain up, please!" and thereafter warns actors when he is told to do so by the stage manager. Successive acts will be called half way through the intervals: "Beginners Act II, please!" and so on. In recent years "call girls" have been introduced in some theaters. A CALL BOOK is used by the call boy when he has many calls to make, and the approximate times of these are noted in his book. Many leading players began their careers in this capacity for excellent opportunities are given to "look and learn." In U. S. calls are: "Half hour please!" "Fifteen minutes please!" "Five minutes please!" "Places please!" and in musicals "Overture!" Call boys are not used in the Amer. professional theater and calls are made by the stage manager or his assistant.

call out. To demand a curtain speech from the leading artist at the end of a performance. He is *called out* of the setting to make his acknowledgments in front of the fallen curtain. The "tabs" are parted for him. (American)

call over. The daily check of outside bookings which the box office manager makes with the theater ticket agencies, and libraries. He marks the booked seats on his seating plans, the unbooked ones being available for sale.

calls, pinch. See PINCH A CALL.

call, train. A *train call* is the time at which a touring company leaves one town for the next on the tour list. For the convenience of actors the business manager gives the times of arrival, and departure, from the changing-places, and the time the company reaches its destination. This enables actors to make arrangements for hotel accommodations.

callithumpian. Noisy, discordant music. Also a member of a *callithumpian band.* From the Greek *kallos*, beautiful + thump.

calypso. "A ballad-like improvisation in African rhythm, often a satire on current events, composed and sung by the natives of Trinidad, B.W.I. at annual festivals." (*Webster's New Collegiate Dictionary, 1945.*) Calypso singing has become increasingly popular in vaudeville, and radio shows.

calypsonian. A singer of calypsos.

cameo. A character part so well portrayed that it stands out in front of the other small parts. Very often such parts are actor-proof and cannot fail to bring prominence to the player. It is not that the actor obtrudes his personality but that the lines in the part, or the situation in the play, make the role particularly noticeable.

campus play. A play given by a college dramatic society at an American university. Latin *campus,* a meadow, hence a close, or quadrangle of a college.

campus theater. American university dramatic societies.

can can. A stage dance in revue, or cabaret, which originated in Paris about 1830 but went out of favor within a few years. The dance was revived in the 1930s. Its main feature is the frill, and limb-revealing high-kick.

canes. Small canes inserted in a wooden disc and revolved at varying speeds on an electric motor, thus making the sound of wind. 2. One cane in each hand smacked quickly and smartly on a leather cushion produces the effect of rifle, or machine-gun fire.

canvas theatre. (Brit.) A large markee in which plays are presented at galas. E.g. The Festival Tent-Theatre at Pitlochry in Scotland.

carbons. Rods of compressed carbon dust used for arc projectors. The rods, hand or electrically fed, burn away in incandescence.

card, on one's. Free admission to a theater on presentation of an actor's professional *card*. A traditional privilege, though less popular from a managerial point of view than formerly, owing to its abuse by many people on the fringe of, rather than in, the profession. In U. S. one employs the euphemism *courtesy of the profession*.

caroon. (Brit.) Parlyaree for a five shilling piece, which it is considered unlucky to receive in a pay-envelope. The term may be directly from Romany (the Welsh variant is *kurune*) or the standard Italian *corona*, a crown. Eric Partridge suggests that if the Parlyaree and Romany terms do not corrupt *crown* they may derive not from Italian, but from the old French *couronne*. (Essay on Parlyaree in *Here, There, and Everywhere.* 1950.)

carp. An American nickname, and vocative, for the Stage *Carpenter*.

carpenter. (of 'scripts). To alter a play to suit different types of audience. Cf. DOCTOR, and ADAPTATION.

carpenter scene. The obsolete term for a *front cloth scene*. A duologue carried on while the carpenter and his men erect the next scene.

carpet-cut. A hinged board running along the setting-line. It lifts to trap the down-stage edge of a carpet or stage cloth, and keeps it in position.

carpet-cut ring. A brass ring inserted flush with the carpet cut and used for the purpose of lifting the cut.

cast. The DRAMATIS PERSONAE; the company of actors. 2. v. To assign parts to actors or actresses.

casting couch. A jocular, if indelicate, reference to the settee in a a theatrical manager's or agent's office.

casting director. One who supplies the cast of plays or musical comedies.

cast iron comic. (Brit.) A comedian whose "gags" and business a blasé audience finds *hard* going. A laboured technique by an outmoded artist.

cast out of type. Assigned a part unsuitable for one's personality, or physique. Such casting is inevitable in repertory companies where actors' work has to be evenly distributed if undue strain is not to be imposed on "types."

cat calls. Uncomplimentary noises of disapproval by an unruly or dissatisfied audience. Cf. RASPBERRY, and BIRD.

catch a cold. To do a bad week's business in a provincial town. As a rule there is some factitious reason for this unless a piece is thoroughly bad. A play featuring, say, a train smash—as in *The Wrecker*, a successful London thriller of the 1920s—would catch a severe "cold" if playing in a town where such an accident occurred, as actually was the case with the play cited. The crash took place on the eve of the company's visit and, naturally, very poor business resulted. The catch-phrase probably originated in the days of DRY-UP COMPANIES when clothing was often left in a theater in lieu of payment to save a company being stranded.

catch on. (Of a play) To attract public notice; find favour. "That new show at the Princes' has caught on in spite of the bad Press."

cater for oneself. (Brit.) Touring actors either take apartments on the "all in" (full board) tariff, or cater for themselves. By the the latter arrangement the landlady charges a fixed rate for rooms and attendance, which includes the cooking of any food brought in by her "lets" or she herself buys what they order and adds the cost to her bill at the week-end. Cf. ALL IN.

catever. Bad business (in the *fit-up theatres*.) (Brit.) A Parlyaree corruption of the Italian *cattivo*, feminine, *cattiva*, bad. Often *multy catever* (Ital. *multo*, very; much). The term can be applied to any disastrous occurrence, e.g. the stranding of a company. Few fit-up companies remain on the road and the term is obsolete.

catharsis. The emotional relief caused by the witnessing of a tragedy. The reference is to Aristotle's *Poetics* (*VI*): "Tragedy, then, is the imitation of an action . . . with incidents arousing pity (*eleos*) and fear (*phobos*) wherewith to accomplish its *catharsis*, or purgation, of such emotions." (Bywater's translation). Aristotle regarded pity and fear as forms of pain which could be purified (*kathairo*, to cleanse) through the realms of art. Literally, *catharsis* is a purgation in the medical sense. In the Aristotelian sense it is, as F. L. Lucas has pointed out, in his admirable lecture on *Tragedy* (published as No. 2 of the Hogarth Lectures), the human soul that is purged of its excessive passions, rather than the passions that are purged of their impurities.

catwalk. A narrow bridge communicating the two fly-galleries above and below the proscenium arch.

cavatina. An operatic air that is shorter and simpler than an aria. The diminutive form of *cavata*, an air. (Italian.)

ceiling cloth. A plain white cloth set above the flats of a chamber, or other interior setting. Cf. CEILING PIECE.

ceiling piece. Is the same as a ceiling cloth.

celestials. The occupants of the "GODS" q.v. The gallery gods.

cellar. The under-stage space. Often the band room is situated here.

C.E.M.A. (Brit.) Short title of the *C*ouncil for the *E*ncouragement of *M*usic and the *A*rts.

centage. (Brit.) The English Telegraphic Code word for *Per Cent*, the amount divided between the lessee of a theater and the touring company playing thereat.

center-aisle. The middle gangway from the back of the auditorium to the orchestra pit on the ground floor. From the back to the front of the balconies in the dress, upper circle, and amphitheater upstairs. This gangway is insisted upon by law to facilitate escape in case of fire.

center line. The line taken from the center of the footlights to the the middle of the back wall on the stage. It is used as a guide when setting scene. 2. the center one of a SET OF LINES.

center opening. The center opening in a setting, e.g. French windows, double doors, and the like.

center piece. Scenery that is set in the middle of the stage.

center practice. Part of a ballet class that has advanced beyond the BARRÉ.

center prompt-box. A hooded box set under the apron. It is used more in Grand Opera, and musicals than in general productions. A conductor follows the score throughout.

center stage. The center of the acting area. The focal point of the leading players, and so, jealously guarded.

chaîne. A short fast turn performed in a *chain,* or line, across the stage in a ballet.

chairman. (Brit.) The compere in the old-fashioned music hall entertainment. He announced the turns and kept order. Cf. AIR-MAN-CHAIR.

chair warmer. A (woman) super who merely sits on a chair in a scene.

chalk a scene. In the early stages of a rehearsal chalk lines are drawn on the bare stage to indicate the dimensions of the setting, and odd chairs are positioned to indicate furniture. Thus an idea of the acting area is presented and movements can be made as they would be in the actual setting.

chamber set. Any interior set; e.g. drawing room, bedroom, etc. Cf. oak set.

chandelier cloth. A ceiling cloth with a hole in the center to take the light cable that fits into the fly-dip to feed the chandelier.

change an act. To strike one scene and set another. Cf. CHANGE A SET. Also known as an *act* or *scene change.*

change a set. See the above entry. A *change* of scenery.

character comedy. (Brit.) Is colloquially known as a "gag" show. A plot is drawn round a number of speeches (by the leading man), and stock characters, or situations, and the players provide the extempore dialogue appropriate to the theme. This used to be a common practice in the *fit-up* days.

character, go out of. This used to be a common habit in melodrama companies when the leading man would "step out of his character part" to reprove a rowdy, or facetious audience.

character, in. See IN CHARACTER.

character juvenile. A "juvenile" actor playing a slightly older part than the customary "boy" roles associated with him. Cf. JUVENILE JOHN.

character lines. Age-lines traced on the face with a lake-liner by a youthful actor playing an old man. See entry at CLAPHAM JUNCTION.

character man. An actor specialising in the portrayal of such roles as Doctors, Lawyers, and professional men generally. The term distinguished him from a JUVENILE MAN. In U. S. frequently a misnomer for a player of *eccentric* parts.

character names. Often actors will be addressed at rehearsal by the producer, or stage director, in the names of the characters they are playing. "Will Elizabeth and George move right when Robert goes off, it will give Mrs. Phelps a better entrance."

character old man. Frequently a very young man who portrays such parts. His performance, however, sometimes betrays his youth by a springy step, or a straight back. Middle-aged actors usually play these roles in repertory companies. In U. S. professional theater type casting prevails and virtually no opportunity exists for "youth" to play "age."

character old woman. An actress specialising in senile parts. In repertory companies such characters are assigned to young women but it is never a satisfactory policy, for youth "will out" and few of their performances convince.

character part. Since all parts are "characters" this term is somewhat tautological, but it means a role other than the lead, or juvenile lead. Typical character parts are: the family doctor, the rich uncle, the "heavy," or genial father, the hunting squire, etc. In U. S. term *eccentric* is considered apt.

characters in order of appearance. The customary order on the program.

charade. A dramatic representation, the solution of which is guessed by the audience.

Charles James. (Brit.) A theatre box. Rhyming slang on Charles James *Fox*, the fighting statesman (1749–1806), third son of Henry Fox, first Lord Holland. "Ring me up and I'll fix you up with a *Charles James*." (an old managerial term, now obsolete.) Rhyming slang is still very prevalent in the music halls.

chaser. The last turn on a variety bill. It *chases* the rest. 2. the last item played by the orchestra at the end of a performance. Usually, however, in Cinema theatres, to chase out the audience.

chatsby. (Brit.) A nonsensical word used when the correct term is momentarily forgotten, or never really known. An elaboration of *chat*, a thing. Cf. COMBINED CHAT for a fuller definition of this curious word.

check takers. Ushers—usually members of the Corps of Commissionaries—who take the tickets in front of the house. In U. S., *gate man, ticket taker.*

check the house. To dim out the houselights (Brit.) 2. To check the box office booking sheets with the counterfoils of the tickets sold.

check the returns. The same as check the house, 2.

cheesecake. The photographs of young actresses showing more than is strictly necessary of their bodies to attract the attention of the "tired business men." (American coinage.)

chef d' orchestre. A Musical Director, or conductor. Obsolescent in the English theater.

child star. A "minor" who makes a success in "kid" parts. E.g. Shirley Temple, and Jackie Coogan in films.

chin armour. A crepe hair beard. (American.) Cf., TIN BEARD.

china crash. Acts in the same way as a glass crash. Pieces of broken china are poured from one vessel into another to produce the effect of falling crockery. See GLASS CRASH.

chip, to. Adversely criticise (a fellow actor; the audience; the theater, in fact, anything of which the speaker disapproves). From the general slang verb *chip*, to reprove, to inveigh against, which Sydney J. Baker records as Australian slang.

chironomy. The art of gesture. Literally hand movements on the stage. From the Greek *cheir*, hand plus *nomos*, law.

chirp. (Brit.) To give the "bird" to a player, or a play. Hence *chirper* one who haunts music halls with the object of guying a performance.

chord in "G." From the orchestra followed any sentimental or "strong" speech by the hero, or heroine in melodrama. "Will nobody save me?" wailed the maiden struggling in the arms of Jasper the villain. "Yes, *I* will," cried a voice off stage followed by its owner's entrance through "gap in hedge." "Who are you?" quavered she. "I'm Barnacle Bill the Sailor" (Chord in "G".) There are few such drama companies touring to-day but occasionally one hears an old trouper murmur "Chord in 'G'" when he speaks, or hears, a line suggestive of the old technique.

chord on; chord off. A chord on the piano at rehearsals of a musical comedy, or pantomime to give an artist his cue for entrance (**on**), or exit (**off**). It is still used as a fanfare to announce the entrance of a star in musical shows, though chiefly in vaudeville.

choreographer. A creater of dance design in ballet. *Choreograph* = a dance plan.

choreographist. A variant of CHOREOGRAPHER.

choreography. Design in ballet dancing. Greek, *chorus*, dance and *graphein*, to write.

chorine. A female member of the chorus. Cf. TERPSICHORINE. (American.)

chorus. The choristers (male and female) in opera or musical comedy. Cf. SINGING LADIES, AND GENTLEMEN, *singing ensemble*. 2. In the Greek sense, a dance performance by a number of persons, accompanied by song. Also a prologue to the drama.

chorus-rooms. The choristers dressing rooms usually on the top landing of a theater.

chow. (Brit.) To grumble, be bitingly critical, or tiresomely garrulous. Compare the slang term *chow the fat*, to talk at length and tediously on one topic. Cf. chip. "You are always chowing about something." (music halls.)

chronicle play. A historical drama, or one written round a well known personality of historical interest. E.g. *St. Joan* by George Bernard Shaw. Daviot's *Richard of Bordeaux*, and the Shakespeare "King" plays.

chucker out. A strongly built commissionaire whose function is the eviction of unruly barrackers, or any members of the audience whose conduct creates a disturbance and who refuse to leave when requested. In U. S., *bouncer*.

circle. The dress, or upper circle.

circle front spot. A caged spotlight in front of the dress circle. Cf. BALCONY FRONT SPOT.

circlers. Patrons of the dress, or upper circle. (obsolete.)

circuit. A section of footlights or any electrical circuit used in the lighting plot. "Check your white circuit, Electrics!" (Brit.)

civic theatre. One run by a town corporation and supported by local citizens.

Clapham junction. (Brit.) The criss-cross lines on the face of a character actor who specialises in "old man" parts. Reminiscent of the multiplicity of railway lines at this famous London junction on the Southern section of the British Railways. Cf. CHARACTER LINES.

claque. A bunch of hired applauders. From the French verb *claquer*, to clap. Echoic of the sound.

claqueur. A member of a CLAQUE.

classic drama. The Greek or Latin plays. They are performed mostly in translation.

clean. (Of comedians and lines) Free from anything to which an audience could take exception, "good clean fun."

clean comic. A comedian who does not rely upon "blue" material for his laughs.

clear. Do not confuse with STRIKE q.v.

clear please! The Stage Director's order to those who are not "discovered" on the stage when he rings up the curtain on the act. All people who "clear" take up positions off-stage for their entrances when cued.

clearer. A Property Master's assistant whose job is to *clear* the stage props before a scene is struck at the fall of the curtain. He takes the properties into the *Prop-room* and brings on those used in the next act. See entry at DEAD.

clearing stick. A very long pole used for clearing borders that foul the battens, or get caught up in a line during a change of scenery. The situation is controlled from the stage. Cf. LONG-ARM.

cleat. A wooden, or iron, piece at the top of a flat over which a line is thrown when setting a scene. 2. To join flats. A line is thrown over the cleat and the flats drawn close together and the line made fast on the tie-off screw. See the general entry at FLAT.

cloak and sword drama. A romantic play in the manner of Anthony Hope's *The Prisoner of Zenda* or Alexander Dumas' *The Three Musketeers*. Plays with a "swagger and dagger" element.

cloths. There are many, from the stage-cloth that covers the bare boards of the stage itself to the several painted cloths that, suspended from battens, are dropped as required by the scene plot. The types of cloth used in the theater will be mentioned throughout this glossary. See STAGE CLOTH; CEILING CLOTH; CUT CLOTH; BACK CLOTH; etc. In U. S. term *drop* refers to non-rigid scenery suspended from battens and raised and lowered as required by the scene plot.

clou. The pivot of the play. It is in its relation to a drama, what the Greeks termed the *omphalos ges*, or navel of the earth. "But you can't drop that scene, it's the clou of the whole thing." (From the French.)

clove hitch. This "knot" is used for tying battens to hanging cloths. It makes "assurance doubly sure" if a seamanlike rolling hitch is substituted. Both, however, are very efficient.

clown. A comedian, or buffoon in a pantomime, or circus. From the Old Norse *klunni*, clumsy, loutish (fellow). The word is cognate with the Danish *kluntet*, clumsy, maladroit.

Cocky. (Brit.) The late Sir Charles B. Cochran, specialist in musical comedy production on the grand scale, and connoisseur, par excellence, of pretty girls, who were known as "Mr. Cochran's Young Ladies." Sir Charles' productions were a feature of English theater life from the 1920s—the era of the "bright young people" (some of whom, by the way, are scintillating still)—to the sober 1940s. The music of Noel Coward and Vivian Ellis was popularized through these shows, the best known being: *This Year of Grace; Bitter Sweet; Bless the Bride, Castles in the Air,* and *Big Ben.* "Cocky" has been called the Ziegfeld of the English theater.

cocoa butter. Is an efficient grease paint remover, and, according to the testimony of "old Pros," good for restoring the hair.

cocoa nut shells. Produce a very realistic effect of horse's hooves. The cocoa nut is sawn in the middle, and the two halves knocked against the stage wall to create the clip-clop sound.

cod. (Brit.) To chaff, "rag," hoax, "pull someone's leg" or to fool a fellow artist. The verb is perhaps connected with the printing trade term *cod*, a fool, and may ultimately derive from the ancient tavern game *Cod*dem, a "guess" contest similar to *bluff* or *brag*, popular in America.

cod version. (Brit.) A burlesque of a well known play.

coda, tap for. The Musical Director on receiving the signal from the stage manager that the curtain is ready to go up, gives two sharp taps on his desk to indicate that the music must end on a coda. 2. Artists are said to *tap for the coda* if their conduct is likely to lead to their being sacked. "That will tap his coda, he was a fool to answer back like that." (Musical comedy term.) *Coda* is Italian for a tail, or tail piece. A short movement that brings a piece of music to a close. A *codetta* is a short coda.

collar work. (Brit.) (Of performances) Striving hard to get one's lines across (the footlights) to a dull, or unresponsive audience. Plugging "gag-lines," or over-acting comic business to gain legitimate laughter. The reference is to the draught horse's collar. "We managed to get the show over but it was collar work all the way."

College show. A musical comedy, play, or revue, usually written and produced by students and often dealing with (American) College life. E.g. the popular *College Rhythm*, in the 1920s, which featured that memorable number "The Varsity Drag." This term must not be confused with a *Campus play* which is a performance by members of the College dramatic society at an American University. *Campus Theater* is generic for all such productions.

Colly. (Brit.) Short for the London Coliseum, the popular variety theater in St. Martin's Lane. Such hypocorisms are common in the theater, e.g. *Pally* for Palace, the *Ally Pally*, Alexandra Palace, a one-time theater, and now the television center of the British Broadcasting Company. *Philly* is the American touring actor's pet-name for Philadelphia. 2. Short for *Columbine* (pantomime artists of the old school).

coloratura. May be described as vocal versatility. Wyld defines it as "florid variations in singing." The Italian meaning is *the art of coloring*, which is of great importance in the rendering of *Da Capa* arias in opera.

color circuit. A circuit of white, amber, blue, or pink "mediums." When colors are unevenly distributed in the footlights one color may invade the circuit of another medium: "Put a couple of ambers in the white circuit."

combination. A *road combination* or touring variety show.

combined chat. (Brit.) A bed-sitting room known in the Profession as a "combined-room." In the old strolling player's language a *chat* meant much the same as the slang term gadget . . . anything. In low slang, however, a chat is a louse, and these pests are not unknown in combined rooms, though not in the houses recommended by the official apartments list. Cf. CONGEALED and CHATSBY.

combined-room. (Brit.) A bedroom and sitting room "combined." One of the "classic" landlady advertisements ran: "I have vacant for next week a large, comfortable combined-room. Piano and lavatory inside."

come back. A successful return to the stage by a "retired" star. One of the notable *come backs* of recent times was that of Gloria Swanson, the screen actress of "silent days" who gave a brilliant performance in the film, *Sunset Boulevard.*

come down from the flies. (Brit.) Corresponds to "come off it," and is addressed to an actor or actress with a tendency to self-inflation over a minor success.

come on. To make an entrance. Cf. GO OFF. 2 (Brit.) To improve in technique, or ability. "So and So has come on a lot lately."

come to cues. (Brit.) To cut short a story; to "cut the cackle and get to the hosses." A colloquial phrase directed at one fond of long-winded narrative, or garrulously explanatory. "Come to cues, old boy, I'm busy."

comedian. A player of "comic" parts. Specifically the leading droll in revues, musical comedy or pantomime. 2. A writer of comedies.

comedies, light. See LIGHT COMEDIES.

comedienne. A female comedian. A comedy actress.

comedetta. A comedy sketch or one-act farce, as distinct from a three-acter. Italian diminutive *etta*, tiny; little.

comedist. A *writer* of comedies, *not* a comedian.

comedy. A light amusing play dealing with contemporary life and manners, often with a satirical slant, but ending on a "happy" note. From Greek *komos*, revel plus *aedein*, to sing. See COSTUME COMEDY and cf. FARCE.

comedy is a serious business. This paradoxical statement should be regarded as extremely important, for comedy is far more difficult than "straight" acting. So much depends on an actor's experience, and sense of humor. Perfect timing, subtle intonation, "telling" facial expressions, and quick reactions—especially in farce—are essential to successful comedy acting. And the old actor who told the tyro that "you can play the fool as much as you like in drama, but *comedy is a serious business*" gave very sage counsel. Serious study has to be given to a comedy part at rehearsal; once the play is produced, and an actor has the "feel" of his part, he can allow himself a little licence.

comedy of manners. A "Society" play in which witty dialogue, and a sophisticated atmosphere prevail throughout. E.g. Wilde's *Lady Windermere's Fan*, Frederick Lonsdale's *On Approval*, T. S. Eliot's *The Cocktail Party*. Cf. CUP AND SAUCER COMEDY.

comer. A play or performer showing signs of "coming on" or being successful.

comic relief. Amusing lines or business which relieve the tension in drama.

Command performance. A play performed at the command of the Royal Family.

commercial play. One written *ad captandum vulgus*, and solely to make money. It has no pretentions to artistry.

commonwealth, on a. (Brit.) A company that acts in a play whose success seems doubtful. The players agree to act for a *pro rata* share-out in the takings after the running expenses have been met. Cf. *twofers*. In U. S. with the permission of Actors' Equity, casts of ailing productions may take cuts in salary to reduce running expenses and stave off closing.

community theater. A non-profit-making theater run by a group, which either for propagandist or tendentious reasons, presents plays. For an interesting discussion of the possibilities of community theater in America see pp. 416–421, *The Stage is Set*, Lee Simonson, Harcourt, Brace and Co., N. Y., 1932.

compère. A revue, cabaret, or concert commentator.

complimentary. A *benefit performance*. The proceeds are presented as a compliment to the actor in whose favor the show is given (American, obsolescent). 2. A free (complimentary) ticket granted by the management. In the plural, tickets distributed to local tradespeople who display advertising matter. They are entitled to free seats.

concert batten. No. 1 lighting batten used for illuminating the stage at rehearsals, etc.

conflict. The basic element that determines the action in a drama. Opposing forces that bring about the crisis.

congealed. (Brit.) A combined-room. "What are your digs like this week?" "Not too bad old boy, I've got a *congealed* which is quite satisfactory" (jocular).

connector box. A box containing several connectors for circuits.

connector, slip. A male or female plug which terminates a flexible cable for connecting.

connectors. Accessories used for connecting one electric circuit to another.

console. "A mobile remote control for stage lighting, resembling, and using, certain of the accessories of the Cinema organ, e.g. stop keys, keys, pistons, pedals, etc. It is suitable for installation in the auditorium or other places in view of the stage" (Strand Electric Company's glossary).

contortionist. An acrobat who is capable of twisting (Latin *torquere*) his body into any number of unnatural postures.

contract. An agreement between the management of a theater and the performer engaged to play a part, or otherwise perform in the theater.

contralto. The lowest of the female voices between F or G below middle C., to E or F, two octaves above those notes.

conversation piece. A dialogue play or other than one of action and excitement. E.g. the plays of Frederick Lonsdale, Oscar Wilde, George Bernard Shaw and, recently, T. S. Eliot's *The Cocktail Party*.

coon. A negro minstrel or one who "goes into black face" for such a part. Cf. the American slang *coon*, a Negro. Coon is aphetic for *raccoon*, or *racoon*, a North American Indian word. The term *coon* is also applied to anyone with a droll disposition. One who is "the life and soul of the party."

cop big. (Brit.) To catch (cop) public favor in a big way. "The new musical has copped big and will probably have a long run." The verb is a North Country broadening of the Old French *caper*, to seize, capture, catch. Cf. the slang phrase "You'll cop it if you don't behave yourself" addressed to unruly children several times a day in English towns in the midlands and the northern counties.

cop the curtain. (Brit.) To take an unusual number of curtain calls at the end of a play.

copper toe. A sheet of copper at the base of a flat to facilitate its "running" and to protect the flat.

coppers, play to. (Brit.) To do very poor business, the cheap seats only being occupied. A reference to the old 4d gallery.

'core. Is aphetic for ENCORE.

cork opera. A minstrel show. From the burnt cork used for blackening the face.

corner, the. *The* Prompt *Corner.* "I hope there'll be somebody in the *corner* during my scene in the third act, I'm a bit shakey in that big speech." In the corner is kept the Prompt Book.

corner boys. See END MEN.

corny. Outmoded allusions or feeble "gags." Either from the rural sense, or the Latin *corneus*, hard as a corn, horny. Such humor being hard to take. "What a show, the corniest gags, and not a titter from the house." Cf. CAST IRON COMIC.

corps de ballet. The dancers in a ballet company.

corpse. To render a fellow performer's speech, or actions, ineffective (dead) by clumsily cutting in on them. Cf. KILL A ROUND. 2. To forget one's lines. To "go dead."

corpse a laugh. The American shape of KILL A LAUGH.

corridor. Literally a cloth painted to represent a corridor in a house. In the days of elaborate drama with many changes of scenes, a corridor served as a front cloth and was hung about six feet from the footlights. See FRONT CLOTH SCENE.

coryphée. The principal dancer in a *corps de ballet*. From the Greek *koruphaeus*, leader (of a chorus in tragedy).

Cosi. The operatic artist's shortening of *Cosi Fan Tutte* by Mozart who wrote the opera while musician to the Emperor Joseph II, at whose bidding he composed the work. This opera is a great favorite at opera festivals.

costume comedy. The plays by Richard Brinsley Sheridan (1751–1816) whose *The Rivals* and *The School for Scandal* have delighted generations of playgoers, as well as actors, for what acting parts are Charles and Joseph Surface, Sir Peter Teasle and Lady Teasle, the egregious Mrs. Malaprop, the foppish Fag (the first part of many now famous actors), Lady Sneerwell, and the host of smaller parts that were so well worth playing in one's stage apprenticeship. The Compton Comedy Company used to tour the Old English Comedies in the provinces until the company broke up in 1924, and how well they performed these plays, especially Goldsmith's *She Stoops to Conquer*. The compiler of this glossary had the honor to serve a short period of his apprenticeship during this last tour of the company, which was founded by that fine actor, Edward Compton, father of the brilliant actress Fay Compton, and that craftsman of letters, Compton Mackenzie, whose play: *The Man in Grey* (adapted from his first novel *The Passionate Elopement*) was in the company's repertoire. Although the term "costume comedy" referred in the main to the "periwig and ruffle" plays, it covers all comedies in which other than modern dress is worn.

costume plot. A list of the cast in a play and the costumes worn by each individual character in every act or scene.

cottage, the. (Brit.) The lavatory (touring actors' slang).

cotton. See SUPERSTITIONS.

cough and a spit. A very small character part. More often this is known as TWO LINES AND A SPIT.

counterweight system. In modern theaters this system has done away with much of the "pully-hauly" work, and simplified the flying of cloths (drops) and scenery. One stagehand is now able to do the work of several. The weight of the scenery is counterbalanced by weights which are added or removed as needed.

country, the. Anywhere out of London, specifically the provincial towns. "The show went well in town but we caught a cold in the country." In U. S., *The road*. Rural summer theaters are known generally as the *Citronella Circuit*.

coup de theatre. A play that is an immediate success and will be certain of a long run. Literally a *theater stroke* (of luck).

couranne. (Brit.) A five shilling (crown) piece. Obsolete.

Court, the. (Brit.) The old Court Theatre, Sloane Square, London, the home of naturalistic acting in the 1890s. The first plays of G. B. Shaw, Ibsen, Chekov and others were first presented here under Harley Granville-Barker's management.

courtesy of the house. The granting of free admission to a professional artist, or playwright.

cover. To understudy a part. An actor may be engaged solely to understudy a leading role. Frequently, however, players of the subsidiary parts cover the more important characters. A *general understudy* (often the Stage Manager) covers most parts after the leading role, who is usually in a class by himself and requires an actor of similar appearance and technique to cover him. In U. S. the stage manager of Equity productions is not permitted to understudy, although his assistant may do so.

covered way. (Brit.) The *foyer* at the Glyndebourne Opera House, Sussex, where fame and fashion congregate during the Mozart Festival in high summer. See GLYNDEBOURNE OPERA.

Columbus circle. Cf. BALLOON TIRE.

C.P. (Brit.) *C*oncert *P*arty. "What are *you* doing this summer?" "I've just fixed for C.P. at Margate."

crab. To pull (claw) a play to pieces; adversely criticize; to disparage generally. 2. To spoil an act by clowning or otherwise distracting the audience's attention from a fellow artist's lines, or song (music hall). The term probably has its origin in the Low German *krabben,* to scratch or claw.

cradle. A kind of "bo'sun's chair" used for men working in positions above the stage which cannot be reached by ladder. It consists of a board with rope supports suspended from the GRID.

crash. *Any* "crash" effect. Splintering glass is known as a *glass crash* and is a bucket full of broken glass poured into an empty one. A door *slam* is a *door crash*; breaking crockery is a *China crash,* etc.

create (a part). To be the first to enact a role. To bring a character to life from the typescript part, as distinct from taking a part in a touring production, in which a player slavishly follows the pattern produced by the original actor who *created* the role in Town.

credit list. The list of acknowledgments of indebtedness to firms who have lent articles of furniture, stage properties, lighting equipment, costumes, etc., to dress the stage.

credits. The CREDIT LIST. 2. Previous accomplishments of an artist as listed in the program.

crepe hair. Is used for stage beards. Hence *crepe hair part,* one needing a beard.

Crewed. (Brit.) Stranded on Crewe railway station in Cheshire, the famous junction where theatrical companies spent many hours waiting for trains on (usually wet) Sundays. A dismal station. Cf. FISH AND ACTORS.

Cri. (Brit.) Short for the *Cri*terion Theatre, Piccadilly Circus, London (artists' colloquial).

cricks. The critics. An American contraction of which *crix* is a variant. *Pix crix*, a motion picture critic.

crime play. A "thriller" featuring murder, theft, or crime generally.

crisis. The turning point in a play or drama.

crit. Short for *crit*ique, or a "notice" of a new play.

Critics Circle. (Brit.) Was founded in May, 1913, to promote the art of criticism, to foster and safeguard the professional interests of the members and to provide social intercourse among them. The headquarters were at the Hall of the Institute of Journalism, London, E.C.4. American equivalent is the New York Drama Critics Circle.

crossfire. The rapid cross-talk of two comedians. They fire wisecracks at each other.

crossing of the stage. Is not permitted to visitors, or guests of actors unless formal permission has been obtained from the stage manager. Crossing, of course, when the curtain has fallen.

cross-talk comedian. A COMIC and his FEED in a vaudeville turn.

crossover beard. A disguise for an actor who doubles parts. From its use by actors to cross the stage for an entrance from the other side, when no backstage *crossover* existed.

crowd. A theatrical company: "I was on tour with a Shakespearean crowd last summer." (Brit.) 2. Supernumeries engaged for "crowd" scenes in a theater or film studio. 3. The audience: "Did you ever play to a dimmer crowd?"

Crummles. A HAM actor. After Vincent Crummles, a noted theatrical figure in Charles Dickens' *Nicholas Nickleby*.

crux. The problem (in a play). Latin for cross.

cue. The last line of a speech which gives the next player the signal to speak. Either from the French *queue* the tail (of a speech) or the Latin *quando*, when (to speak) or COME IN. Hence ENTRANCE CUE.

cue biter. One addicted to the evil practice of biting cues. See BITE CUES.

cue bound. An actor who is unable to continue a stage conversation unless he receives the exact (verbatim) cue as written in the 'script. Some players become cue bound as an excuse for having forgotten their lines. "I didn't get the right cue."

cue, curtain. See CURTAIN CUE.

cue despiser. One who speaks his lines irrespective of cues thus ruining others' speeches.

cue lines. Those lines upon which one takes up cues. 2. The electric cables leading from the stage manager's cue board to the various parts of the stage where sound, or other effects are carried out.

cue list. A special list of cues (apart from the actual plot) kept by stage managers, electricians, property men and others who are concerned with the carrying out of effects.

cue, miss a. To be late for a stage entrance, or not to hear a spoken cue on the stage. Colloquially, to miss the point of a story.

cue sheet. A list of cues used for effects, lighting, etc. Cf. PLOT.

cue struck. A player who has to be given the exact word is so described. Cf. CUE BOUND.

cues, pick up. See PICK UP CUES.

cued. Past participle; given the cue for entrance (of an orchestra, the cue to begin playing). "The band has been cued."

culmination. The coming to a climax in a drama. From the Latin *culmen*, summit.

cup and saucer comedy/or drama. One performed in a drawing room setting. A "Society play." Tea is usually served in one of the acts. The term is obsolete and has been superseded by *cocktail drama*.

curtain cue. The lines or business which bring down the curtain. Cf. TAG.

curtain, fake. See FAKE A CURTAIN.

curtain, good. See GOOD CURTAIN.

curtain music. A few bars played after the entr'acte music to create an atmosphere before the rise of the curtain on the next act. This music is usually played after the lowering of the house lights.

curtain quick/slow. According to the atmosphere, or tension in a play the curtain falls either quickly (as in farce) or slowly where there is a dramatic PICTURE at the end of a scene.

curtain raiser. A one-act play lasting about half an hour. E.g. J. M. Barrie's *Shall We Join the Ladies?* It usually precedes a play that falls short of the customary length. Cf. LEVER DE RIDEAU, an opening piece, and ONE-ACTER.

curtain speech. Words spoken by a leading player after receiving an ovation. 2. A long speech in a play that "brings down the curtain" at the end of an act or play. 3. A prologue as in E.g. *Edward My Son*. 4. In weekly repertory companies a short speech that advertises the following week's production (Brit.).

curtain-taker. A conceited leading lady, or leading man. Fond of taking calls and making curtain speeches.

curved backcloth. Is sometimes used as a substitute for a cyclorama to give an illusion of distance which it can do most effectively if cleverly lit. See CYCLORAMA.

customers. (Brit.) The music hall comedian's term for his audience. "Now, listen, customers" is a favorite gambit with provincial "comics" in touring revues.

cut cloth. A cloth forming the background scene may have a doorway or window space in front of which an actual door, or window, piece is set.

cut in. To cut into a fellow actor's speech by anticipating a cue, thus killing the efficacy of his lines.

cut out. To eliminate risqué or offensive lines in the 'script. To remove "gags" that have misfired on trial. 2. To omit a speech or line and so occasion a DRY-UP.

cut-out piece. See PROFILE.

cyclo. = CYKE = CYCLORAMA.

cyclorama. A permanent cyclorama is a domed wall at the back of the stage but few theaters are fitted with them, so a curved backcloth is substituted. The main object of a cyclorama is to give depth or distance which can be very well produced by means of skillful lighting, and the use of CUT-OUTS, GROUND ROWS, and CUT CLOTHS lowered in front of the cyclorama. Plastic models have become very effective lately, especially in PANTOMIMES (Brit.). They can represent trees, balconies, chimney pots, eaves of houses, even hay stacks made to scale in relation to the distance suggested by the director. Set in front of the "cyke" these props are extremely realistic. Deriving from the Greek *kuklos*, a circle, and *horama*, sight, the cyclorama came to the English theater from Germany in 1913.

cyke. Short for CYCLORAMA.

D

Da Capo aria. Also known as the *grand aria*, is one in which the first subject is followed by another contrasting with it in mood and treatment, after which the first is repeated (operatic).

daddy. The man who plays "elderly" comedy parts in a repertory company. The jovial, rich uncle, the comic father, the ingénue's guardian and such roles. 2. The usual nickname of a provincial actor manager who is "daddy" to his company of BOYS AND GIRLS. See SUGAR DADDY.

daisy. The Victorian precursor of the present-day *honey*. The term came to England from the United States about 1880. It was quoted in a newspaper as applied to Wilfred Denver, the hero of the drama, *The Silver King*, and became a synonym for any popular favorite. "Have you seen Edna May in . . . she's an absolute *daisy*."

damager. The manager. He allegedly *damages* the play and the actors' prospects.

dame angle. The feminine angle of a play. Dame being American slang for a woman.

Dame May. The late Dame May Whitty, the English actress who did so much for theatrical welfare. She was the first actress to receive the honor of Damehood, and never was an honor more richly deserved. Her early stage career was spent in the company of such great stars as Sir Henry Irving and the Kendals, and of the many memorable parts Dame May created during her long career, perhaps the best known was that of Susan Throstle in Sir James Barrie's evergreen *Quality Street*. But to modern playgoers her New York success as the mother in *Therese Raquin*, and Mrs. Branson in the London production of *Night Must Fall* will be cherished memories. The latter part of Dame May's life was spent in Hollywood where she made films that owe much of their success to her own performances. With her husband, Ben Webster, Dame May worked assiduously to better the lot of the rank and file of the profession, and it was in the Whittys' flat in Bedford Street, Covent Garden, that British Actors' Equity Association was founded, and the dining table, round which many discussions took place, is enshrined in the Council Room at Equity Headquarters in Imperial Buildings, Kingsway, London. Prior to the formation of Equity, Dame May was on the Council of the Actors' Association which died on the inauguration of the new movement. After her death a memorial service was held for Dame May Whitty at St. Paul's Church, Covent Garden.

damn the show, to. (Of critics) To adversely criticize; to SLATE generally. Hence in U. S. a captious critic is known as a *drammer dammer*.

damper. Means the same as the above. The reviewers put the *damper* on the show.

dance director. The official in charge of the dancers in musical comedy productions. He arranges the pattern of the dance and supervises the rehearsals of the dancing ensemble. Cf. CHOREOGRAPHER.

dance interlude. A dancing act put on during an interval in a drama, or a film.

danseur. (Feminine *danseuse*) A stage dancer.

dark. A theater is said to be dark when it is closed pending a new production. There is no front-of-house illumination or sky-signs. "The Playhouse is *dark* until next month so we might be able to have the stage for rehearsals of the Sunday show."

dark blue evening dress. Many leading actors prefer to have their evening suits made of very dark blue material as this color appears black under stage lighting and looks exceptionally smart FROM THE FRONT. There is also a superstition that to wear black on the stage is unlucky.

dashing hero. The leading man in romantic drama. Full of dash and vigor (obsolete). Cf. JUVENILE JOHN.

date. A theater booking. A town on the company's TOUR LIST.

date, pencilled. See PENCILLED DATE.

day of play. Production day, full of FIRST NIGHT NERVES and chaos.

dead. As a verb *dead* is used by stage carpenters and flymen. When adjusting borders to mask light-battens it is necessary for the carpenter, or one of his henchmen, to stand in the auditorium and call instructions to the men on the ropes that support the battens on which the borders are fixed. The men work on the fly-platform and hoist or lower as directed. The battens are supported by a SET OF (three) LINES: short, center, and long, which are rove through blocks (pulleys), and when adjusted the ropes are cleated or *deaded* to the fly-rail. "Up on your long; drop your short slightly; now just a strain on the center line. Right! *dead* it at that."

dead. (noun) An electric circuit which has failed. 2. A piece of furniture or stage property, spot or flood light, sound effect, etc., is said to be *dead* when it is no longer required by the plot. During a change of scenery all *dead* properties are taken to the Property Room unless they are to be resurrected in some later scene. "Put that telephone on the stand-by table, it is *alive* for the last act." 3. Applause is dead when it is not of sufficient strength to warrant a curtain call. 4. In U. S. said of an actor who *muffs* a performance. Also refers to a scene that fails to *come off*.

dead act. = dud act = an act that is bad to the point of insulting an audience.

dead! dead! and never called me mother! Lady Isabel's poignant cry on the death of little Willie in the sentimental play *East Lynn* by Mrs. Henry Wood. The line is a theatrical classic and much quoted by people outside the profession.

D.B.O. Short for *dead black out*, a direction on the lighting plot. "The act opens in a D.B.O."

dead front board. A stage switchboard having a front panel which conceals the live parts.

dead heads. People on the FREE LIST, e.g. bill displayers. As far as the box office is concerned they are dead.

dead letter perfect. (Of a player in a part) The desideratum at dress rehearsal and, it is hoped, at the opening performance. Cf. WORD PERFECT. *Letter perfect* or *up in the part* are U. S. equivalents.

dead pack. A stack of flats not in use.

dead pan face. Utterly expressionless. Of comedians who perform the craziest antics and crack the craziest gags without a change of expression. Hence a *dead pan singer* who has the same technique. In U. S. also *cold-pan, poker-face,* opposite of *mugging* or *taking it big.*

dead season. The summer season in London or New York, which is said to be *dead* theatrically. Most people are out of town on seaside, or country vacations. Thus, the *off season.*

dead stick. A situation on the stage where all the performers are unable to continue the dialogue. It is usually caused by a contretemps so dire as to paralyze the cast. A general DRY UP.

dead wood. Unsold theater tickets. Nobody occupies the (wood) seats. Cf. THE WOOD FAMILY.

début. A player's first appearance in public.

decencies. Pads used to conceal outline when wearing costume in e.g. Shakespeare or Old English Comedy (a Victorian term now obsolete).

deck hand. A scene shifter; stagehand. The term is an American one borrowed from the sea, the wooden boards of the stage suggesting the *deck* of a ship. Cf. GRIP HAND.

décor. Scenery and stage decoration generally. Adopted from the French in recent years.

Deli-board. (Brit.) Short for *Deli*color control *board.* See DELICOLOR CONTROLLER, *infra.*

Delicolor Controller. (Brit.) An apparatus that facilitates changes of color in stage lighting. Working on the dimmer principle the color changes can take place at any desired speed. A dial indicating the standard range of color media can be operated by moving a pointer to any color required by the lighting plot, and the master change lever at the side of the Deli-board is operated to merge the colors from the lighting circuits controlled by the unit. By moving the indicator to any color medium, and working the side lever, the controller of the unit can brighten or reduce light, and change any circuits he pleases. Blues in the footlights can be changed to amber, amber to pink, etc., by this simple method. A more technical description of the function of the Delicolor controller can be found in any up-to-date manual on stage lighting. An admirable book is *The Tech-*

nique of Stage Lighting by R. Gillespie Williams (Sir Isaac Pitman & Sons., Ltd., London).

delivery. An actor's stage voice. It is pitched somewhat higher in volume than in conversation off stage in order that it carry to every part of the house. In some theaters there is a soundboard at the back of the auditorium which helps the acoustics, and much use is made of amplifiers in large theaters. But any actor worthy of the name ought to be able to *throw* his voice to any part of the theater without factitious aid, or any strain on the vocal chords. The training in voice production provided by touring repertory companies (especially in Shakespearean productions) cannot be valued too highly. Theaters of every size were visited by these companies and an actor used his voice accordingly.

'delphi, the. (Brit.) Aphetic for the *Adelphi* Theatre, Strand, London, commonly applied to the original Adelphi Theatre of drama fame. See ADELPHI DRAMA.

demet. (Brit.) Cheap material used for window curtains in stage settings.

dent the lid. To applaud vociferously and loudly. The simile comes from the beating of an ash-can lid by street urchins. They dented the lid.

Denville actor. (Brit.) One whose work is exclusively under the management of Alfred Denville in repertory. The Denville stock companies have been an institution in the English provincial theater for many years.

Denville Hall. (Brit.) A hostel for aged actors, founded by Alfred Denville.

deportment. Bearing upon the stage, carriage, movement, repose, etc. Beginners seldom know what to do with their hands and have a tendency to shuffle their feet and hold themselves too stiffly. The old Costume Comedy Companies were excellent schools for deportment. Actors were deprived of that easy way out of the hands difficulty, the trouser pockets. There were no pockets in costume.

deus ex machina. Latin, a god from a machine (crane). An artificial solver of a dramatic problem. The Greeks used to lower a god onto the stage.

DIALOGUE

dialogue. A conversation between two or more persons on the stage. Hence stage conversation generally. The Greek *dialegesthai*, to converse, talk.

diamond horseshoe. The fashionable audience at the first night of the opera season. Their jewels glisten in the horseshoe shaped dress circle.

diction. This term is applied to *language*, not to *speech*, therefore it is incorrect to refer to an actor's diction as being good or bad, when the DELIVERY is what we are trying to criticize. In U. S., dictionaries authorize secondary meaning of diction as *distinctness of utterance; enunciation* in speech and song.

die standing up. To fail to "register" with the audience. To bore them. "So and So is dead standing up, he'll never get over in that part." (American originally but common in the English theater nowadays.)

digger, the. The grave-digger in Hamlet.

digs. (Brit.) Short for *diggings*, or theatrical apartment. The term was born during the "gold rush," the huts being built round the *diggings* of the gold searchers.

digs, fix. (Brit.) See FIX DIGS.

digs quarter. (Brit.) That part of a town where the PRO DIGS are situated. Cf. ROOMS.

dim. To lower the lights on the stage or in the auditorium.

dimmer. The electrician's word for a rheostat or resistance. It reduces the voltage in a circuit and so *dims* the light according to the requirements of the plot. Dimmers vary in type but the commonest in use today employs a moving contact arm which varies the amount of resistance wire in series with a circuit. This type of dimmer is wire wound and can be of the rotary, radial or slider type. The old-fashioned liquid dimmers, though still used in the older theaters, are obsolete. There is also a resistance called a *reactance dimmer* which uses an electronic valve to control the voltage. In U. S. *variable rheostat* continues to be most used (corresponds to British *wire resistance*) dimmer in professional theater.

dimmer board. Self-explanatory.

dinarly. (Brit.) As occasionally heard among "old Pros." It is Parlyaree for money, though more often as *nanty dilarni*, no money, and it is a corruption of the Italian *niente*, nothing and *dinaro*, money. In this sense it means that the ghost has not walked and the speaker is anxiously awaiting TREASURY. See general entry at PARLYAREE.

dinner interval. The long interval for dining at the Glyndebourne Festival of Mozart and Classical Opera. Those who remember the Glyndebourne wines of pre 1939–45 War days are not likely to forget them. These wines were, alas, sold during that disastrous war. The wine list, embellished with appropriate quotations, from the Greek Anthology, was stimulating reading. After the meal guests paraded the exquisite gardens until the bells summoned them to the auditorium. See entry at GLYNDEBOURNE OPERA HOUSE.

dip. A small trap in the stage floor hiding light plugs to which spot, flood, and projector lights are connected. In U. S., *pocket*. 2. A varnish used for coloring, or frosting vacuum-type lamps in the old-type footlights.

dire. (Brit.) The uncomplimentary adjective used by professional artists, to describe a bad performance by a fellow player. The word is traditional.

director. One who superintends the rehearsals of a production and is responsible for its entity. Corresponds to British *producer*, as opposed to the American *producer* who is primarily a *money raiser* and *presents*.

dirty make-up box. See SUPERSTITIONS.

disappearing footlights. Those that sink into a well and are not visible to an audience.

discipline in the theater. Outside the Naval service there is no discipline so necessary—or so strict—as that in the theater, and, in many respects, a theatrical company resembles a ship's company. The maxim "a happy ship is an efficient ship" can be equally applied to a theater, for a well disciplined company is a happy one. Discipline spells efficiency and it is essential, once the curtain has risen on a performance, that the strictest routine is observed by everybody from the star to the callboy. In a ship all live in one hull, as all artists work in one building, and it is incumbent upon each one of the company to take a full share in the success of the production. Loyalty to the management and fellow artists, respect for "seniority" (in experience, or in the literal sense), the recognition that such notices as *Silence*, and *No smoking* mean what they say, and the observance of courtesies (e.g. to the stage staff and the callboy who, if his call is not acknowledged, cannot be held responsible for a missed entrance). Whatever happens the show must go on. Private troubles or grievances are not obtruded in the theater, and players have been known to give flawless performances when extremely ill. To complain is not the "done thing," all that matters is that the production runs as smoothly and efficiently as a well run ship. Punctuality is especially desirable and artists are expected to be on the stage in time for their entrances, or the curtain calls at the end of the play. All these things can be classed as discipline and the more strict the management the better the production. Cf. the SHOW MUST GO ON.

discovered. A single player, or several, on the stage at the rise of the curtain are said to be *discovered*. Cf. AT RISE.

divertissement. Literally, a diversion or interlude, either as a sketch or a short ballet between the acts of a drama.

divine Sarah, the. The great French actress Sarah Bernhardt. (Rosine Bernard, Mme. Demaha, 1845–1923.)

divot. A toupee. From the golf sense. A tuft of hair, on the head, resembling a sliced turf in the grass caused by a bad stroke.

do as Garrick did. The advice given to a disgruntled star who is upset by an adverse Press notice. The great David Garrick is said to have written his own notices.

dock-doors. The doors of a scenery dock, or as it is commonly called, scene-dock.

dock, scene. See SCENE-DOCK.

doctor. To edit a typescript of a play or adapt one for, say, twice-nightly presentation. To make judicious cuts without detracting from the value of the play as a whole. Cf. VET.

dog town. A date where a play is tried on the dog before presentation in the metropolis. A TRY-OUT town.

dog, try it on the. See TRY IT ON THE DOG.

dog's letter. See LITTERA CANINA.

dome. That part of a cyclorama curving over the top of the setting. 2. The position of the front-of-house projectors known as dome spots, or dome arcs. 3. Beerbohm Tree's room in the dome of His Majesty's Theatre. This room is a "show piece" and is surrounded by magnificent tapestries depicting all Shakespeare's characters.

domestic drama. Plays about "ordinary people" ("like you and me"), dealing with every-day situations and problems in the average home. Uncomplex in plot and dialogue. Typical of this type of play is *George and Margaret*, the great success in the London theater just before the Second World War.

dominant lighting. The main lighting on the setting. Cf. SECONDARY LIGHTING.

domino. A false note played on the piano. A *clinker*.

domino thumper. One who plays the piano on the stage as a SINGLE TURN. From the black and white keys.

Don, the. Short for *Don Giovanni*, the opera by Wolfgang Amadeus Mozart (1756–1791). The opera was first performed in 1787 following upon the tremendous sensation of FIGARO.

door slam effect. A heavy piece of wood hinged onto another and dropped at cue. Or a door set in a frame off-stage and slammed at cue.

door space. That in a flat in which a door frame is set.

double. To play two parts, one straight, the other in character and so disguised by a beard, or other effective camouflage. (Of furniture) To use, say, a settee for two scenes by changing the covers. Often a divan can be VAMPED by means of ginger-beer boxes, cushions, and a length of chintz.

double-act. Two vaudeville artists, cross-talk comedians, or singers, e.g. Weber and Fields, Amos 'n' Andy, etc. A *double turn*.

double crown. (Brit.) The most commonly used playbills measuring thirty by twenty inches. The type seen in theater booking agencies, or shop windows.

Doughnut, Bobby. (Brit.) The punning nickname bestowed upon the famous stage and screen star Robert Donat by members of Sir Frank Benson's Shakespearean Company, in which he served his apprenticeship.

downstairs. The ground floor section of the auditorium.

downtowners. Down town theaters. (U. S.)

drag part. The part of a woman played by a man. He *drags* his skirt across the stage—or he did when this term was first coined—in the 1800s. A typical drag part was the lead in *Charley's Aunt*, who wore the bonnet and long skirt of that era. "My dear, he came to the Chelsea Arts (Ball) in *drag!*" The term *drag* is much favored by homosexuals.

drain, go down the. (Of a line or gag) To fall flat, be wasted on a dull audience. "What a house! all the best gags went down the drain." (Music halls.)

drama. A prose or verse composition in dialogue form to be enacted upon the stage. Dramatic art generically.

drama company. A theatrical company playing a repertoire of melodrama, or one touring the traditional drama of the evergreen variety like *East Lynne, Maria Martin, Uncle Tom's Cabin*, et hoc . . . few of these plays are performed to-day.

drama den. (Brit.) A Provincial theater specializing in the presentation of heavy drama. The term is pejoratively used to-day of an old theater where only the poorest companies are booked.

drama house. (Brit.) A more dignified name than the preceding. These theaters in the Number 3 towns employ stock companies to act the time honored plays that were popular at the Adelphi theater in its hayday. The standard of acting is extremely "ham," and the audiences are mainly rustics or artisans. Few such theaters remain since the advent of the talking films.

drama man. (Brit.) A stock company actor. One following the Vincent Crummles tradition.

drama of development. One that starts with its CONFLICT and develops therefrom, as opposed to a drama that leads up to the CRISIS.

dramactor. A contraction of drama actor.

dramagedy. A telescoping of drama and tragedy. A tragic drama.

dramateurs. Amateur actors who perform the old dramas. Cf. SHAMATEURS.

dramatic agent = theatrical agent.

dramatic artist. A fanciful term for an actor or actress.

dramatic critic. A reviewer of plays.

dramatic line. The orthodox principle on which a drama is constructed: the initial incident, rising action, climax, falling action, and denouement, catastrophe, and conclusion.

dramatis personae. Literally the persons in the drama. The cast of a play as it is printed on the program IN ORDER OF APPEARANCE.

dramatist. Originally a writer of *dramas* but now applied to anyone who writes for the theater, though playwright has superseded the term in recent years.

dramatize. To prepare, or adapt, a novel, or other work, for stage presentation. 2. To bring out the dramatic element in a part. To give color to a showy role. Hence *dramatization*.

dramaturge = a playwright.

dramaturgy. The writing and production of dramas. From the Greek *dramatourgos*, drama-working. (drama + *ergein*, to work.)

drame. A French tragic play containing some humor in contrast with the tragic tone.

drammer. Melodrama (actors' jocular usage). Hence the heavy pun *drammertures* applied to amateur dramatic societies attempting such plays.

drapes. Short for *drape*ries, curtains of velvet or fabric used in place of scenery in revues or in repertory productions.

draw. An attraction. "Whatever might be said about this play, Blank will be a *draw*."

draw-name. A box-office name. The player draws the audiences to the theater.

drencher pipe. Is fitted near the top of the safety (fire) curtain and can be turned on in case of fire to flood the IRON and so prevent overheating.

dress, Basil. See BASIL DRESS.

dress circle. The first tier above the pit. So called because patrons holding these seats wear evening dress. In some provincial theaters it is, however, considered ostentatious to do so, and even in the metropolis fewer people are "dressing," which is regrettable.

dress rehearsal. The final rehearsal in costume, with the full stage settings and lighting as will appear at the opening performance. These rehearsals are run through as performances and nobody is pulled up by the director. Criticism is made afterwards. The Stage Manager makes notes of any shortcomings in the lighting, scenery, or make up of the actors. On the following morning the company will be "called" onto the stage to hear the director's comments and suggestions. See IT'LL BE ALL RIGHT ON THE NIGHT.

dress the house. See PAPER THE HOUSE.

dress the part. To wear clothes appropriate to the character.

dress the stage. To decorate the stage in consonance with the period of the play. To fix curtains, carpets, light brackets, chandeliers, etc., and generally furnish the scenes.

dress well on and off. (Brit.) The rider in an advertisement for artists which is often seen in theatrical newspapers. Touring, or resident, repertory companies expect artists to look immaculate on the stage as well as "in the street." The advertisement usually runs: "Wanted artists for Repertory; all lines; dress well on and off." A variant of this requirement is: "Good modern wardrobe essential."

dresser. A male, or female, who assists a leading player during the changes of costume, and generally acts as valet, or maid. 2. A *walker-on* who has a good appearance and is impeccably tailored. He helps to *dress* the stage.

dressing room lawyer. A redresser of the wrongs of others and preventor of his, or her, own. On the analogy of *sea lawyer*, or *barrack room lawyer*. Since the advent of the Actor's Equity Association there has been less abuse of actors' rights, and a clearer understanding as to what constitutes those rights. Still, however, the dressing room lawyer persists in the smaller companies.

dressing room order. When allocating dressing rooms the Stage Manager does so in order of seniority. The principals occupy the rooms nearest the stage and the second leads and supporting cast, on the first and upper landings.

dressing room, star. See STAR DRESSING ROOM.

drinkers save stamps. (Brit.) This warning was sometimes seen in advertisements for stock companies in the Victorian days, and even to-day it is occasionally found. They need not trouble to write.

drop scene. A cloth is *dropped* in front of a setting which has to be struck and changed during the scene that is played in front of the cloth.

dropsy. (Brit.) A gratuity or "tip." From the *dropping* of money into the open palm of the recipient. "We'll have to give out the *dropsy* at the end of the week, the local staff is one of the best we've struck this tour." The term was borrowed from Cockney. 2. Salary (music halls).

drugget. Cocoa matting or an old stair carpet, placed at the back and sides of the stage, behind the setting, to reduce the noise of actors walking during the action of the play. From the French, *droguet*, is cognate with the Dutch *droog*, dry. Ernest Weekley suggests that the term may have applied to material manufactured without water.

drugget pin. A nail with a large brass, flat head to keep druggets in place. It is easily removed.

drum roll. Is used in thrillers in much the same way as curtain music in plays. It creates an eerie atmosphere before the rise of the curtain.

Druriolanus. Drury Lane Theatre, London. From the nickname EMPEROR AUGUSTUS, q.v.

Drury Lane. Is synonymous with heavy drama technique.

dry up. To forget one's lines. 2. To cause others to pause, or otherwise become incapable of speech on the stage by introducing extraneous lines or amusing business. "That new gag of Henry's dried us all up." 3. Noun, a sudden silence following a forgotten speech.

dry-up company. (Brit.) A small touring company under a dubious management. One likely to find itself stranded. Such a one is admirably described by J. B. Priestly in his best-seller *The Good Companions*, and several in the equally readable *Playing to the Gods* by John Drummond, an author who writes with wit on theatrical vicissitudes and customs.

dude. A languid, immaculately clad light-comedian who usually wears a monocle and speaks with a drawl. He acts in the best tradition of the Victorian "silly ass" swell as exemplified in such artists as the late George Grossmith. Though American slang in origin, the term derives from the German *dude*, a fop, an inept person, ultimately from the Low German *dudendop, dudeldop,* or *duden-rop,* a lackadaisical fellow.

dumb it down. To eliminate subtleties and to stress the obvious in dialogue. Generally to broaden a performance and play down to the level of the *dumb* blondes and dim-witted males of a backward audience.

dumb show. Expressive eye-play and gestures in a wordless drama. See MIME and contrast MUSSITATE, and GOLD FISH.

dungeon. The cellar under the stage where are the bandroom, odd store cupboards and the like. It is very gloomy and dark and full of booby-traps for the unwary, for odd pieces of scenery, wardrobe baskets and light cables feeding cues, are strewn about.

duologue. A conversation for two persons. A short sketch so written.

E

early doors (Brit.) Doors leading to the cheaper parts of the house (e.g. the pit and gallery) that are opened earlier than those of the more expensive section of the auditorium.

early doors this way! (Brit.) The direction by the doorkeeper to patrons of the pit and gallery.

eat a play. (Of audience) To appreciate every line or situation. The answer to the artist's prayer. They *eat it up*.

eat the ginger. Play the leading part, or one with good lines and a chance for "showy" acting (American adoption).

eccentric dancer. One who dances in an unnatural and grotesque manner, usually in revues or musical comedy.

ecstasis. A term used in elocution for the pronouncing long of a vowel that should be short. The literal Greek meaning is a stretching out.

Edinburgh Festival. The yearly festival of music and drama in the "Athens of the North." Starting under the artistic management of the Glyndebourne Society the season has become increasingly popular with the years and is the most brilliant assembly in Europe. Much of its success is due to the energetic work of Rudolf Bing, the present manager of the Metropolitan Opera House, New York, and formerly of the Glyndebourne Opera. The finest orchestras under the world's most talented conductors appear at the festival and opera is performed by the Glyndebourne Company under the artistic direction of Fritz Busch and Carl Ebert who have so long been associated with the brilliant productions of Mozart operas. Plays are presented with leading artists at the local theaters and the atmosphere is one of cultural and aesthetic pleasure. Cf. BATH ASSEMBLY.

effects. The NOISES OFF. Door bells, and slams. Street noises, the revving of car engines, horses' hooves, thunder, rain, sea waves over shingle, etc. Many of these effects can be produced on a panatrope, but lots are still used in the old-fashioned way. Disc and slide projectors are used for optical illusions, fireworks are employed for other spectacular effects. Ossidue, the surplus from gold leaf, can be blown into practical fire effects to produce sparks. But there are many ways in which reality can be approximated on the stage and any handbook on stage effects can be consulted. Throughout this glossary such methods are explained in their alphabetical order.

effects man. Is euphemistically known by the title *Effects Director*. He is responsible for all stage illusions and off stage noises, and is often the ingenious inventor of new methods of producing a desired effect. In *The Wrecker*, a successful train wreck thriller of the 1920s there were hundreds of noises and lighting effects plotted, and an effects crew worked almost ceaselessly throughout the play. At the "high spot" when the express thundered past the signal box, twenty men worked the effect under the "baton" of the Effects Director who conducted the noise in the manner of an orchestra. Each man came in "on the beat" and the effect was a masterpiece of concerted action, earning a tremendous round of applause at every performance.

effects projectors. Produce rain, snow, lightning, clouds, sea waves, etc. The stereopticon is especially useful for scenic effects.

e-flat revue. A touring revue of the cheaper sort.

élancé. The darting movement in ballet dancing.

electric lighting. Was first used in the English theater in 1881 at the performance of the Gilbert and Sullivan opera *Patience* at the Savoy Theatre. In U. S., California Theatre, 1879. (See William Winter's *Life of David Belasco*, Moffat Yard and Co., 1918.)

electric sticks = LIGHTNING STICKS.

elevator stage. A lift-operated stage. Cf. SINKS.

elevators. Are placed inside the shoes of short-statured artists to give them height.

elocution. The art of public speaking. It embraces articulation, delivery, intonation, inflection, modulation, pronunciation, tone, pitch, pace and rhythm. To speak effectively on the stage easy movements and correct breathing are essential. From the Latin *eloquor*, to speak out. See EYES LEVEL WITH THE DRESS CIRCLE.

emote. To display *emotion* in a dramatic scene. To TEAR A PASSION TO TATTERS.

Emperor Augustus. (Brit.) The late Sir Augustus Harris, manager of Drury Lane Theatre, London, for many years. Cf. DRURIOLANUS and AUGUSTUS DRURIOLANUS.

enceinte. The enclosure of a theater. "Opinions were divided as to the place in the enceinte of the magnificent theater." From the French *enceindre*, to gird around, enclose (obsolete).

enchainement. A sequence of steps in ballet dancing making up a phase in the dance.

encore. A request for the repetition of a song or sketch. Usually shortened to *'core*. 2. The repetition given in response to the audiences' acclamation. From the French. Cf. BIS.

end men. The two comedians on the flanks of the blackface chorus in a Negro minstrel troupe. Cf. CORNER BOYS.

endearments. *Dear* and *darling*, as forms of address, are common in the theater, no intense feeling being implied.

engagement. The conventional term for a SHOP on the stage. In U. S., a *booking*, *date*.

English Horace, the. Ben Jonson (1572–1637), believed to have been so called by Thomas Dekker, his contemporary. An intimate friend of Shakespeare, Jonson had Horatian wit and his best known play, frequently revived, is *Every Man in His Humour*. Ben Jonson wrote the famous lyric "Drink to Me Only with Thine Eyes."

English Salzburg. John Christie's beautiful Opera House at Glyndebourne, Lewes, in the heart of the Sussex downland. See the entry at GLYNDEBOURNE OPERA.

enunciation. Clarity of utterance and correct pronunciation of words.

en route. (Brit.) A column in *The Stage* newspaper thus headed which gives the whereabouts of all touring companies for the current week and their destination for the following one. E.g. *Kiss Me Kate:* This week, Opera House, Birmingham; next, Pavilion Theatre, Bournemouth. 2. In the general sense, on tour.

E.N.S.A. The short title of the *E*ntertainments *N*ational *S*ervice

Association, a British wartime organization for producing plays and concerts for the armed forces of the Crown. ENSA did a splendid job and found its way into all the theaters of war: in dangerous as well as safe areas. Few units were unvisited by an ENSA company.

ensatainment. Entertainment provided by ENSA. An infelicitous pun with a pejorative implication. See BASIL DRESS.

ensemble. The general PICTURE, the artist in the setting. The assembled company acknowledging the applause at the end of the play. In U. S., the chorus of singing and/or dancing boys and girls.

en sourdine. Music played gently throughout a "love" or other quiet scene. From the French, *muted*.

entr'acte. An interval between the acts.

entr'acte music. That played during the ACT WAIT.

entrance. An old player is seldom said to "come on" the stage but to make an entrance. He usually does this with a flourish and so ensures his welcome ROUND (of applause).

entrance cue. The lines which bring an actor onto the scene. Contrast, however, the SILENT CUE.

entrechat. In ballet, a jump in which the feet change position several times, the heels being struck together.

enunciation. Clarity of utterance and the correct pronunciation of words. The Latin *e*, out, and *nuntiare*, announce.

epilogue. A short poem, or speech, at the end of a play. Greek *epi*, in addition + *legein*, to speak.

Equity. Short for Actors' *Equity* Association, labor union of actors affiliated with American Federation of Labor.

eternity, Hamlet in its. See HAMLET IN ITS ETERNITY.

etiquette. See STAGE ETIQUETTE.

exeunt omnes. The stage direction for *all go out* (Latin). Cf. EXIT.

exit. He, she, or it goes out (theatrically, off the stage). Latin stage directions were common in Classical plays. See OMNES.

exit cue. The line that takes one off. See THAT TAKES ME OFF.

exit lights. Those that, by law, must be kept burning in the auditorium.

exit line. An effective speech or single line that takes a player off the stage.

extravaganza. A fantastic musical show. From the Latin *extra*, outside and *vagari*, wander. To go beyond the orthodox in dramatic or musical productions.

eye black. Mascara used in stage make-up for darkening eye lashes. Cf. HOT BLACK, SPIT BLACK, and WATER BLACK.

eyes level with the dress circle. Is the rule for keeping up the chin and ensuring clarity of speech. There is a tendency with young performers to drop the chin and, in consequence, become inaudible. From the stage the dress circle is exactly level with one's eyes (an old theater rule).

F

Fabulous, the. The name given to the Sadlers Wells Ballet Company during its successful tour of the United States of America in 1951.

factory, the. Artist jocular name for the theater, because of the hard work and general drudgery therein.

fade out. To dim the lights to a dead black out. Cf. D.B.O. and CHECK THE HOUSE.

fake a curtain. To agitate it so as to give the impression to the audience that it is going up for another call. It renews the applause, and the curtain is thus successfully PINCHED.

fall on one's arse. (Brit., of comedians) If every gag fails to raise a laugh, this action will guarantee one.

false calves. Leg padding in an actor's tights to improve the shape. Resorted to by actors in costume plays in which physical defects are mercilessly revealed. In U. S., *symmetricals*.

family box. One reserved for family parties.

family pass. See the following entry.

family ticket. A free admission pass for the entire family.

fan. An enthusiast for the theater, or a particular player. Short for *fan*atic.

fan mail. Letters received by stars from their fans. In the case of a very popular player this mail can be fantastically large and has been known to be delivered in sacks.

farce. Short for farcical comedy which is played at a quicker tempo and on broader lines, than pure comedy. Originally *farce* was that interlude of buffoonery, or patter, "stuffed in" between the acts of a heavy drama. The French verb *farcir* is to stuff (food), from the Latin *farcire*. Modern farce, or broad comedy, is an elaboration of the original sense.

farcette. A short farcical sketch, as a variety turn.

farceur. A jester, buffoon.

fat part. A showy role with plenty of *meaty* lines and good opportunities to shine. A leading artist's dream.

Father of Vaudeville. Olivier Basselin (1400–1450) of Vau de Vire in Normandy. See VAUDEVILLE.

fauteuil. An arm chair. In the plural, the stalls of a theater (French).

feed (or feeder). A comedian's foil. A butt or general target for his gags. A good foil can do much towards making a comedian's reputation. 2. A cable that takes electric current (i.e. *feeds*) to a fixture. 3. A man operating a carbon arc *feeds* it when he closes the electrodes.

feel of the house. Within a few minutes of the rise of the curtain a player has what he calls "the feel of the house." The reception of his first lines will indicate sympathy or otherwise, and he will play his part accordingly. An audience is unpredictable, it will eat out of your hand in one town and be inimical to freezing point in another. The reasons are mental, environmental, and sociological. The injudicious booking that takes a smart, sophisticated comedy to an industrial town where people work hard for their living will hardly spell success. A crude comedy or drama, played in a fashionable provincial theater, will meet with similar treatment from an insulted audience. Such bookings are inevitable where there is a gap in a tour list and the booking is made as a FILL-IN-DATE. Even in metropolitan theaters there is this tendency for audiences to vary in their receptions. "What are they like to-night?" "As hard as nails, you'll have to throw it at 'em." Or the answer may be: "They are lovely, they'll eat anything." A player's performance is greatly affected by this *feel of the house*.

female impersonator. An actor who portrays woman parts. The term is a clumsy one (contrast MALE IMPERSONATOR). After the first World War an all-male concert party, *Splinters* became the rage of the English music halls. The "girls" in the chorus were quite sensational.

festival theater. One devoted to performances of Classical plays, or Opera. E.g. the Shakespeare Memorial Theatre at Stratford-on-Avon. The Malvern Theatre which presented the works of George Bernard Shaw in the summers before 1939.

Festspielhaus. A festival playhouse. E.g. Salzburg, and Bayreuth, which are associated with performances of Mozart, and Wagner, operas. From the German.

festoon. A border of foliage, flowers, etc., used in woodland scenes.

festoon curtain. One that can be looped into one or more folds. It is also known as a SWAG curtain.

Figaro. Short for *The Marriage of Figaro*, the favorite Mozart opera which was produced in the year 1786 and brought Mozart his first success, following a period of acute financial embarrassment. Yet, such was his generosity and improvidence that Mozart died in poverty although he was to make money for others.

figure, the get out. See GET OUT FIGURE, THE.

fillet. The narrow section of the stage floor between the lifts.

fill-in-date. One taken as a *pis aller* when a company is faced with a WEEK OUT.

filly. A member of the dancing troupe. An obsolete Victorian term for a very pretty young girl. Literally, a lively young (female) foal.

filter frame. The frame in front of a magazine compartment footlight into which the gelatines and frosts are fixed.

finale. The end of a performance or piece of music. Italian, from the Low Latin *finalis*, the end.

fine-box. (Brit.) The forfeit-box kept by the stage manager who imposes *fines* for unpunctuality or any infringement of theater discipline. E.g. smoking on the stage at rehearsals, talking loudly in the wings, or generally incurring the censure of the management. The offenders are mulcted of a coin.

fireplace backing. The conventional backing for a stage fireplace, painted according to the type of grate used in the setting.

fireproof. To paint scenery and inflammable furniture, properties, etc., with any efficient fireproofing solution. It is the law of the land that such fireproofing be carried out, and the theater fireman will usually test the scenery by applying a match to the edge of flats. He considers scenery to be fireproofed if his match causes a smoulder. Should a flame result then there is a bad time coming for the stage management, which is responsible for fire precautions. Any properties likely to catch fire must be frequently proofed during the run of a play, also scenery for, after a time, the proofing loses its efficiency.

firing step. (Brit.) A hollowed platform in the flies where the slack of the running gear (ropes) is coiled down. As many flymen are ex-sailors the flies resemble the deck of a sailing ship. Cordage is neatly cheesed (coiled in landlubber English), rope-ends are whipped to prevent fagging, weak strands are efficiently spliced and a general air of shipshapeness prevails in this department of the theater.

first night. The opening night of a play in the metropolis, or a first night performance anywhere, though one usually associates it with a Town production.

first night nerves. Symptoms displayed by all sensitive artists before the rise of the curtain on a first performance. This feeling is not confined to novices but is common to any player worthy of the name. Some of the greatest actors and actresses suffer agonies of apprehension every time they face a first night audience. Cf. BUTTERFLIES IN THE STOMACH.

first night wreckers. (Brit.) A gang of thugs who, in the Victorian era, attended first nights with the deliberate intention of "stopping the show," or, at least, *drying-up* the cast in any way whatever. They cat-called, shouted insulting remarks (some of which were repeated in the Press on the following day and did more to encourage, than suppress, the hooligans) and generally became a serious menace. They were bested in the end by friends of the managements who mingled in the audience and forcibly ejected them.

first-nighter. An enthusiastic playgoer who never misses a first night of a Town production. Cf. GALLERY FIRST-NIGHTERS.

fish and actors. (Brit.) The contemptuous observation made by railway porters at Crewe (or any other big railway junction) when he sees a carriage and truck drawn into a siding. There are few travellers on a Sunday and most of the traffic through the junctions are freighters or slow trains containing theatrical touring companies and fish trucks. Hence the term *fish and actors* (in order of importance).

fish and chip tour. (Brit.) A tour of the small dates (the Number Threes) on a small salary, just enough to enable the players to support life on a diet of fish and chipped potatoes. The term is a jocular prolepsis, for such engagements often turn out far better than anticipated. "I've just been offered a *fish and chip tour* for the Spring." Cf. WOOLWORTH CIRCUIT.

fit-up. (Brit.) A portable theater that is fitted-up in the village green or fair ground. Known as booth theaters or one night stands they were quite common at the turn of the century but few are seen to-day.

fit-up actor. (Brit.) One playing in such a theater.

fit-ups. (Brit.) Small dates where booths are fitted-up for from one to three nights. Cf. ONE NIGHT STAND.

five and nine. (Brit.) The Number Five and Number Nine sticks of grease paint which used to be the standard foundation for a male make-up. Cf. FOUNDATION.

five minutes, please! The call made *five minutes* before Curtain Time.

five positions in ballet dancing. The basic positions of a ballet dancer's feet from which all movements start and in which they end.

fix digs. (Brit.) To obtain apartments in a town. "Have you fixed digs for Blackpool next week?" As a rule theatrical landladies "write in" to a local stage manager who places their communications on the Call Board inside the stagedoor. These letters arrive at the beginning of the week and they state what accommodation is available and the terms. Players who have not already "fixed" can answer such letters as seem reasonable. As a rule such bookings are satisfactory, the "dud" apartments being reported upon to the stage manager who places them on his black list. There is an *official* lodgings list provided by Actor's Equity. See PRO DIGS.

flash powder. A chemical substance through which is passed an electric current producing a flash and a cloud of smoke. Used in plays for explosive effects.

flat. A canvas-fronted unit of scenery usually about eighteen feet high by six feet wide. The vertical sides are called stiles and the cross pieces—set in toggles—the rails. A foot or so from the top of each stile are cleats, and sashes, by means of which flats are joined together to form a setting. When cleated together the lines are made fast to the tie-off screw. To reinforce a setting, braces are fixed behind the flats. 2. Slang for a bad actor. He is as wooden and inanimate as a flat. 3. A listless performance of a play.

flat, door. A door flat has an opening to take a door frame.

flat, French. A large folding flat that, when battened out, forms the back piece of a box-set. This unit can be flown and dropped when needed. Cf. TWO/THREE-FOLD FLAT, infra.

flat-man. A scene-shifter; a *grip*. He runs the flats during the act changes (American).

flat marking. Stencilling markings on the canvas at the back of the flats to facilitate packing. E.g. P.S.I. (Prompt side. Act I), O.P.3.2. (O.P. side. Act 3, scene 2). Flats thus marked can be stacked at the sides of the stage and easily run on to form the settings. In U. S., the designations R., L. (right and left) are used.

flat, two/three-fold. Flats hinged together which can be used either to form the back of a setting, or as a backing piece.

flat, window. A flat with an opening to take a window piece.

flea pit. A small or very old theater reputed to be verminous. Quite often, however, the term is libelous. It is probably a theater that has lost popularity owing to the building of a larger house in the vicinity and has, in consequence, become a second rate date. Cf. BUG HOLE.

flesh diversion. An underdressed revue or cabaret. A LEG SHOW.

flesh pedlar. A theatrical agent. He deals in "bodies" (i.e. actors and actresses).

flies. Platforms which run from the proscenium arch to the back wall of the stage. Here the flymen work on the ropes to hoist or lower the cloth and border battens, and the stage curtain. In old theaters there is only one platform, usually on the Prompt side. 2. In America, the wings.

flies, come down from the. See COME DOWN FROM THE FLIES.

float spot. A spotlight used in the footlights (floats).

floats. Footlights. Originally these were wicks that floated in a trough of tallow. In U. S., *foots*.

flock. A group of people on the stage. Part of a CROWD.

flogger. A canvas strip tied to a pole for dusting flats before painting (scenic artist's term).

flood-bar. Has the same function as a SPOT BAR, q.v.

floor mopper. An acrobatic dancer.

floor stands. Telescopic stands for spot, or flood lights. They are from five to seven feet in height. Tripod stands are also used.

flounce. A line of black painted on the edge of the lower eyelash which helps to accentuate the eye in the glare of the stage lighting. Originally a "Society" term during the Second Empire, it was adopted by the theater with the flounce itself.

fluff. To forget, or stumble over, lines. The term is said to originate in the story of an actor who, after vainly trying to attract the attention of the prompter, called off-stage: "Major MacFluff, where the devil's Major MacFluff!" One waits for a prompt and *fluffs* pending the line. Cf. PONG.

fluffy. Uncertain of one's lines. Anything but DEAD LETTER PERFECT.

Flute, the. The Mozart opera, *Die Zauberfloete* (The Magic Flute), produced in 1791 and still a favorite with opera lovers (opera artists' abbreviation).

fly. To hoist out of sight unwanted borders or cloths.

fly-ladders. Ladders on each side of the stage, behind the proscenium, by which the men reach the fly-platforms. Cf. CATWALK.

flyman, head. The "leading hand" in charge of the flymen.

flymen. Men who work in the flies raising and lowering the battens which support cloths and borders and, when not counterweighted, the stage curtain.

fly-plugs. Light DIPS situated in the fly-floor, used for auxiliary overhead lighting.

fly posting. The illicit posting of playbills, or other advertising matter. It used to be the common practice in the days when fit-up companies flourished. Either from the slang sense of fly, artful, or the literal sense of leaping (flying) over fences to stick bills on barn walls, or outhouses. More probably, however, it may be the pasting of a *fly-sheet* (poster) in any conspicuous position where such advertising is forbidden.

fly rail. The wooden rail that runs along the fly gallery to which the ropes are made fast. The pin-rail.

flyings. Drops and borders, ceilings, flats, etc., that are flyable.

F.O.H. manager. *F*ront *o*f *h*ouse manager. The manager whose job is in front of the curtain as opposed to the Stage Manager whose concern is BACKSTAGE.

F.O.H. staff. *F*ront *o*f *h*ouse workers, e.g. box office keepers, bar tenders, program sellers, ushers, doormen, linkmen and others who work on the auditorium side of the curtain. As distinct from the BACKSTAGE STAFF.

fold. (Of a production) To end its run. To close prematurely.

foliage border = wood border, q.v.

folk play. A Medieval play produced at village festivals.

follow. To keep an artist in a spotlight. 2. A music hall and vaudeville technicality, referring to the *spot* on the *bill.* "We *follow* the dog act."

following. A faithful audience. "The show will do well with Henson in the lead, he has a big following."

foot a flat. To lift a flat that is lying on the stage, one man places his foot on the bottom rail while his mate lifts the top and "walks his hands" until the flat is upright and can be run into the desired position on the stage, or into the scene dock. Cf. WALK HANDS.

footlight Fanny. A girl in the chorus who, in the backrow, thrusts herself to the front.

footlight favorite. A popular player, or entertainer (obsolete).

footlight well. The narrow trough in front of the stage into which the light compartments are fitted.

footlights. The row of lights at the foot of the stage. They are set in compartments which have a reflector. The front of the compartment contains a color frame set in a groove so that the gelatine medium can be fixed according to the colors required by the lighting plot. The footlights are wired in circuits and a different color can be used for each circuit if necessary. They can also be dimmed independently, or controlled from the DELI-BOARD.

foot music. The rhythm of tap-dancing.

foots. Short for footlights. Cf. FLOATS.

Forces' sweetheart. (Brit.) Vera Lynn, the British vaudeville artist and singer was a great favorite with the troops in the 1939–45 war, hence the sobriquet. Miss Lynn traveled extensively in the war zones at home and abroad and never let the troops down when a concert had been promised to them. A good, and popular TROUPER.

fore stage. That portion of the stage that juts out beyond the proscenium arch. Cf. APRON, and BLACK.

fork. The u-shaped bracket that supports a lantern. It can be tilted at any angle.

Fortuny. An Italian system of stage lighting (c. 1902) in which light is thrown upon colored silks which reflect it on to a "sky dome" and from thence to the stage. From its inventor, the Italian designer, Mariano Fortuny.

forty-two weeks in the year. In the "good old days" when, before the advent of the films, touring companies could rely upon forty-two weeks work in a year.

forfeit-box = FINE-BOX.

Forum, the. The local name for the Town Hall in the City of Birmingham, Warwickshire. Concerts are frequently held there and the local people are extremely jealous of this term. "Earl Granville, who was received with most enthusiastic cheers, said: 'I rise a stranger in this famous Town Hall . . .' (cries of No!) . . . 'known in Birmingham, I believe, by a still more classical name'" (The Bright Celebration, Birmingham, in June 1882, quoted by J. Redding Ware).

foundation. Any "basic" make-up. E.g. the combination of Nos. 5 and 9 grease paint which forms a *foundation* for a male make-up. 2. Foundation cream. Nowadays *foundation* is sold in pots, the tint being already blended.

fouetta. A ballet movement consisting of the turn on one leg and a whipping movement of the other. A *multiple fouetta* is a quick repetition of the movement.

foul. A tangled fly rope. "Drop your long line; it's fouled the batten." The line is lowered and cleared.

fourth wall. The space formed by the proscenium arch through which the audience sees the performance. In a BOX SET the back piece and side flats form the other three walls.

foyer. The promenading space in the hall of the theater where people smoke and drink at the adjacent bar and discuss the play. From the French for hearth or home.

frame cloth. A cloth stretched on wood. Cf. PAINT FRAME.

freakery. A "freak" show in vaudeville or in a carnival.

free admission. The complimentary seats granted by the courtesy of the house to members of the theatrical profession and people who advertise the fare. Cf. FREE LIST, COMPLIMENTARIES.

free list = FREE ADMISSION.

free list entirely suspended. (Brit.) When the business is unusually good and the advance bookings preclusive of complimentary tickets, a notice is often displayed saying: "Free List entirely suspended."

French brace. A right-angled, triangular brace attached to a flat or screen. A specially constructed metal weight keeps the brace in position.

French curtains. Fully-swagged curtains.

French's edition. The printed "acting" version of an established success. Such plays are printed with the full stage directions, scene, property, and lighting plots as used in the metropolitan production. They are published by Samuel French, Limited, 26 Southampton Street, London, W.C. 2, and 25 W. 45 Street, New York.

French flat. A folding flat.

French tabs. French *tab*leau curtains, which draw right across the stage from left to right. Also known as TRAVELER CURTAINS.

fret = PROFILE.

from the front. The audience's point of view. For instance a "tired" suit may look extremely smart *from the front* of the house. A speck of dirt on an evening shirt may not be noticed. However there is a regrettable tendency in lazy players to rely too much on this and inexcusably "tatty" garments have been inflicted on the public in provincial towns by repertory artists.

front cloth. A painted cloth, a street scene, garden scene, or any appropriate picture before which a scene is played while the next act is being set behind it. Often in spectacular dramas the scene was played "broad" to disguise the bumps and thuds made by the scene-shifters behind the cloth. Cf. CARPENTER SCENE.

front cloth scene = DROP SCENE.

front, in. *In front* means in the audience; in front of the curtain. "I hear Noel Coward is in front to-night."

front of curtain call. An acknowledgment of the applause taken in front of the TABS, either by a single artist or the entire company.

front of the house. Anywhere in front of the proscenium, the auditorium, foyer, bars, offices, etc. Cf. BACKSTAGE.

front of the house manager = company manager. Cf. RESIDENT MANAGER.

front piece. A piece of false hair stuck on the forehead to cover the receding portions of the natural hair, thus giving the effect of youth. Cf. TOUPEE.

frost. A square of frosted gelatine which is placed in front of a naked lamp to diffuse the light. Frosts soften light and help to eliminate shadows. 2. (Of plays) A failure.

frou frou. The short ballet skirt said to have been originally designed by the great Camargo (1721) who shortened the skirt to enable dancers to jump and beat. Cf. TUTU.

full set. One occupying the entire stage leaving little space at the back for artists to cross or for the staff to stack furniture or flats.

full West End cast. (Brit.) The often mendacious billing of a touring cast. Cf. ALL BROADWAY CAST.

full up. (Of lights) Every light on the plot brought in on cue. E.g. "Full up floats, battens, and spot barrel, perches, and wall sconces."

funny man. A comedian, a term that refers mainly to musical comedy or vaudeville. Cf. COMIC.

funology. Comic entertainment. On the analogy of LEGOLOGY (American).

funster. A variant of funny man. Cf. GAGSTER.

furniture. Is usually hired for the run of a play which, if very successful, is an uneconomical business, for the furniture could be bought for far less than the accumulated hiring fee.

furore. A frenzy of enthusiastic cheering at the end of a play that has gone well. "What a furore there was on the first night of *Oklahoma.*"

fusible link. "A connection that, at high temperatures, melts and causes a skylight to open and creates an outward draught on the stage in case of fire." R. Gillespie Williams: *The Technique of Stage Lighting* (Pitman, London).

fustian. The florid, bombastic, ranting style of play associated with MELODRAMA and FIT-UPS at the beginning of the present century. This form of drama has virtually ceased to exist although the writer remembers seeing a ludicrous and sorry performance in a hall in a picturesque Devonshire village just before the Second World War. Perhaps a few of these companies still exist. John Drummond, the novelist, writes amusingly on these companies in *Playing to the Gods*, a book worth the attention of all theater lovers.

G

gaff. (Brit.) An old term for a portable theater, the name was given to the first Drury Lane Theatre which was erected on the site of a cockpit, the *gaff* being the iron hook with which the cocks were goaded to fight. *Penny gaff* is pejorative for any FIT-UP, or cheap theater. From the original price of admission.

Gaff Street. (Brit.) Shaftesbury Avenue, London, or any street containing a number of theaters.

gaffer. (Brit.) A stage "old man," especially a country yokel. *Gaffer* is rural English dialect for any old man. Probably a contraction of grandfather. 2. An actor who plays in the fit-up theaters, or penny-*gaffs* in which sense it is obsolete in the English theater.

gag. An impromptu line, or piece of business, introduced by a player with the object of raising a laugh, or generally brightening a dull moment. From the rare slang term meaning imposture, a hoax, joke, comic effect generally. The word may have some relationship with the German *geck*, a fool, from which the Scottish dialectal *gegg*, a simpleton, may be derived. 2. In U. S., also, to *hoke,* from *hokum,* nonsense, low comedy material introduced in a play or revue for laughs.

gag show. A crude play having a sketchy plot but no written dialogue. This is provided (i.e. *gagged*) by the company. Usually the leading man has a number of long "set" speeches round which the plot is written and the company back him up, or rather fill in the "breathing pauses."

gagster. One addicted to the introduction of comic business or, in his opinion, amusing lines.

Gaiety girls. (Brit.) Members of the famous George Edwardes's choruses at the Gaiety Theatre, London, in the gay 1890s. Many married into the peerage.

gala performance. (Usually) the last performance of a seaside concert party at the end of the season. The stage and auditorium are decorated and an *en fête* atmosphere prevails. Often this is also a benefit night.

gallery. The highest, and, therefore, the cheapest, seating in the auditorium. In many of the old theaters the seating is extremely uncomfortable for it consists of long backless forms.

gallery check. (Brit.) A metal disc given to patrons in return for payment at the gallery pay box. It is given to the attendant at the door upstairs and returned for checking next morning at the box office.

gallery first nighters. An association of ardent theater lovers who attend all possible first nights and sit in the gallery.

galleryites. Patrons of that part of the house. A loyal, if sometimes noisy, class.

gallery line. A strong, sentimental line of dialogue, pitched in a key likely to reach the back of the gallery and so call forth a round of applause.

gallery, play to the. Act "broad." To be quite blatant in courting the favor of the GALLERYITES (music hall artists' technique).

Gang Show. (Brit.) This, now famous, British Boy Scout revue is a feature of the London theater. It was instituted in 1928 by Ralph Reader, a brilliant producer who writes the "book" and composes the music. The productions are elaborately and expensively staged, and the cast numbers from 100 to 150 boys. There is a freshness and originality about these *Gang Shows* that insure full houses during the fortnight's run. The 1950 performance at the King's Theatre, Hammersmith—the first since the war—packed the theater at every performance, and the teen age House of Commons sketch will be long remembered. In this production 2500 costumes were worn in the various scenes.

garden cloth. A painted cloth (in U. S., *drop*) representing a garden scene. Used for such plays as Shakespeare's *A Midsummer Night's Dream*, or as an exterior backing for French windows of a country house. It can also be a CUT CLOTH (*cut out drop*) in front of a cyclorama.

Garden, the. (Brit.) Short for the Royal Opera House, Covent Garden, the home of Grand Opera in Great Britain. This theater was built in the year 1858 on a site occupied by a theater since 1733.

Garden Party, the. (Brit.) The annual theatrical garden party given by members of the Profession to help swell the funds of theatrical charities.

garland. A border or festoon of foliage, or artificial flowers.

gauze cloth. A net cloth of very fine mesh used for special stage effects. A "gauze" can be plain or painted and, when lit from the front, it has an illusion of solidity. If lit from behind it is transparent and reveals the setting behind the cloth.

G.B.S. The initials of George Bernard Shaw (1856–1950), the Irish playwright, dramatic and music critic, socialist and wit. His early writing career was hard-going, five novels being rejected in four years, though they were all published after he became famous. As literary and art critic his work had a sting that quickly caught the attention of the *cognoscenti,* and his music criticism, written under the pseudonym Corno di Bassetto, was of a stimulating trenchancy. A member of the Fabian Society, Shaw wrote propagandist tracts and was a fervent speaker in the cause. His success, however, began with the publication of *The Perfect Wagnerite,* and *The Quintessence of Ibsenism.* Shaw plays, with their brilliant and provocative prefaces on social, religious and biological themes, became the rage. *Mrs. Warren's Profession* (1893) was banned on the grounds of immorality until 1902, when its production caused a sensation and gave food for much thought. *Candida* (1894) was successfully produced in January, but his great success was the 1902 production of *Man and Superman,* after which any play by G.B.S. was assured of success. *Pygmalion* was the first play to have the adjective *bloody* spoken on the stage (cf. NOT PYGMALION LIKELY), and what a sensation Mrs. Patrick Campbell caused when she said it. Perhaps Shaw's greatest plays were *Back to Methuselah,* and *St. Joan.* Most brilliant was *The Apple Cart,* a satire on dictatorship which was produced in 1929. George Bernard Shaw lived to the age of 93 and, but for the accident that hastened his end, he might have attained his century.

gelatines. Color "mediums" in frames that slide over footlight compartments, or compartment battens (in U. S., *X-rays*) to diffuse light. As supplied by the Strand Electrical & Engineering Company, Ltd., London, the colors are numbered as follows: *White* No. 30, clear; No. 31, light frost; No. 29, heavy frost; *Yellow* No. 50, pale yellow; No. 1, yellow; *Ambers* No. 3, straw; No. 2, light amber; No. 4, medium amber; No. 33, deep amber; No. 8, salmon; *Orange* No. 5, orange; No. 5a, deep orange; *Pinks* No. 51, gold tint; No. 52, pale gold; No. 53, pale salmon; No. 9, middle salmon; No. 7, light rose; No. 54, pale rose; No. 36, pale lavender (also known as "surprise pink"); No. 10, middle rose; No. 11, dark pink; No. 12, deep rose; No. 13, magenta; *Red* No. 6, primary red; No. 14, ruby; No. 26, mauve; No. 25, purple; *Blues* No. 17, steel blue; No. 40, light blue; No. 18, middle blue; No. 32, medium blue; No. 19, dark blue; No. 20, primary blue; No. 15, peacock blue; No. 16, blue-green; *Greens* No. 21; pea-green; No. 22, moss green; No. 23, light green; No. 39, primary green; No. 24, dark green; *Neutral* No. 55, chocolate tint; No. 56, pale chocolate; No. 60, pale grey.

The Centry Lighting, Inc., of U. S. A., produces tints of which the following numbers are obtainable:

1. frost. 2. light flesh pink. 3. flesh pink. 4. medium pink. 5. pink. 6. rose pink. 7. dark rose pink. 8. deep pink. 9. Dubarry pink. 10. light magenta. 11. medium magenta. 12. dark magenta. 13. rose. 14. rose purple. 15. dark rose purple. 16. violet. 17. special lavender. 18. medium lavender. 19. dark lavender. 20. light purple. 21. purple. 22. royal purple. 23. medium purple. 24. dark purple. 25. daylight blue. 26. light sky blue. 27. light blue. 28. light navy blue. 29. special steel blue. 30. light blue special. 31. medium sky blue. 32. medium blue special. 33. medium blue. 34. medium navy blue. 35. dark sky blue. 36. non-fade blue. 37. dark blue. 38. dark navy blue. 39. urban blue. 40. light green blue. 41. moonlight blue. 42. Nile blue. 43. light blue green. 44. medium blue green. 45. blue green. 46. dark blue green. 47. light green. 48. medium green. 49. dark green. 50. light lemon. 51. medium lemon. 52. dark lemon. 53. very light straw. 54. light straw. 55. medium straw. 56. dark straw. 57. light amber. 58. medium amber. 59. amber. 60. dark amber. 61. orange. 62. light scarlet.

GELLIES

63. special light rose. 64. light red. 65. medium scarlet. 66. pink red. 67. fine red. 68. pure red. 69. special chocolate. 70. chocolate. 75. grey.

gellies (pronounced jellies). Short for gelatines.

general understudy. An actor or actress engaged to COVER most parts in the play.

gentlemen supers = WALKING GENTLEMEN. (Brit.) Supernumeraries engaged to *dress* the stage.

gentlemen ushers. (Brit.) Men of good appearance and deportment who act as stewards at a festival Opera House, or similar theatrical function.

George. The traditional nickname for the stage door keeper. In U. S., *Pop.*

George Spelvin. The American WALTER PLINGE and of equally obscure ancestry. Spelvin has the distinction—unique, I imagine —of playing 210 parts (20,000 performances) in a period of three years. This information is owed to a correspondent in *John o' London's Weekly*. Exhaustive research, however, has failed to trace the birth of Spelvin or Plinge as a program name.

Gerald. (Brit.) The late Sir Gerald du Maurier, actor and producer. He was the son of George du Maurier (1834–1896), the pictorial satirist of Punch, and author, and illustrator of the famous novel *Trilby* which was successfully made into a play and provided in *Svengali*, one of the finest acting parts for a leading man. Sir Gerald du Maurier was a master of modern stage technique. His polish, timing, and zest in his work made him the most popular figure on the English stage. His superb performance in *Diplomacy* was one of the finest pieces of acting of the century. But Sir Gerald will best be remembered for his portrayal of the leading characters in "thick ear" plays during the 1920s. His most famous part being that of Drummond in Sapper's popular play *Bulldog Drummond*. Du Maurier was very popular in his profession and he treated star and stagehand with equal courtesy. *Gerald, a Biography*, was written by his daughter Daphne, the popular novelist.

gesture. See CHIRONOMY.

get in, bad. (Brit.) An awkwardly situated scene dock whose doors are at right angles to, say, a narrow passage. It means that the scene shifters have to make a tortuous journey which takes twice as long to dock the flats and baggage.

get in, good. (Brit.) A *good get in* is a theater whose dock doors are in such a position as to make it easy for the scene shifters to run pieces of scenery into the scene dock from the lorry ("Touring carpenters" term).

get in. To get into the cast of a Town production. Also, in a general sense, to get into the right theatrical circles and so become known to influential people who can "pull strings" with managements.

get out figure. The weekly running cost of a touring show. The term has its origin in the figure needed at the box office to enable a company to leave the town without surrendering their baskets and properties. In U. S., the *nut*.

get out. The ability to leave a town with all expenses paid. In the old days of dubious managements it used often to be a serious problem how a company would get out (of the town) after a week's poor business. And it often fell to the cast to accept part salaries in the hope that the money would be made up in the following week. The term is still used jocularly in the modern theater when the house is thin. "Do you think we shall get out this week?"

get out on. The amount of the landlady's bill. "What did you get out on, last week?" (touring artists').

Gibus. (Brit.) A collapsible opera hat that is worn with a tuxedo (dinner jacket) but *never* with "tails." It is named after the inventor.

Gillivan. A *Gil*bert and Sul*livan* opera. An American contraction.

girls, the. Chorus girls in a musical play, or pantomime. The *line* of show girls or dancers.

give it a drink. A cat-call of disapproval directed at a bad singer —or actor.

give me the last line. A request from an actor at rehearsal who has not heard the CUE LINE of the last speech.

give the ticket. (Of managers) To sack an artist. (American) Cf. the English GIVE CARDS (i.e. the unemployment and national health cards which are held by an employer).

ghost walks on Friday, the. In the theater TREASURY (pay day) is on Friday, and this expression has been used for at least a century and has spread to other professions. According to Charles Earle Funk (in *A Hog on Ice*, 1950) it is credited to an actor who, in *Hamlet*, had the part of the ghost of Hamlet's father. According to the story, when Hamlet spoke the lines, "I will watch tonight, perchance t'will walk again," the actor playing the ghost, off stage, shouted back, "I'll be damned if he will unless our salaries are paid."

ghost walked yet, has the? There being, as a rule, no set time for payment of salaries, this is a stock question in the theater on Friday. In some theaters, however, there is a TREASURY CALL, the time being stated on the Call Board. See the entry at TREASURY CALL.

glam. Short for *glam*or. Hence, *glam up*, a variant of *tart up*, to dress up with object of impressing managers or agents (British chorus girls' colloquial).

glass crash. Broken glass poured into an empty bucket makes a startlingly realistic crash. It is used in farces when the comedian is supposed to have fallen through the roof of the greenhouse when escaping out of the bedroom window. Cf. CHINA CRASH.

glass slipper. In the pantomime *Cinderella*, the story of which came to us from the French, an error in translation made the slipper glass, *verre*, whereas the slipper was described as *pantoufle en vair*, a slipper made of fur.

glaze. To give a sheen or gloss finish to a painted surface by spraying on lacquers, varnish or shellac. Metallic powders may be dry-brushed into scenery. See SIZE.

glissade. A sliding step (ballet). From the French, *glisser*, to slide.

gloomy Dane. The part of *Hamlet*, Prince of Denmark. Cf. MOODY DANE.

Glyndebourne Opera House. The unique theater adjoining *Glyndebourne*, the home of Mr. John Christie, near Lewes, Sussex. Now in the twelfth year (1951) it has regained something of the pre-war glamor which characterized the Festivals of Mozart under the brilliant management of Rudolf Bing, the artistic direction of Carl Ebert, and the conductorship of Fritz Busch. Those who remember the pre-war Glyndebourne will regret the passing of many personalities at these superb performances. During the war years Glyndebourne was closed, but reopened in 1946 with a season of Benjamin Britten's *The Rape of Lucretia* given by the British Opera Group, followed in 1947 by a further season and the production of Britten's *Albert Herring*, and several performances of the exquisite *Orfeo* by Gluck, the first hint of a return to the old regime of classical opera. Economic difficulties, and a return to austerity, again closed the Glyndebourne Opera for two years, during which plans were made to revive—when possible—the festivals of Mozart on prewar lines. In 1950 the Opera House reopened with performances staged in the grand manner, and that pleasant institution, the Glyndebourne dinner, was revived. Glyndebourne lovers will miss the debonair figure of Mr. Rudolf Bing, who resigned his management to take over the Metropolitan Opera House, New York.

go. To be successful (of a play): "The show didn't *go* too well last week, but you'll have a more intelligent crowd in front at this place." "We'll have to alter this scene, it doesn't *go* well."

go back on. Repeat speeches at rehearsal. "Go back on those lines, Mr. Plinge, I can't hear you from where I'm standing. Speak up, please!"

go behind. To *go behind* the scenes. Visit friends on the stage. Cf. GO ROUND. In U. S., *go back*.

God bless you both. The ironic aside (*sotto voce*) when a "thin" laugh greets a comedian's best gag. Cf. IT MUST BE THE LANDLADY.

gods, play to the. To court the applause of the gallery patrons by over-acting or addressing "meaty" lines to the upper part of the house.

gods, the. The gallery of the theater, the Olympian heights. "The place was full, we couldn't even find standing room in the gods."

go for. Criticize; attack in the newspapers; disparage; generally to SLATE a performance or player. "The critics went for the show bald-headed."

going up! The final warning from the Stage Manager that he is about to ring up the curtain. Cf. PLACES PLEASE!

go into black face. To enact a role requiring negroid make-up. "I have done everything but *Othello*, and I have no burning desire *to go into black face* and have the stage stolen from me by some young and brilliant Iago." A confession of Sir Laurence Olivier, quoted in Milton Shulman's *How to Become a Celebrity* (Rheinhart & Evans, 1950). In general application, to play the part of a negro minstrel in a concert party or in a music hall act.

goldfish. To make a pretence of singing by *mouthing* sounds in the manner of a goldfish in a bowl. "If you can't sing, goldfish, it'll look the same from the front" (music halls).

gold program. The much coveted gilt program presented to guests at the Glyndebourne Opera at the first two Festivals.

gone dollars, the. A parody on the title of the Gilbert & Sullivan opera *The Gondoliers*. It was coined by John Stetson, the American producer, who put on the opera at a Chicago theater where it did very poor business. He changed the theater billing to *The Gone Dollars* in rueful reference to his losses over the production, and, according to legend, the show began to do well.

go off. To leave the stage at the end of a scene, or to make an exit. Cf. COME ON.

go on for. Play the part one is understudying. "You will have to go on for *George* tonight. Melville has the flu."

go over big. Make a hit, to delight an audience by brilliant acting, singing, or dancing. Cf. SMASH HIT and WOW.

go over bits. Rehearse scraps of dialogue that are apt to cause confusion in a performance. Repetitive cues and the like. The "tricky" monosyllabic speeches that so often trip one up.

go round. To visit an artist in the dressing room. The visitor *goes round* to the stage door from the front of the house. "Come round after the show, my dear." Cf. PASS DOOR.

go up on one's lines. To dry up, balloon, or MAKE AN ASCENSION (American).

good/bad house. A good (i.e. full) or bad (i.e. empty) theater.

good curtain. The ending of a scene or act that has good lines, or a situation that evokes applause.

gram. (Brit.) Short for radio*gram*, or panatrope whereon sound effects are produced, or which may be used in a small theater in place of an orchestra. In U. S., radiogram = radio-phonograph.

grand. (Of artists) Rather UP-STAGE; conceited as a result of a minor success. "So and So has become rather *grand* since he had that notice in the *Telegraph*." "She's too *grand* to know any of her old friends since she got into Town."

Grande dame part. That of a lady of rank and bearing. E.g. the traditional stage duchess.

grand drapery. Velvets at the top and sides of the stage. The top part is known as the *teaser*, the side parts as *tormentors*.

Grand Guignol. Blood-curdling, one-act dramas full of horror and sensationalism. They are an elaboration of the French puppet drama in which *Guignol* was the principal character. The Grand Guignol plays were started in Paris in 1897. There was a season of these dramas at the Little Theatre, Adelphi, London, in the 1920's.

grand old man of the stage. Several popular artists have had the title bestowed upon them, those in the present century being the late George Arliss, Cyril Maude, and the stage and film star, Sir C. Aubrey Smith, all beloved in their profession.

grand opera. Essentially a tragic opera that has no spoken dialogue.

grave trap. The trap door on the stage that is used for the *graveyard* scene in *Hamlet*, and also for the entrance of the *Demon King* in pantomime.

gravy. Easy laughs from a friendly audience. 2. Good lines, or business, in a farce or comedy. In U. S., profit, *easy money*.

grease. Any grease paint foundation, or remover. E.g. Boot's theatrical cold cream, cocoa butter and even Trex, a kind of lard which before the war of 1939–45 was popular with repertory actors. In U. S., cold cream, mineral oil, albalene, etc.

greaseball. An artist who uses an inordinate amount of powder to tone down a heavy (grease paint) make-up (adopted from America).

grease paint. A composition made up in jars, or sticks, used for making-up the face. It is manufactured by several firms, the best known being Leichner. In U. S., Max Factor, Stein, Revlon, etc. An excellent book on the art of make-up is Yoti Lane's

Stage Make-up (Hutchinson's Technical Library, London). 2. Generic for actors and actresses. "There seems to be a lot of *grease paint* in front this afternoon." Cf. PROS.

grease paint Avenue. (Brit.) Brixton, a suburb of London, noted for theatrical lodgings. The abode of music hall artists.

grease paint, the smell of. Has an overpowering attraction for actors, especially those who are out of work. The phrase connotes that nostalgia for the stage felt by all who have worn make-up and acted on the professional stage. Cf. ONCE AN ACTOR, ALWAYS AN ACTOR.

grease rag. A cloth used for removing grease paint.

great B.P. The great *British Public*, as fickle as any public in the world.

great divider. (Brit.) Wrinkles. Cf. CLAPHAM JUNCTION.

great profiles. Those of the late Rudolf Valentino, the film actor; John Barrymore, the Broadway star; and Ivor Novello, the English musical comedy star, composer and impresario.

greedy. Artists are said to be greedy when they seek the center of the stage, or generally draw attention to themselves by such actions as killing fellow artist's laughs, or masking them so that all the limelight is on themselves.

green. The stage. "How long have you been on the green?" (i.e. in the profession). Of the many suggested origins the claim to simple rhyming slang is the most legitimate: greengage = stage. The term is a very old one, used mostly by VAUDEVILLIANS.

green card. An identity card held by a member of E.N.S.A. during World War II. It enabled an artist to move in "closed" areas where entertainments were given to the troops. It also exempted the owners from other forms of national service to which they would otherwise have been directed.

green fat. (Brit.) Jokes and good lines with comic business in an actor's part. Cf. GRAVY.

green lime, please! A melodrama villain indicated his diabolical intentions in the light of a green lime. At rehearsals when mouthing his lines he used to remind the stage manager that he would require the green limelight in that speech, "on the night." The phrase "green lime, please!" is sometimes murmured today when a line savors of melodrama.

green rag. The stage curtain. Cf. GREEN, and RAG (music halls).

green, red and cerise. (Brit.) The color design in the tie worn by members of the Green Room Club. The colors were suggested by the initials G.R.C.

green room. A retiring, or waiting, room at the side of the stage. At one time green rooms were fairly common but few remain today. There is one at the Theatre Royal, Bath, and a very superior one at the Glyndebourne Opera House, and at one or two town theaters. In U. S., obsolescent.

Green Room Club. (Brit.) A theatrical club in the West End of London to which the leading members of the profession belong. In U. S., Lambs and Players are leading New York clubs for professional actors.

green room gossip = STAGE GOSSIP.

Green Room rag. A performance given yearly on a Sunday evening by members of the Green Room Club. It is a light entertainment in aid of charity. *Rag* is English Public School and University slang for a practical joke, a lark, hence its application to a burlesque performance.

green room talk = greenroom gossip = theatrical shop.

Grey Lady, the. (Brit.) The ghost that is said to haunt the backstage of the Theatre Royal, York. See HAUNTED THEATERS.

grimacery. The slang term for facial expression.

grip-hand. An American STAGE-HAND. He *grips* the flats.

grips. Short for the preceding.

grommet. A length of sash line attached to the top of a cloth (drop) to which working lines are made fast.

gross. The *gross* receipts of a performance include all advance bookings and box-office takings. "What did we do gross, tonight?"

ground rent. Is payable to landowners of the ground on which a portable theater, or tent, is erected.

ground row. A piece of scenery representing a bank of grass, a hedge, a low wall, or anything required by the nature of the setting. 2. A row of lights that illumines the foot of a backcloth, or any cloth that needs lighting. 3. A light-trough mounted on a trolley having the same function as sense 2. The trough can also be used vertically to light wings, or backings. In U. S., *horizon strips* or *cyc. foots*.

group. To form supers into symmetrical groups for a stage picture, or to form an effective crowd in a spectacular drama. 2. An assembly so arranged.

G-string. A minute piece of covering worn about the loins of some showgirls in musicals and revues, which can easily be likened to the G-string of a violin.

guide lines. The two perpendicular steel *lines* behind the proscenium which guide the curtain up and down.

H

habit, the theater. That of regular playgoing. "The Jones' seem to have the theater habit this year, they are always gadding somewhere."

hack. A play doctor hired by a repertory company to lick poor plays into actable shape (obsolete).

half, the. The call made by the call-boy *half*-an-hour before the OVERTURE. "Has the half been called?" Cf. QUARTER, FIVE MINUTES, and OVERTURE AND BEGINNERS.

half-crown brigade. (Brit.) Out of work actors who, meeting more prosperous friends and acquaintances, try to borrow *half crowns* from them "for old times sake." In U. S., *moocher, sponge.* Cf. TOUCHER.

half up. Lights checked to half power. When the light plot orders *half up* it usually means that at a cue the lights will come to FULL UP.

halls, the. The vaudeville theaters, as opposed to legitimate houses. Short for *music halls*. Hence, *on the halls*, acting as a variety artist.

ham. As in ham-fatter, connotes inferiority and is used adjectivally for crude technique in acting or production. Several guesses as to the origin of *ham* have been made by eminent professionals but of all the most likely is that the term is short for *ham-fatter*, a crude, rustic (*ham*let) actor. Its origin is said to derive from the old nigger-minstrel sing *The Ham-fat Man* and is of U. S. coinage. A ham-actor is one associated with the fit-up companies. A ham-fatter who used ham fat as a basis for, or the removing of, grease paint make-up.

ham-actor. See HAM, *supra*.

hamartia. The element in a tragic character that causes his misfortune. The Greek meaning is error or sin, and Aristotle held that it was this moral flaw in the character that made the ideal

HAMBONE 96

tragic hero: "a man not pre-eminently virtuous and just whose misfortune is brought upon him not by vice or depravity but by some error (hamartia)" (*Poetics II*).

hambone. An amateur actor.

Hamlet in its eternity. Actors' jocular phrase descriptive of a performance of Shakespeare's *Hamlet* in its *entirety*. It goes on for ever.

hand props. Any properties that the artist carries with him onto the stage. They are usually placed on a STAND-BY TABLE (PROP TABLE) in the wings near the entrance. Literally properties that are *hand*led, as distinct from ornamental props such as vases, pictures, curtains, etc.

hands. Applause. The clapping of the audience's hands. Cf. ROUND.

handline. Any rope used for hauling, or lowering—a curtain, cloth, border, etc.

hardened artery. Broadway, New York, where theaters often have hard-boiled audiences.

hardy perennials. The evergreen Xmas pantomimes, or favorite farces, children's plays and the like. E.g. *Peter Pan, Treasure Island, Toad of Toad Hall, Where the Rainbow Ends, Charley's Aunt,* etc. Their popularity never wanes.

Harlequin. The principal character in the pantomime *Harlequinade*. He is the servant of Pantaloon and in love with Columbine, except to whom he is invisible, as is she to all but him. Harlequin wears a parti-colored costume, a black mask and carries a wand with which he frustrates all interferers with his designs. The name derives from the Low Latin *Harlequinus*, a demon, whence Italian *arlecchino* (Dante has *Alichino*). Doctor Joseph T. Shipley, in his erudite and illuminating *Dictionary of Word Origins* (Philosophical Library, New York, 1945, 2nd edition), suggests Old High German *erle*, sprite plus *König*, king, *harlequin*, king of the sprites.

harlequinade. The old pantomime feature that is seldom seen in modern performances. It was a madcap affair between Harlequin, Columbine, and Pantaloon.

harmonica. A modern application to the mouth organ of a term that was, according to the Anglo-American philologist Logan

Pearsall Smith, coined by Benjamin Franklin, the American statesman and inventor (1706–1790). Perhaps the greatest exponent on the modern harmonica is Larry Adler, who was born in Baltimore in 1914 and won a prize in his teens for harmonica playing. He appeared in the Cochran revue, *Streamline,* in London at the Palace Theatre in 1934 and was a tremendous sensation. Adler remained in England for a number of years, touring the provinces in vaudeville; then he toured the Colonies. On his return to the United States he gave recitals on the harmonica, arranged from music for the violin and oboe. His playing of the oboe part in Mozart's *Oboe Quartet* and, with the violinist, *Bach's Concerto in D Minor,* were remarkable. The original sense of *harmonica,* as coined by Franklin, was a musical glass.

has-been. A supernumerary who might well retort to his detractors that it is better to be a *has been* than a "never was." A facetious critic, reviewing a revival of one of Bernard Shaw's (a noted vegetarian) plays, punned: "Mr. Shaw no longer lives on beans, but has beens."

haunted theaters. Several playhouses are said to possess ghosts. At the Theatre Royal in old York, England, which is built on the site of a monastery, the wraith of a nun appears at intervals, and courageous artists have remained in the theater all night in the hope of seeing this Grey Lady, as she is known by the stage staff. Several London theaters, notably the Adelphi (see entry at ADELPHI DRAMA) and His Majesty's, are credited with ghosts.

have line, to. Possess a graceful figure (obsolescent).

have the needle. To have stage fright which often produces that extremely uncomfortable and irritating sensation known as "pins and needles."

have you fixed? (Brit.) This question may mean: "Have you fixed an engagement?" or "Have you fixed digs?" (touring artists).

he/she can't touch the part. The part is beyond the player's ability. "It was a fine part, but she couldn't touch it."

he/she will be through the back cloth in a minute. Said of a player with a tendency to move up stage with each line he utters.

heavies. Heavy parts.

heavy father. The old-fashioned pater familias of melodrama; the "Roman," unforgiving father, who turned his erring daughter out of doors to "bear her shame alone."

heavy man. An actor who is usually cast for the villain in drama, or the *heavy* (i.e. "Roman") father.

heavy merchant = heavy man.

heavy part. A stage villain in melodrama or dramatic role in a modern play.

heavy woman. Plays parts similar to the heavy man (obsolete).

hick. Connotes rurality. Hence a *hick audience*, a simple, unsophisticated, country crowd. The derivation is obscure, unless it is a shortening of *pohickery*, a native Virginian name of the 17th century, which sense is suggested by Ernest Weekley.

hide away. The American version of a FIT-UP. A date hidden away IN THE LONG GRASS.

high kick. A frill and limb-revealing kick in, say, the CAN CAN dance, or the LINE DANCER in a revue or cabaret.

highlight. A leading role that stands out above the rest of the characters. 2. To give prominence to an artist in the billing or newspaper publicity matter (in U. S., *headline*); a build-up of a show or individual artist. "In spite of the highlighting the piece FLOPPED." 3. In make-up, to accentuate prominent areas (e.g. cheekbones) and thus effectively contrast the shadows or hollows of the face.

high part, the. The gallery, or upper circle (Irish theaters).

High Priest of Music. The "maestro of maestros," Arturo Toscanini, who was for many years conductor of the National Broadcasting Company's orchestra of New York. He achieved fame overnight, at the age of 19, when he deputized for a conductor in Brazil. From that time Toscanini has been a public favorite. He conducted at La Scala Opera House, Milan, and at the Metropolitan Opera House, New York. A dynamic and despotic conductor, Toscanini's word is law and musicians all over the world have testified to the feeling of terror under his baton. Nevertheless, to have been conducted by the maestro is regarded as a badge of honor.

Hipp. (Brit.) Short for the London *Hipp*odrome, Leicester Square, W.C. 2.

Hippodrome corner. That corner of Leicester Square where it meets Charing Cross Road. Cf. POVERTY CORNER.

hit. A success achieved by a play, or the personal triumph of a player. Hence, SMASH HIT, a FURORE. The applause *hits* the roof, or *knocks* the audience. Cf. KNOCK 'EM. In U. S., *wow 'em.*

hit the nut. Do good business, be successful (of an artist). From the hitting of a cocoa nut on the fair ground. See entry at NUT. In U. S., to meet the weekly operating cost of the production.

hit the tanks. Tour the American small towns.

hog the stage. *Steal the limelight.*

hokum. Comic business that never fails to get over, or sentimental dialogue. A trashy plot, melodramatic situation, etc. The Oxford English Dictionary (Supplement) suggests a telescoping of *hocus pocus* and *bunkum.* Perhaps rather the "Latin" neuter of *hocus* (short for *hocus-pocus*). It is American theater slang.

hold (a scene). To keep the stage position at the end of a scene, or act, in order to take a PICTURE call. 2. Hold an audience, keep their attention. Also (of a scene), "You can play it broad enough, it'll hold!"

holdover. A play or movie with an extended run because of good business. Of American origin.

home from home. (Brit.) An actor's expression for some of the digs in which he stays when touring the provinces. Originally the meaning was literal, now it is mostly jocular, and rueful. Theatrical landladies, when advertising their apartments, used to add: *every home comfort,* or *a home from home.* Cf. QUOTH THE RAVEN.

Home of Variety, the. (Brit.) The slogan of the London Palladium, Oxford Street, where the leading *variety* artists appear.

honey. A *sweetie* (short for *sweetie*-pie), a popular person in the theater, or anywhere. "Isn't James Mason (James Stewart, or any other players popular with the women) a honey?" It is also said of a good part: "I've got a honey of a part in next week's show" (female repertory artists).

hoofer. A dancer. Hence *hoofer act*, a dance act, and *hoofers*, a dancing troupe.

horizontal floods. Are used for lighting the CYCLORAMA. Horizon strips.

horizontal line of sight. This is usually marked on the stage and the setting made accordingly. But where no line is shown a careful check for visibility has to be made from the house, especially from the side seats.

horn tower. A portable tower containing a loud speaker unit.

hot-black. An eye-lash cosmetic that has to be heated to produce the EYE-BLACK for *beading* the lashes. A taper, or candle, is used for this purpose.

hot spot. A bright spot in an area of uneven lighting. A pool of light.

house = audience. "What sort of house did you have last night?" 2. The auditorium. 3. The theater. Cf. DRAMA HOUSE.

house! Short for "house-lights," the order from the stage manager to the electrician to black out the house just before the curtain goes up, and to bring them up at the end of an act when the curtain falls. In some theaters, however, there is a bell that communicates with the electricians' perch from the prompt corner.

house author. A play doctor, or playwright, employed by a theater to supply plays or adaptations for presentation in the program provided by the managements. The term is obsolete but was common enough when stock companies flourished at the end of the last century.

house lights. All lights in front of the curtain which are dimmed out during a performance, except those made obligatory by law, such as exit lights over doors, etc.

house, front of the. Any part of the theater in front of the curtain.

house, full. The notice outside a theater when all seats are sold, and there is not even STANDING ROOM.

house full boards. Are placed outside a theater when seats are SOLD OUT.

house seats. Seats withheld by the management for the use of the producer, star and friends.

hunch. (Brit.) To dance (on the stage). From the hunched-backed technique of eccentric dancers, or the Standard English sense of the verb, to arch, bend, or form a hump.

I

Iago. A crafty, deceitful type of person. From the name of the archetype in *Othello* (obsolete). Cf. JOSEPH SURFACE.

Ibsenity. Lines reminiscent of those in Henrik Ibsen's morbid plays.

I had 'em in the aisles. See AISLES.

I knew it in the bath. An actor's jocular lament when he dries up at rehearsals. Like so many stage catch-phrases it is probably true.

illegitimate laughter. That which is not called for by the lines or situation. It is evoked by the overacting of a tense scene, or by out-moded dialogue. In *King Richard the Third*, the solemn line "Bring in the bier" invariably causes a titter. As one of the bearers, the writer took this laugh as an entrance cue. Any reference to *beer* is a sure laugh in the English theater. In a recent revival of Ibsen's *Hedda Gabler,* in London, the *illegitimate laughter* was extremely embarrassing though the performance of Jean Forbes Robertson as Hedda was superb. It was just that the "gloom" was too much for the modern sense of humor to endure. People do not indulge in gloom for its own sake nowadays. But the plays of Ibsen, and Strindberg, have always caused this out-of-place laughter. Cf. IBSENITY.

illusionist. A conjurer; sleight of hand artist.

impersonate. Portray a stage character. Cf. CREATE.

impresario. A promoter of the higher form of entertainment, particularly opera or musical plays. He organizes production, discovers talent wherever it may be, and generally works "for the good of the cause." Frequently he is manager of an important theater. A model impresario is the brilliant, and internationally famous, Rudolf Bing of the Metropolitan Opera House, New York. From the Italian *impresa,* undertaking, enterprise.

impromptu. Extemporaneous lines or business interpolated when an actor has DRIED UP, or a play needs broader technique to get it over to a dull-witted audience. Gagged lines, or an unexpected curtain speech demanded by an enthusiastic audience. The leading player speaks without preparation. In the days of the "gag-shows," and more demonstrative audiences at melodramas, impromptu speeches had no terror for the performers who more often than not gave impromptu performances. See GAG-SHOW.

improvise. See entries at PONG and VAMP.

inaudient. (Of audiences) Those who refuse to listen to the words of a bad play and simply BARRACK or CAT-CALL.

in character. Appropriate to the play and period. Free from anachronism.

independent switch. One operated on its own. A "practical" switch worked by an artist on the setting, as distinct from one that is operated from the electrician's perch off stage. See PRACTICAL.

independents. Light circuits that, by virtue of their functions in the play, have to be operated *independently* of the main lighting group, blackout, and other controls. Each is connected to a separate board.

ingénue. The female juvenile lead; she was originally known as "the singing chambermaid" in the days of melodrama. An old story credited to John Stetson, the American theater manager, and quoted by the author of *Humour in the Theatre*, which must be known to all "pros," is that of his retort to his Stage Manager of whom he had enquired about the progress of a juvenile girl he had engaged for his company. "I think she is a perfect ingénue, sir," answered the S.M. "Oh, *is* she? Then call a rehearsal tomorrow morning and tell her about it."

in production. (Of a play) *In* rehearsal and general preparation for *production*. A DARK theater sometimes has a notice stating that "this theater is closed; a new play is in production."

inset scene. A small setting inside a large one. It is often "flown away" at the end of the scene and dropped for a later one.

interchangeable rep. The system of putting on plays for a fortnight instead of a week. It is common where repertory companies are playing in adjacent towns, or suburbs, the companies playing on the football system of "home, and away." They produce two plays and change theaters at the end of the week's run. Thus, the artists have a fortnight's rehearsal for each play.

intermission = INTERVAL (American), hence INTERMISSION MUSIC = ENTR'ACTE MUSIC.

interpret. To create a part. To interpret the author's "message" through the portrayal of the character. The term is usually in reference to leading roles.

Interval Club. A theatrical residential and social club at 22 Dean Street, Soho, London. It was formed to provide meals and rest to artists during *intervals* in rehearsals or performances. The *residential* address is at 1 Soho Square, London, W. 1.

interval music. The same as ENTR'ACTE MUSIC.

in the long grass. Touring the small town dates which are very much off the beaten track. "We have been in the long grass all the summer." Adopted from the American theater.

intimate revue. A smart, topical revue played in a small (intimate) theater.

intimate theater. A small theater in which the audience is very close to the players. Also a semi-private theater where a type of play suitable for its clientele is usually presented. *Intimate theater*, however, usually refers to a house where revues or "plays of ideas" are presented.

in Town. Acting in a metropolitan theater. "Did she play the part in town or was she engaged for the tour only?"

intrigue. The intricacies or machinations in the plot of a drama. From the Latin *intricare*, to entangle, perplex.

in vaudeville. The American equivalent of being ON THE HALLS.

iron's down, the. (Brit.) Becoming obsolete, this catch-phrase means a bad or unresponsive audience. When the *iron* safety curtain is lowered the audience cannot be heard on the stage.

is it my turn to utter? An exaggeratedly comical catch-phrase meaning "do I speak next?" It is usually said of one who has not been paying attention at rehearsals and is caught "off."

Italian nightingale, the. The late Angelica Catalani. Cf. SWEDISH NIGHTINGALE.

it dries me up! Said of anything that deprives the hearer of speech. It corresponds to "I give up!" "It beats me!" To be too exasperated or annoyed for words. "It dries me up when I think of the terms he offered for the part."

it must be the landlady! An ironical catch-phrase used by actors receiving faint applause on a line that usually gets a good hand (touring artists). Cf. GOD BLESS YOU BOTH.

it wasn't there. A reproof addressed to a stage manager who PINCHES a curtain call on a dead house. The applause wasn't there.

it will hold. A director's phrase addressed to an artist who feels that he has made too lengthy a pause in the dialogue. It means that the audience will not become restive because of it.

it'll be all right on the night. This assuring phrase from an inveterate forgetter of lines has become a theatrical gag. Experience, however, proves that what goes persistently wrong at rehearsals seldom is *all right on the night*.

it'll look well on the train call! In the days when the Sunday trains were full of touring companies and changes *en route* were frequent, the parading of golf clubs, the carrying of fur-collared overcoats, etc., gave an air of opulence to the company, and a harp displayed on the station platform by a musician set a hallmark on a musical comedy troupe. The catch-phrase greeted any request to tour an awkward piece of luggage. "It'll look all right on the train call, I suppose."

J

Jack's come home. A theatrical lodging house (Australian actors'). An adoption of the nautical "Jack's come home from sea; anything'll do for him." The reference is to indifferent rooms.

Jasper. The traditional name for the villain of the piece in melodrama.

jell. Short for jellup, solidify, jellify; hence to get over, to establish one's personality. (Of a play) To cohere, become an entity. "The show was well cast, magnificently mounted and acted, yet it didn't jell."

jeune premier. The juvenile lead. Cf. JUVENILE JOHN, and INGÉNUE.

Joey. The traditional nickname for a clown in pantomime. It commemorates Joseph Grimaldi (1779–1837), the greatest clown in the annals of the stage. Son of Giuseppe Grimaldi, a dancer, and one-time ballet master to David Garrick at Drury Lane Theatre, the boy's childhood was far from happy, for his father was severe to the point of cruelty. Indeed, so ill-tempered was he that his fellow artists nicknamed him *Grim-all-day*. From the age of two, when little Joey made his first public appearance, he accompanied his father on tour and appeared as the cat in pantomime at Drury Lane in 1783, nearly losing his life when he fell down a stage trap onto the stone floor of the cellar beneath. This was followed by an equally narrow and miraculous escape when, playing the part of a monkey, the chain with which his father would swing him around the stage, snapped, hurling young Joey across the footlights to land—luckily for him—onto an obese and shock absorbing gentleman in the pit-stalls. Grimaldi's apprenticeship was hard and penurious, but his talent obtained him pretty regular employment at Drury Lane and the Sadler's Wells theaters. He worked hard and, even at that age, he showed the originality and initiative that were to prove him later to be the greatest artist in his line. At the age of nineteen he married the daughter of one of the proprietors of Sadler's Wells. But poor Joey was destined to be a real life *Punchinello* for, within a year of his marriage, his young wife died, and for some time he despaired of his reason. In fact, the only thing that kept him sane was his work, to which he devoted his mind and energy. His supreme artistry won him the acclaim of London and the provinces. Charles Dickens, the popular novelist of that time, gave an enthusiastic account of the clown and houses were full at every performance. However, in spite of the fame his work brought him, Grimaldi's life was one of sorrow and trouble, and before he reached his fiftieth year he was stricken with an illness that made him a permanent cripple and he was obliged to retire from the stage.

Joseph Grimaldi, name that is still revered, did not live long in retirement; his life came to an end in May, 1837.

jog. A narrow flat used to give an illusion of depth to a wall or other piece of scenery.

jogar. (Brit.) A street-singer, or queue entertainer. From the Italian verb *giocare*, to play, jest, entertain generally. Cf. BUSKER.

John Audley. (Brit.) To conclude; bring (a performance) to a close. The term dates from the 18th century. A manager of a touring company, named Shuter (an appropriate name indeed!), used to spin out a performance until an audience sufficient to fill the theater for a "second house" had gathered, then someone in front of the house would call out: "Is John Audley there?" whereupon the show ended abruptly. Hence, "to come the John Audley" was to "pull a fast one." (Lord John Audley was sentenced to death for cheating in 1631.) Another version of the term is that John Audley was a showman and this signal, "Is John Audley there?" was given by the doorman to indicate that there were enough people outside the theater to fill the house a second time, and the first show ended. In the days of gag shows the performances *could* end any time.

John Scarper. (Brit.) The act of doing a scarper. To leave theatrical apartments without paying the landlady's bill. See PARLYAREE.

Johnny in the stalls. (Brit.) Like the Stagedoor Johnny he haunts theaters where there are plenty of showgirls (obsolete). See STAGEDOOR JOHNNY.

join. Where the flats meet when cleated together. Joins have to be carefully watched as occasionally frames warp through damp, or long storage, and do not join closely. This causes a slight gap through which backing lights are apt to show. 2. Where a wig joins the forehead. Cf. BAD JOIN.

joint. (Brit.) An engagement of a husband and his wife on a *joint* salary. "We have just fixed a joint in concert party." They receive one pay packet.

Jonah. A player who is certain to bring bad luck to a play or members of the company.

Joseph Surface. The name applied to a hypocrite. From the arch hypocrite, Joseph Surface, in Richard Brinsley Sheridan's play *The School for Scandal* (1777). "He is a proper Joseph Surface; I wouldn't trust him if I were you" (old actors, seldom heard in this sense today). Cf. IAGO.

juggler. One specializing in legerdemain; "the quickness of the hand deceives the eye" feats, on the stage. Conjury, ball-tossing, jesting, etc. all come under juggling. From the Latin *joculator*, jester.

juice. Electricity. "These floods simply *eat* the juice" (electrician's).

jump a rail. To place an additional rail on a flat to carry electrical fittings on the painted side. E.g. wall brackets.

jump lines. To speak several lines ahead, thus causing momentary—if not acute—embarrassment to one's fellow actors. A jump often occurs when cues are very much alike, though it happens more in repertory performances than in a "run" of a play. And, having jumped, it is very difficult to go back, especially if it is a big leap ahead. A jump can also cut out an important entrance cue.

juvenile. Short for juvenile lead.

juvenile business. The portrayal of juvenile parts. A juvenile means any age from callow youth to near-forty; and is usually applied to "lovers," or the dashing heroes of "hearty" drama.

juvenile John. The nickname for any juvenile lead. Cf. INGÉNUE.

juvenile lead. A player of standard "young man" parts.

juvenile troupe. (Brit.) Children engaged as dancers for a Christmas pantomime.

K

Kapellmeister. The conductor of an opera orchestra. The literal translation from the German is master of the chapel.

kathakali. Dance drama in the India theater.

keep it clean! A comedian with a tendency to "crack blue gags" is so enjoined when a theater audience is likely to take offense.

keep it down! A request from the stage manager to artists who raise their voices in conversation off-stage while the play is in progress.

keep that in . . . and at the matinee! This greets the introduction of any felicitous gag or business that amused the company at rehearsals, or was tried out successfully during a performance. The rider is employed if the gag is exceptionally brilliant. Cf. THAT'S OUT.

keep to the 'script. To speak according to the book and not introduce extraneous matter for the sake of laughs or effect. To give the exact cues.

Kenny B. (Brit.) The affectionate nickname bestowed on Sir Kenneth Barnes by students of the Royal Academy of Dramatic Art, Gower Street, London, of which Sir Kenneth is President. See RADA and PRADA.

kid show. A performance in which children predominate.

kill a baby. To cut out a *baby* spotlight from the lighting plot.

kill a laugh. To start a fresh line before that laugh evoked by the preceding one has died down. Often this is deliberately done when an actor has been instructed to speed up playing-time. But, as a rule, lines are so well timed in good productions that it is only in case of an inexperienced player that laughs are killed.

kill a round. To deprive a fellow artist of a well deserved *round* of applause by speaking on top of the line that earned it. This is not often done, though a case of extreme professional jealousy, or spite, has been known to kill applause.

kill a shadow. To soften a hard line of spotlight by frosting it, or introducing a floodlight which has much the same effect. See FROST.

killing line. A comedy line (speech) that makes the audience "nearly die with laughing" (Victorian).

Kings, the. (Brit.) The *King's* Theater, anywhere. In London, however, it means the King's Theatre, Hammersmith.

Kirby Flying system, the. A system of weights, pulleys, and ropes invented by one named Kirby to give the illusion of flying. The player is suspended by piano wire of very high tensile strength attached to a specially constructed safety harness.

klunk. To fall heavily on the boards of the stage.

knife. To cut a play. To excise lines that might offend, or to reduce playing-time for a twice-nightly performance. "You surely aren't going to *knife* my part?"; "My dear fellow, I'm going to *carve* it!" The term is obsolescent, but was common in the Victorian era when tedious "wordy" plays were the rule.

knitting. See SUPERSTITIONS.

knock-about act. (Brit.) A tumbling turn, or rough burlesque. The artists *knock* each other *about* during their act.

knock-about drolls = KNOCK-ABOUT COMEDIANS = ATHLETIC DROLLS. (Brit.) Funny acrobats.

knock 'em. (Brit.) A music hall, and Cockney, term for winning an audience. The performance *knocks them* silly. From that great little comedian, Albert Chevalier's famous song: "Knocked 'em in the Old Kent Road." In U. S., wow 'em.

L

lace. To bring two flats close together by lacing the sash-line through a number of screw-eyes in the stiles of the flats. This method is adopted where there is a bad join, and the flats require a stronger lashing than the orthodox method of cleating.

laddy! The Old Pros' mode of address: "Laddy! when I was with Irving at the Lyceum, we used to . . ." In the present century "Old boy!" has superseded "Laddy!" Cf. ACTOR LADDY.

lake liner. A lake-colored lining pencil used to indicate age lines in character-old-man parts (a crimson pigment).

Lancashire comic. A Lancashire comedian who predominates in English touring revues, which usually WORK the North country dates. Their broad humor, accents, and esoteric gags would be lost on most southern audiences, although many such companies appear in this region. But it is in his own territory that the Lancashire comedian is most successful.

land a spot. To obtain an engagement. To land a *spot* of work. Adopted from U. S. Cf. SHOP.

land of promise, the. Hollywood, the goal of the ambitious, and frequently disappointed, stage artist. Although a number of front rank players are successful in their break into pictures, many fall by the wayside.

Lane, the. The famous Drury Lane Theatre, London. Originally built in 1663 and rebuilt in 1812, the history of the theater has been admirably written by that thorough historian of the English theater, Macqueen Pope.

lapse of time curtain. The lowering of the stage curtain for a second or two to denote the passage of time in the action of a play. The house-lights remain dim.

lapsus memoriae. A dry up; literally a lapse of memory (on the stage).

Larry. (Brit.) The nickname of Sir Laurence Olivier, the English stage and film star. Larry is a shortening of Laurence.

La Scala. The famous Opera House in Milan, the mecca of Italian opera. Here the performances have a finesse and *ampleur* that pale emulative productions into insignificance. Toscanini, Bruno Walter, Felix Weingartner and other leading conductors have reigned during the opera seasons here. The operas of Verdi and Puccini are notable performances at La Scala.

last line = TAG. See GIVE ME THE LAST LINE.

last minstrel of the English stage. The dramatist James Shirley (1596–1666). A prolific writer, his most successful plays were: *The Brothers, The Wedding, The Lady of Pleasure, The Cardinal,* and *The Traitor.* With the suppression of the theater, in 1642, James Shirley's fortunes were broken.

latecomers. Those unpunctual and exasperating people whose entrance into the stalls (orchestra) and circle, after the rise of the curtain, is as distracting as it is insulting to the artists on the stage. This discourtesy cannot exist at operatic performances, since such people are not admitted into the auditorium once the curtain has gone up on a scene.

laughter assignment. A comedy part (American colloquialism).

laughter emporium. The American version of the English FUN FACTORY.

laugh line. A good comedy line that never fails to get its laugh.

lay the skid. To sabotage a player's lines, or business, by cutting in before the speech or business is over, thus killing whatever laughter there might be. An act of professional jealousy. The agent of this nefarious business lays the grease on which his victim slips . . . skids. In U. S., *put the skid under.*

lead, play the. Have the leading role. Cf. NAME PART.

lead, the. The star part. The plural is employed when male and female *leads* are of equal importance.

leads, first, second, third. The grades of leading parts.

leading business. Leading parts. An artist advertising for work in a theatrical newspaper often insists on *leading business only.*

leading lady. She who plays the principal part.

leading light. The star artist in an opera, musical comedy, or play. His name leads the rest in the sky-sign.

leading man. The male star-lead, or other leading part.

left. In a stage direction, means the left hand side of the stage facing the audience. The actor's left. In most theaters this is on the PROMPT-SIDE.

leg curtain. Is used to mask the side of the stage. *Legs.*

legit. Short for *legit*imate stage. The orthodox theater as opposed to a music hall, vaudeville and burlesque theaters.

leg mania. Stage-dancing (of stage-struck girls who long to be dancers). In U. S., *legomania*, dance craze.

leg-tosser. A dancer in a stage troupe. Cf. TORSO-TOSSER, and LINE DANCER.

legology. The science of stage dancing (American). On the analogy of FUNOLOGY, sexology, etc. (Jocular.)

Leichner stick. A stick of grease paint manufactured by the firm of Leichner, Ltd., of Acre Lane, Brixton, London, S.W. 2. Leichner is a favorite in the make-up box.

leitmotiv. A leading motive that recurs throughout an opera or musical play, in association with a particular person or situation. The German *leitmotiv*, lead motive. Cf. THEME SONG.

length. A number of lamps fixed on a short wooden batten used to light a backing or, set behind a ground-row, to illumine the bottom of a cloth. For lighting door backings the length is hung on the frame of a flat. In U. S., horizon strips or cyc. foots.

les pointes. The tips of a ballet dancer's toes.

letty (usually in the plural). (Brit.) Lodgings, especially theatrical apartments. The term is obsolete and is a survival of the "rogues and vagabonds" period of theatrical history and derives from the Italian *letto*, a bed, plural *letti*.

lever de rideau. A curtain raiser, a one-acter (French).

libretto. The text of an opera or other extended vocal composition.

lift. To plagiarize, either lines from another play or an artist's line of business. The material is *lifted* out of a work without permission of the holder of copyright.

light check. (Brit.) A dimming of lights. Do not confuse with check lights (to a prescribed degree, on resistance).

light and shade. The niceties of intonation, inflection, modulation, etc., in the reading of a part.

light comedy. Stands between HIGH COMEDY and FARCE. Hence:
light comedian = light comedy actor. One who portrays light-hearted young men in such comedies.
light comedy merchant = LIGHT COMEDIAN. He *sells* comedy.
light rehearsal. This, under the direction of the Stage Director, drills the Electrician and his staff in the running of the lighting plot. Cues, checks, and dims are tried out, and all off-stage lighting is correctly positioned. Often such rehearsals take hours, especially in musicals and pantomimes. 2. A LIGHT RUN THROUGH, *infra*.
light relief. A variant of COMIC RELIEF.
light run through. (Brit.) A purely WORD-REHEARSAL, no stress being laid on lines or acting. In U. S., line reading.
lightning call. (Usually in the plural) Rapid curtain calls taken by a greedy leading artist. An inveterate pincher. Cf. PINCH CALLS.
lightning-change artist. The more usual QUICK-CHANGE ARTIST, one who imitates (takes off) a number of well known personalities. Brandsby Williams, the English actor, assumed several Dickensian characters in his Protean act on the music hall stage.
lightning-sticks. A primitive but most effective method of creating the effect of lightning. Two metal sticks (with insulated handles) connected directly across the main electricity supply that spark brilliantly when touched together.
lights, put up. To bring up the house lights on the fall of the curtain in an interval, or at the end of the play.
Like Charley's Aunt, still running. Said of a very successful play that is out to emulate the record-running old farcical comedy, *Charley's Aunt*, who, in the play, spends most of "her" time being pursued round the University quadrangles by the lovesick Spettigew.
lime juice. The limelight. Lime light provided by the *juice* (current) of the electricity.
limelight, fond of. Greedy for notice. One who claims the center of the stage. "She is pretty good at her job, but rather too fond of the limelight."
limelight man. Is in charge of the limes (*follow spots*) and car-

bon arc projectors. He adjusts the carbon rods and generally regulates the feeding of the arc.

limes. Short for *lime* lights. In U. S., *follow spots*.

limited run. A play—often a revival—that is put on for specified number of weeks as a fill-in when a theater has a new play in production. "They are putting on *Journey's End* for a limited run."

line dancers. Stage dancers (e.g. the Tiller troupe or Jackson girls) who dance in a *line* in musical shows.

line, have. See HAVE LINE.

line of sight. A line taken from any angle in the auditorium that will ensure unobstructed vision. Scenes must be set within these lines of sight, and it is necessary to see that borders are not too low to obscure vision from the gallery. See HORIZONTAL, and VERTICAL, lines of sight.

line please! A request for a prompt. It is far better to ask boldly for this than to flounder, and embarrass the other artists in the scene. If the man on the book is attending to his job he will see that the line is given before the request for it is necessary.

line, the. A *line* of stage dancers in a musical comedy or a revue.

lines = dialogue. One's part. 2. Ropes that support battens on which the cloths (drops) and borders, flats, etc., are tied. 3. The thin "signal halliard" lines on flats which are frapped and cleated when setting scenery.

lines, set of. The three lines (short, long, and center line) that support a batten. "Send down a set of lines for this cloth" (stage carpenter to the flyman).

linnet. (Brit.) A little BIRD, or faint noises of disapproval in the auditorium. The first flutterings of the BIRD.

linty. (Brit.) A sprite. Like the *gremlin* of Second World War coinage, it is blamed for any untoward happening in the theater. From the Scottish *lintie*, a pet name for a linnet, a bird regarded as unlucky.

liquid board. A liquid-dimmer control board. See the general entry at DIMMER.

literary play. One that reads better than it acts. Usually an adaptation of a wordy novel, having little action to redeem it from flatness.

lithos. Double-crown *litho*graphic pictures of a salient point in a play, and used for advertisement display.

littera canina, or dog's letter. A trilled *R* which sounds somewhat like the growl of a dog.

little Willie. The pathetic child character in Mrs. Henry Wood's sentimental play *East Lynne*. It is an axiom in the theatrical profession that a man cannot call himself an actor unless he has played this part as a boy. See DEAD! DEAD! AND NEVER CALLED ME MOTHER!

live. Electrical equipment that is connected to the main switchboard or, indeed, to any switchboard. Cf. ALIVE.

live show. An interlude, short sketch, or variety act, given between films at a cinema. A personal, rather than celluloid, appearance.

live stage. One set, and lit, ready for the curtain to go up on the performance. A *dead* stage is one that is either in complete darkness, or lit by a pilot light.

live a part. To have complete absorption in it. To *be* the character portrayed.

lodging list. A list of the addresses of theatrical landladies in London, and the provincial towns, compiled for the convenience of members of British Actors' Equity Association. These apartments have been recommended by artists themselves and submitted to the editors of the list. It is, therefore, very reliable. In U. S., similar lists of acceptable hotel accommodations are available through Actors' Equity Association.

loge. A box, or stall, in the theater. From the French.

logical accent. That which is placed upon the significant words in a player's lines. The stresses that appear natural and logical to one.

London Player's Guild. A society of London-theater understudies, and small part players which produces "Sunday shows" as a means of introducing talent to managements. To quote the prospectus, the Society was formed "for the purpose of bringing to the notice of managements, in particular, and the public, in general, understudies and small part players unknown in London."

long-arm. A long wooden pole used for clearing borders, ceilings,

LONG CARRY *118*

etc., that foul the lines in the flies. Cf. CLEARING STICK, and WOODEN ARM.

long carry = LONG HUMP. An expression used when the distance from the scene dock doors to the nearest point where a lorry can pull up is a long one, and all scenery has to be carried (humped) by hand.

long hump = LONG CARRY (stage carpenters' and stage hands').

longueur. A period of dullness in a play; "longiloquence" (French).

look at the house. It is considered unlucky for an artist to look through the curtain at the audience.

lounge suit opera. The "musical drama" (the Broadway phrase, 1950) entitled *The Consul,* by Gian Carlo Menotti, which ran for a year in New York and was brilliantly performed by Patricia Neway and ten supporting artists. Set in a dictator-state, the action takes place in the Consul's office and tells of a woman's attempt to obtain a visa to go to another country. She fails and commits suicide. The clothes worn in the opera are as somber as the theme. The opera failed in London when produced by Sir Laurence Olivier at the Cambridge Theatre. It ran for nine weeks.

lowest of the arts, the. Acting. This questionable dictum dates from the 1890s.

lowest terms for actors. There is a story that an actor of the old school, when seeking apartments at the seaside at the height of the summer season, asked a landlady what were her lowest terms for actors. B......s, was her reply.

lucky to drop powder. Chorus girls, when they drop powder on the dressing room floor, dance on it in the belief that it will bring them good luck and quick jump to stardom. See SUPERSTITIONS.

luxury opera. The Glyndebourne Opera, q.v.

Lyceum, the. The old Lyceum Theater, the home of melodrama. Sir Henry Irving staged many Shakespearean productions here, but the theater was mainly associated with "spectacular" drama. Hence *Lyceum technique* is descriptive of overacted, ranting drama. *Ham*-like performances as they would seem to playgoers of the present time.

M

Ma. (Brit.) As a mode of address to a theatrical landlady this is frowned upon by the up-stage artists who invariably address her by her proper name. The term "Ma" has been current for at least a century, and is still used by vaudeville artists and less formal people in straight companies. "What's for supper tonight, Ma?"

Mac. (Brit.) The late Charles Macdona who toured his *Macdona Players* in a repertoire of Bernard Shaw plays. His brilliant company introduced Shaw to provincial audiences and he ran a season in Paris at the Albert Premier Theatre and in the Dominions. The Macdona Players were very popular, and their visit to a local theater was an event.

machine-made. The unindividual style of acting. A one-pattern technique.

magazine compartment footlights. In this method of stage lighting each lamp is set in its own compartment with lamp, reflector, and filter frame, complete.

maillot. Tights. From the name of the inventor.

maître de ballet. A ballet master. A choreographer, or teacher of ballet technique.

maize country. CORNY dates hidden away IN THE LONG GRASS of the country. American in origin, the term has reached the English theater, especially the touring companies whose lot frequently falls in such territory.

make it more pear-shaped. A completely unintelligible instruction given to an artist by a certain director who, quite obviously, had not the vaguest idea what he was talking about and of very little else besides. A stupid cover for his lack of knowledge. The term, however, caught on and spread to other theaters, and is used with heavy sarcasm by repertory producers when players give a poor representation of their ideas at rehearsal. "I suppose it's all right, but can't you make it a little more pear-shaped?" In U. S., an unfortunate bit of vocal imagery designed to produce *roundness* of tone, which inevitably provokes the classic sally: "more pear-shaped? Certainly, which end of the pear?"

make fast = MAKE OFF = TIE OFF. A flyman's term borrowed from the Navy.

make off. To secure a line, or lines, so that they are finally made fast (tied off) to a prescribed position. Cf. DEAD.

make the play. By an outstanding performance, or all round excellence of acting, redeem a poor play from failure. "The *acting* made the play." An intrinsically good play can succeed even when the acting is indifferent, but a mediocre play must have good acting—provided the play *is* actable—to keep it alive.

make-up. The materials: grease paints, powder, rouge, wigs, etc., used in the art of facial make-up for the stage. 2. The act of preparing for an appearance on the stage, the painting of the face with grease paint appropriate to the type of stage lighting used in the play. Make-up embraces costume and transformation generally and is a highly technical and complicated business, so much so that a special artist is sometimes engaged for a theater, as in a film studio.

make-up box. Contains compartments to hold sticks of grease paint, etc., but most artists use a cigar box, the elaborate make-up boxes are regarded as a sign of the amateur. It is a superstition in dressing rooms that make-up boxes should never be "cleaned out" as this is said to bring bad luck.

make-up man. An artist employed to *make up* actors, particularly in motion picture and television studios. Stage performers are usually responsible for their own *make-ups*.

Malapropisms. Solecisms in pronunciation and polysyllabic words. Mrs. Malaprop, the character in Sheridan's *The Rivals* (whose "nice derangement of epitaphs" for *nice arrangement of epithets* is a classic quotation), and Dogberry, in Shakespeare's *Much Ado About Nothing*, are the archetypes.

male impersonator. This somewhat misnomic term means a *female* who impersonates a *male*. E.g. the English music hall artist, Hetty King, famous for such parts. Cf. FEMALE IMPERSONATOR.

man of parts. A versatile(?) actor. "He plays *Hamlet, Romeo, Shylock,* and snooker. He plays snooker best" (old theater "crack").

management, go into. To form a theatrical company. "So and So doesn't act any more, he has gone into management."

mark the 'script. This is the stage manager's, or his assistant's, job under the supervision of the director. As the stage directions are given to the cast, and business is suggested, so these directions are marked in the Prompt book during rehearsals.

mask. To stand between a fellow artist and the LINE OF SIGHT, thus *masking* him from view.

mask in. To set a scene in accordance with the lines of sight, thus preventing an audience from seeing outside the setting to the undressed part of the stage.

masque. Short for *masque*rade, an old-fashioned play of which the most frequently revived, and typical, is John Milton's *Comus* which has been played in recent years at the Open Air Theatre, in Regent's Park, London. Milton's, however, was an elaboration of the early type of court entertainments, folk plays, and the masques made popular by Ben Jonson, James Shirley (cf. THE LAST MINSTREL OF THE ENGLISH STAGE), and others.

Master of the Greensward. (Brit.) He in charge of the "stage" of the Open Air Theatre, Regent's Park, London, where Shakespeare is presented in a perfect pastoral setting (when the weather is good!) and performances are of high quality.

matinée days. The artists' pet aversion. Usually on Wednesday and Saturday, though some theaters have Tuesday and Friday. Since the Second World War matinees are sometimes given on Thursdays. In U. S., usually two matinees per week, Wednesday and Saturday or Thursday and Saturday.

matinée feeling, that. That after-lunch lassitude that always seems to make matinee performances so much less vital than evening ones. At least, so it appears from the artist's point of view.

matinée idol. A "romantic" actor popular with women who attend matinee performances in the West End of London. The term is obsolescent, as there are few plays written for this type of lead-

MECHANICS 122

ing man today. Usually very handsome, and impeccably tailored, his part fits him like the proverbial glove. A perfect example of the matinee idol was the late Owen Nares who played these parts for some years. Nares was a real idol whose technique was the envy of his would-be imitators. He abandoned this type of role in the 1930s and proved himself an excellent character actor. Sir Gerald du Maurier, though portraying the more virile parts, was also a great matinee favorite.

mechanics. The mechanical movements made in the first stages of a rehearsal. "Let's go over that scene again, but don't act it, just the mechanics."

M.D. Short for *Musical Director*, the *conductor* of a musical comedy, or revue.

medium frame. Holds the gelatine color filter in front of a light. In U. S., *color frame*.

med opera. Short for *medi*cal opera, a play dealing with medicine. One in which a doctor is the leading character or the theme is medical. E.g. Brandon's play *The Outsider*, the "quack" play that had a long run in London in the early 1920s, or Doctor Harold Dearden's *Interference*, which starred Herbert Marshall.

medza caroon. Half a crown (parlyaree). Cf. CAROON.

medzer (usually in the plural). (Brit.) Coppers, hence *nanty medzer* penniless. A Parlyaree variant of DINALI. From the Italian *mezzo*, half, hence *medza*, a half-penny in Parlyaree. Edward Seago records this term in his delightful *Circus Company*.

melocution. That "mellifluous" articulation associated with melodrama villains. A telescoping of *melo*drama and elo*cution*.

melodrama. Sensational plays spiced with strong sentiment, and interspersed with song or musical interludes. The dialogue is highly bombastic and sentimental. During the act waits the soubrette of the company gives songs, or one of the male characters entertains with juggling or tells "funny stories." See CHORD IN "G."

melos. An operatic song. "A term used by Richard Wagner for the local melodies in later musical dramas, to exemplify vocal phrases which have not the quality of symmetry characteristic of earlier opera songs" (Otto Ortmann, in *An Encyclopaedia of the Arts*, The Philosophical Library, New York, 1945).

menagerie. The slang term for an orchestra. From the zoo-like noises that emanate from the bandroom instruments when the musicians are tuning up for the overture.

men aside. (Brit.) In all stage productions there are a number of men to work each side of the stage during the act changes. They are responsible for the moving of the flats on their side of the stage, and shifting furniture that is stacked there. In touring productions the plots are sent ahead to the next date on the tour list, and such details as the required number of stage hands given to the local union contractor so that he can make arrangements for calling his men, according to the needs of the production.

mezzanine. The under-stage space. From the Italian, *mezzanino*, a diminutive of *mezzano*. In U. S. theater, lower balcony.

Michael Angelo of Buffoonery, the. Joseph Grimaldi, the great clown (1779–1837). See entry at JOEY.

middle comedy. Greek comedy which burlesqued stories from mythology and introduced typical characters. No pure examples of this type of comedy, which flourished 388–338 B.C., have survived (H. T. E. Perry's definition in a *Dictionary of World Literature*, edited by Dr. Joseph T. Shipley, Philosophical Library, Inc.).

midnight matinee. A performance of a metropolitan success, played at midnight to an invited audience of fellow professionals who, by reason of their being engaged at other theaters, are not able to see the show in the ordinary way. These midnight performances are great fun as the "all Pro" audience stimulates the cast to surpass themselves, especially in comedy or revue where plenty of lattitude is allowed for gags, etc. In U. S., "pros" see their colleagues in the Sunday benefits for the Actors Fund of America. This is a convenient arrangement since benefits are frequent and other shows do not usually play Sundays.

mike fever. A feeling similar to that of acute stage fright which sometimes overcomes an artist when facing the *microphone* in broadcast performances of plays, or when "airing" alone. In U. S., also *mike fright*. Cf. MONOPHOBIA.

milk an audience. To over-act. PLAY FOR A ROUND.

mime = DUMB SHOW. 2. A play performed without speech, gestures being employed instead. From the Greek *mimos*, a buffoon.

mimodrama. An elaboration of sense 2 of the above. 2. A puppet show.

minnow. A small part. From the very small fish so named. Such parts, however, are not to be despised, as they often provide good acting opportunities or have telling lines that draw attention to an artist. Cf. TWO LINES AND A SPIT.

miscast. Cast out of type. Given a part beyond a player's power to sustain. A role unsuited to an artist's physique or temperament.

mise en scène. The scene and artists grouped together. The general "set-up" of a production (French theater).

my name was spelt wrong in *The Stage*. This is "the unkindest cut of all"; one of the worst things that can happen to a young and sensitive beginner who needs all the publicity he can get. *The Stage* is the mouthpiece of the English theatrical profession and is regarded with a mixture of affection and ridicule. See the entry at *Stage* newspaper.

moko. "A type of oil-bound distemper to imitate high gloss finishes where an enamel or cellulose would be forbidden under fire regulations. It is also used to withstand outdoor weather conditions." A scene painter's term, quoted from Strand Electric's admirable small glossary of *Technical Theatrical Terms*. Cf. GLAZE.

money-spinner. A successful play, or artist. E.g. the American musicals *Oklahoma*, *Annie Get Your Gun*, and *Kiss Me Kate*, or the phenomenal Ivor Novello's *Dancing Years*, *Perchance to to Dream*, and *King's Rhapsody*.

monkey pole. A long stick which has a line threaded through the top, used to cleat two adjacent flats. By use of this pole the line can be quickly taken over the top cleat on a flat. When the line is cleated it remains attached to the pole.

monodrama. A play written for one player.

monophobia. The fear of being alone on the stage. There are players who, excellent in a general scene, are nervous of having the stage to themselves. This phobia extends to broadcasting *alone* in a studio.

monopolylogue. An entertainment by one person who impersonates several well-known characters in life or fiction. E.g. the Brandsby Williams' sketches from the works of Charles Dickens, or Miss Ruth Draper's brilliant work. The Greek *monos*, alone + *polus*, many + *legein*, to speak. Cf. PROTEAN ENTERTAINER.

monthly rep. A Repertory Company whose plays run for a month, instead of the weekly or the fortnightly "change-about" system.

moody Dane. A variant of GLOOMY DANE, the part of Hamlet.

morality play. A medieval allegorical drama, of the 15th and 16th century. Cf. SOTTIE.

more on/off stage. The direction to a player to move more toward the center, or toward the side of the stage. In a lateral direction. Cf. UPSTAGE.

mostly paper! Said of a house that has been generously *papered* with complimentary tickets. Mostly paper; little money taken at the box-office.

mount. (Of a play) To dress and produce it.

moves. Movements on the stage as laid down at rehearsal by the director, whether standing, walking, sitting, or even reclining on a settee. "You have forgotten a move, old boy, you cross down right to the fireplace and sit at the desk."

movie version. The motion picture version of a Broadway or London success.

Mrs. Pat. Mrs. Patrick Campbell, the celebrated English actress whose sharp wit and fiery tongue were respected by many contemporary leading players of the early 20th century. She was a brilliant actress and the first to use the adjective *bloody* on the stage when playing Eliza Doolittle, the cockney flower-girl, "guinea pig" of the Professor of phonetics, in George Bernard Shaw's *Pygmalion*. Mrs. Pat's best remembered plays are *The Thirteenth Chair*, and *Magda*. Late in her career she went to Hollywod to work in films, but she never felt satisfied with the medium. The correspondence—scintillating with wit and wisdom—between Mrs. Patrick Campbell and George Bernard Shaw, entitled *My Life and Some Letters*, by Mrs. Patrick Campbell, should be read by all who are interested in the history of the theater of which Mrs. Pat was the *aura popularis* of her time.

multicore. As the word implies this flexible cable has several insulated cores protected by a strong asbestos covering. It is used between the light battens and the FLY-RAIL.

multiple wing floods. Trolly-mounted units of several flood boxes.

mum. To act. See MUMMER, *infra*.

mummer. An actor or actress. Literally one who wears a mask (low German *mumme*, a mask), acting in dumb show. Cf. the Dutch *mommen*, to mask, and the old French *momer*, to act in dumb show. The term is a professional colloquialism today.

mummery. The art of acting. Colloquial, from MUMMER.

Mummersetshire. (Brit.) The *lingua rustica* of the stage. Dialect plays are exceedingly difficult to cast, as few actors are able to produce the authentic idiom of the regional dialect required by the play. As a rule, consistency is impossible, and an adviser on regional dialect helps the cast to reach a mean which has earned the jocular nickname *Mummer*setshire, or actor's dialect. It is an admixture, at best, with North Country (broad vowels) and Somersetshire (where *s* supposedly becomes *z* in rural areas) predominating. Theatrical Mummersetshire—rhyming on Somersetshire—has a dialect which is as near as most players can approach authenticity. Regional theaters which specialize in dialect, e.g. the Irish Players, are, of course, impeccable. And one of the finest productions in dialect was the Dorsetshire company of amateurs that performed Thomas Hardy's *Tess of the D'Urbervilles* in Dorchester, under the eye of the author himself. Cf. SEVEN UNKNOWN LANGUAGES OF THE STAGE.

music drama. An opera that has flowing rather than discursive music; the works, say, of Wagner as opposed to Verdi.

music hall. Now called a variety theater, was instituted in England in *circa* 1850—at the Canterbury Music Hall in Westminster Bridge Road, London. *The Grand Order of Water Rats and Lady Ratlings*, a variety artists' charity organization, celebrated the century of the English music hall in an all-star program at the London Palladium in November, 1950. See entry at VARIETY.

music hall technique. A farcical comedy, or comedy sketch, played on broad, almost crude lines after the manner of a music hall COMIC of the early days.

musical. A musical comedy or revue (American).

musical comedy. An operetta, a light comedy set to music. There is a song motive running through the play, and good parts for the heroine, hero, and comedian.

musical comedy country. See RURITANIA.

musicomedy. A contraction of *musical comedy* (American).

mussitate. To move the lips in simulation of speech, no sound being uttered. Cf. GOLDFISH.

must speak the King's English. The rider sometimes seen in the *Wanted Artists* column in a theatrical newspaper. Usually the advertisements are inserted by small drama managements: "Wanted Artists, all lines, for resident repertory company. Must speak the King's English, and dress well on and off."

mystery. The obscure or puzzling element in a drama.

Mystery play. A religious play dealing with incidents in the life of Christ. These plays, also known as *miracle* plays, are presented at Christmas, Easter, and at church festivals. Several of the old Mystery plays were revived during the Festival of Britain in 1951, a particularly spectacular one being produced in the cathedral city of York.

N

name in lights, have one's. To have achieved success, one's name appearing in the electric sign in front of the theater. Such fame can be disconcertingly, and heartbreakingly, evanescent.

name part. The role which bears the *name* of the leading character (*part*) in the play. E.g. Drummond, in Sapper's *Bulldog Drummond*. Cf. TITLE ROLE.

natural. A part that it is *natural* for an actor to play, or want to play. E.g. *Hamlet*. In U. S., 1. A role that is *tailor-made* for an actor. 2. A play that can't *miss*.

naturalistic acting. The art of portraying character "to the life," the "free from artificiality" technique introduced by Sir Harley Granville Barker in England at the beginning of the present century. Although this technique looks perfectly natural from the front it is far from easy to acquire. It is a case of art concealing art. Sir Gerald du Maurier was one of its finest exponents.

nature's darling. The name given to William Shakespeare by Thomas Gray (1716–1771) in *The Progress of Poetry*.

near the bone. Said of a salacious play, or risqué line in revue. "The nearer the bone the sweeter the meat." Cf. BLUE STUFF, and BLUE GAGS.

negro minstrels. A musical or variety entertainment originating in the United States, and made popular in the theater by E. F. Christy who started his famous Christy Minstrels in 1842. The "set-up" consisted of a blackface chorus who "doubled" the part of "interlocutor." Two corner boys (end-men) who, on the flanks of the chorus, supplied the comedy business and were the target of the interlocutor-cum-compère.

newel. The handrail at the foot of a stage staircase. Often called a *newel-post*.

night, the. The opening *night* of a new production. Cf. IT'LL BE ALL RIGHT ON THE NIGHT.

nix. To ban, censure (a play). From the German *nicht*, not (to be).

noises off. Effects heard off-stage. The approach of a car, voices, sleigh bells (*The Bells*, a Lyceum drama, was one of those that helped to make the name of Sir Henry Irving), horses' hooves, and other noises incidental to a play.

nom de théâtre. A stage name. These were adopted at the time when connection with the stage was not considered respectable.

non-copyright plays. Old plays whose copyrights have lapsed with the passage of time and which can be acted by repertory companies or amateurs. They are performed without payment of fees.

non-practical. Stage fittings and parts of the setting that are merely there as scenery, and are not PRACTICAL, q.v.

none of your fancy fours and fives. (Brit.) A remark alleged to have been made by an agent to a leading touring actor when being offered a part in a play, meaning "you can have the part provided you'll accept a reasonable (sic) salary." No four or five pounds a week. It is now a catch-phrase in the provincial theater.

no play; no pay. An old clause in a touring contract. Artists were paid for their appearances before the public and received no pay for weeks out.

nose out. To discover (a play, or artist). "How did he get on Broadway?" "A talent-scout nosed him out in a travelling show" (American).

nose paste. A putty-like substance that becomes malleable when warmed in the hand. It is used principally for altering the shape of the nose in character parts. E.g. *Shylock*, the *Dromios*, and *clown-parts*. In U. S., *nose putty*.

not a hand. No applause. Said of a line, or exit, that fails to earn a ROUND. Cf. HANDS.

not according to 'script. Extraneous lines, or gags, that are introduced during a long run of a play. Cf. NOT IN THE BOOK.

not a dry eye in the house. The reception of a sob scene, a WEEPIE.

not a dry seat in the house. An indelicate catch-phrase meaning that the scene or comedian was so funny that the audience was utterly helpless with laughter. On the analogy of *not a dry eye in the house*.

not in the book. (i.e. 'script) Gags, or lines interpolated during a performance. "That gag dried me up, it wasn't in the book!" (complaint by a CUE-BOUND player).

not Pygmalion likely. Euphemistic for not *bloody* likely, from the use of that adjective in Bernard Shaw's play *Pygmalion*, by Eliza Doolittle, the cockney girl.

notice. The newspaper critique following a first night performance. 2. That which tells a theatrical company of the termination of the run of their play, and ends their contracts. Also used of an individual case of dismissal for incompetence or bad conduct.

noticed, be. To have one's talent spotted by an important manager who happened to be in front. To be recognized by the Press. "A consummation devoutly to be wished," but seldom realized.

number. The poor relation of the operatic *aria*. A song, dance-tune. "Let's try your new number Miss Gay." 2. A number (figure) that goes on the side of a music hall stage to indicate the turn on the program. Cf. ARIA.

number 1 date. Bookings in the English provinces are graded according to the size of the population, and the importance of the town. *Number 1's* are cities the size of Manchester, Birmingham, Glasgow and Edinburgh, and some of the London suburbs like Golder's Green and Streatham.

number 2 date. A seaside holiday resort or inland Spa, cathedral, or small industrial city or town. Also known as *seconds*.

number 3 date. One in a rural, industrial, or mining district. E.g. the market towns in the "broad acres" of Yorkshire, the pottery district, or the mining towns of south Wales. There are also a number of these dates in Somerset, Devon, and Cornwall. Cf. SMALLS and FIT-UPS. Also known as *thirds*.

number of dressing room. A dressing room number is determined by the importance, or otherwise, of the artist in the company. *No. 1 D.R.* is given to the star-lead, and the supporting cast is graded accordingly.

number the dressing rooms. The job assigned to the assistant stage manager of a touring company when he gets the baskets, and personal properties, into the theater on Monday morning. He numbers the rooms in order of seniority, then orders the men to place the props in their appropriate "homes" for the week.

nut, the. The weekly operating expense of a production (American).

O

Oakley, an. A complimentary ticket (American). Annie Oakley was a famous female sharpshooter who toured with Buffalo Bill's circus in the 1880s, and was the central figure in the recent musical comedy hit *Annie Get Your Gun*.

Oberammergau. See PASSION PLAY.

oblique. To set scenery at more or less right angles to the center line of the stage.

offer up, to. (Brit.) To show the producer the position of a picture or ornament for approval before fixing it permanently, particularly mirrors which reflect the stage lighting. 2. Carpenters offer up doorways to fit into the door-frames, in fact they offer up anything before it is approved. The term is used by carpenters outside the theater and is peculiar to their trade.

off. *Off* the stage, i.e. the setting. In the wings, or in the dressing-room. Cf. OFF STAGE. 2. To have missed an entrance cue. An artist being *off* when he, or she, ought to be *on* (the stage).

off-set. To erect a piece of scenery at an angle to another, not necessarily at right-angles.

off stage. See entry at ON STAGE.

off-stage lines. Those spoken outside the setting. They usually herald the appearance of the leading player and warn the audience that a round of applause would be appreciated. She, or he, usually gets it. Cf. NOISES OFF.

off-stage space. The amount of space outside the setting. When stacking flats, furniture, properties, etc., at the sides or back of the stage, it is well to know beforehand what stage space is available so as to allow for the free movement of artists, or stagehands, behind the scene.

old boy! As a mode of address this is employed *ad nauseam* by actors. It superseded *Laddy* of the Victorian era.

Old Vic. Situated in the New Cut, Lambeth, London, this famous house was originally named the *Coburg Theatre* and renamed the *Victoria, circa* 1834. Mainly associated with Shakespearean productions, the theater has been a popular favorite with London playgoers and its history—too colorful to be recorded here, but reverently treated by theater historians in recent years—is part of the story of London. Like so much that was dear to Londoners, the Old Vic suffered severe damage in the bombing by Nazi airmen in World War II, which closed the house for several years. The Vic reopened in 1950.

oleo act. A scene played in the forepart of the stage while another scene is being set further back. It corresponds to a front cloth scene. Oleo derives either from *oleo* (ex Latin *oleum*, oil) in the *oil painting* (front cloth) sense, or *olio*, a hotch potch, miscellany; hence a music hall, or front cloth, sketch.

omnes. Latin for all; everybody (on the stage). A collective exclamation, e.g. boos, groans, jeers, murmurs of disapproval or approbation, incredulity and the like. This is a standard stage direction. "There must be a terrific *omnes* when you hear that line."

on. On the stage, i.e. within the setting. Cf. ON STAGE.

on and off artist. One who appears intermittently throughout a play, e.g. a stage butler who comes *on* to announce people, *and* immediately goes *off* "until next time."

on stage. With off stage, this is a somatic adjective. The on-stage arm is the one nearest the center of the stage when an artist faces the audience. Thus, in position *stage left*, the right will be the on-stage arm, and the left the off-stage one. If the artist crossed from left to right, his left arm would become the on-stage arm. The same applies to furniture and properties so positioned. "Bring the settee a little more off stage (i.e. toward the side). Cf. UP-STAGE.

on stage off. This is not as paradoxical as it reads. A player can be on the *stage floor*, but off the setting, waiting for his entrance cue.

on the boards. On the stage, i.e. in the theatrical profession, treading the *boards* of the stage floor.

on the plate. On the *switchboard*. This electrician's term dates from the days of gas illumination and refers to the *plate,* or gas control board.

on the road. Touring the provinces. A column in *The Stage* newspaper gives the whereabouts for the current week of all touring companies. Thus: "*Annie Get Your Gun:* this week, Hippodrome, Newcastle; next, Palace, Manchester." Cf. PLOUGH THE PROVINCES.

on the sheet. The sheet is a rough plan of all the seats in the theater. Seats are marked off as sold to obviate double booking. An artist wanting two seats would say to the Box Office, "Put me on the sheet for tonight." Or, "What does the sheet look like for next week," meaning how many seats have been booked for the following week's performances.

on the stage. In the theatrical profession (cf. ON THE BOARDS). 2. Actually performing on the set.

on top of 'em. A small theater with little space between the stage and the front seats. "We were on top of 'em last week."

once an actor, always an actor. A stage axiom dating from the "rogues and vagabond" days of strolling players.

one-acter. A one-act play. A CURTAIN-RAISER.

one-man show. A variety turn by a single artist who impersonates several characters, or performs an acrobatic or juggling act. A solo musician on an unusual instrument, e.g. one who plays on a saw, or has a *one-man band.*

one-nighter = a ONE NIGHT STAND, *infra.*

one-night stand. A portable theater erected for one night's performance in a village. See entry at FIT-UP. In U. S., a one-performance town. Business does not warrant a longer *stand.*

o-o, the. The *once-over.* A quick inspection by the stage manager of the stage before the curtain rises. He checks the lights and important properties. Just *once* again he looks *over* the scene.

O.P. Short for *Opposite Prompt* (side). Generally this is on the right hand side facing the audience, but in some theaters the Prompt Corner is on the right, in which case the O.P. is on stage left. Units of scenery that have to be set on the O.P. side are marked thus: "Act II, O.P.; Act I, scene II, O.P., and so on. In U. S., designation R, L, right, left, is used.

O.P. Club. (Brit.) A now defunct theatrical club in London. It was popular during the early part of the present century.

open. To open a theater with a new production. Hence OPENING NIGHT, or any first night of a tour. "We open next week at Brighton for a short tour prior to London production."

open cold. To produce a new play in Town directly after rehearsals, instead of having a preliminary run in the provinces. The play hasn't had time to *warm* up.

open in a black-out. An act is said to *open in a black-out* when the curtain rises on darkened scene. The lights go up on a cue, e.g. the entrance of a servant to switch on lights or open curtains to let in daylight. The lights come up according to the lighting plot.

open on. Any door or window that opens onto the stage (i.e. toward the artist). The door is pushed onto the stage by one making an entrance, and pulled after one when making an exit. Cf. OPEN OFF, where the reverse takes place.

open set. OPEN STAGE, *infra*.

open stage. In Classical drama, opera, ballet and such productions as need space for crowd movements, the stage is free of obstructive scenery. Wings, a rostrum—upstage—or such symbolic pieces are all that one sees in an open stage.

opening. The width of the stage across the proscenium archway. 2. A gap in a piece of scenery. 3. The division in tableau curtains.

opening chorus. The chorus that introduces a musical comedy, or concert party.

opening line. The first speech in a play. "I must rush down now, old boy, I have the opening line" (actor to dressing-room visitor).

opening night. A first night of any production.

opera. A drama set to music, dates from *circa* 1594, with the production of Rinuccini's *Dafne* at the Palazzo Corsi in Florence "as an attempt to revive the classical Greek tragedy. Opera was thus first a chanted tragedy, with solemn recitative replacing the tragic declamation. This sense of opera as drama, filled with the spirit of Greek tragedy has persisted throughout its history; it dominates the work of Gluck (18th century) and the reform of Wagner (19th century)" (Max Graf in *A Dictionary of World Literature,* edited by Dr. Joseph T. Shipley, Philosophical Library, New York).

opera bouffa. A semi-comic opera. See BUFFA.

opera comique. A comic opera with spoken dialogue.

opera, grand. Grand opera has no spoken dialogue and is tragic in theme.

opera seria. Literally serious opera, as opposed to dramatic opera, or opera buffa.

opera glasses. A small pair of binoculars used at the opera house by patrons seated in the circles and balcony. They can be hired in the theater.

operetta. A short opera, or musical comedy on operatic lines. *Etta* is an Italian diminutive.

opposition. (Brit.) The rival theater at a provincial date. "What have we at the opposition next week?" (touring actors').

orchestra bell. A warning bell from the Prompt Corner to the bandroom under the stage. It gives the signal to members of the band that they are required in the orchestra pit for the entr'acte music.

orchestra pit. The space in front of, or just below, the stage where the band plays.

orchestra stalls. The seats nearest the orchestra. Cf. FAUTEUIL.

orchestra stands. Are used in the orchestra pit to hold music sheets.

orthoepy. The science of correct pronunciation in public speech. From the Greek *orthos,* straight + *epos,* word.

O.U.D.S. (Brit.) The *O*xford *U*niversity *D*ramatic *S*ociety, known as the "owds." This society, which is social as well as dramatic, was founded by the late Arthur Bourchier, the London actor. Many front rank players learned the rudiments of their art in the O.U.D.S.

Our Gracie. Miss Gracie Fields, O.B.E., the first lady of vaudeville. A brilliant artist, she won the hearts of the theater public by many acts of generosity to fellow artists and charities, in particular the founding of a children's orphanage at Peacehaven, Sussex. An unselfish trouper, she never refuses an appearance when requested, unless there is an insuperable reason for doing so. Miss Fields is a comedienne as well as a very fine singer, and her famous hits: *Granny's Little Bear-skin Rug, The Little Pudden Basin,* and *The Rochdale Hunt* (Rochdale is her birthplace) are always demanded of her. But the most requested are her rendering of *Ave Maria* (a moving one) and *Sally in Our Alley.* Gracie Fields has also appeared on the legitimate stage and in films.

out of town houses. Theaters outside the metropolitan district.

out of type, to be cast. See CAST OUT OF TYPE.

out with. *Out* of London *with* a traveling company. Touring the provincial dates. "Have you seen So and So lately?" "No, he is *out with* a musical."

overparted. Said of a player who is unequal to the performance of an important leading role. Also of a repertory artist who is given too many leading parts in succession. Cf. UNDERPART.

over rehearse. As the term implies, to overwork a player at rehearsal until he becomes stale and irritable.

overture. A short piece played for a few minutes before the rise of the curtain on the first act of a play. 2. The introduction to an opera, or musical comedy.

overture and beginners! The warning call that brings beginners (i.e. beginners in the opening act of a play) from their dressing rooms to take up positions on the stage for the rise of the curtain.

P

P.A. Short for *Press Agent* or *Publicity Agent*. This use of initials spread during the Second World War and the habit has remained.

Pa. (Brit.) The affectionate sobriquet bestowed on the late Sir Frank Benson by members of his Shakespearean Company to whom he acted as "father." Francis Robert Benson was born in 1858 and became interested in acting while at New College, Oxford, where he produced the first Greek play to be performed in the University—the *Agamemnon* of Sophocles—wherein Benson played the part of *Clytemnestra*. On going down from Oxford, Benson adopted the stage as a career, starting with Sir Henry Irving in *Romeo and Juliet* at the Lyceum Theatre. In 1883 he took over the Walter Bentley Repertory Company which had been moribund for some time. His repertoire included Shakespeare and the Old English Comedies. A season at the old Globe Theatre in 1889 was a brilliant success, notably for the perfect teamwork of the artists under R.F.B. (as he was then known) and the presentation of the plays. After an equally good season at the Lyceum in the following year, Benson formed his own Shakespeare Company which was to become famous and gave to acting some of its most celebrated exponents. A brilliant athlete at Oxford, Frank Benson infused enthusiasm for sport into the members of his companies, which may have accounted for the fine bearing and alertness which characterized all Bensonians. The first question asked of an aspirant to his company was "Are you good at games?" A humane, scholarly actor, Sir Frank's performances were always interesting—some sparkling—but there was an unevenness in execution that disappointed his kindest critics. *Hamlet, Lear, Richard II*, and *Petruchio* (an extremely "athletic" performance) were his favorite parts. It was during the tercentenary matinée at the Lyceum Theatre in 1916 that Frank Benson was knighted on the stage by King George V, with a sword borrowed from a theatrical costumer. He died in 1939. Eminent Old Bensonians include: Henry Ainley (THE VOICE), Oscar Asche, Robert Donat, Henry Baynton (see entry at BAY), and many other well known names. Cf. BENSONIAN.

pack. A stack of flats at the sides, or back, of the stage. They are packed in order of setting, all prompt-side scenery being stacked at that side, and the others at the O.P. Flats are marked *P.S.* or *O.P.* with the number of the Act and scene for which they are required. Where possible, furniture is packed at the back of the stage and "run on" when the space is clear of scenery.

pad. In the "make-up" sense, to build up girth by the use of padding material. This has to be done with great skill, especially for such parts as Shakespeare's *Falstaff* or *Sir Toby Belch*. 2. To add gags or lines to a colorless part in order to make it more palatable to an audience.

paint frame. A large wooden mobile frame raised and lowered by a winch, and counter-balanced. Large drop scenes, panorama cloths, etc., are stretched on this frame by the scenic artist who works on a catwalk built in front of the frame. In most theaters it is situated at the back of the stage, level with the fly-floor, and is lit from the sky-light above the grid. In U. S. professional theater all scenery is painted in shops, and paint frames are no longer used in the majority of theaters.

pale week. One in which business has been consistently poor.

pan. To deride, fault find, generally disparage, denigrate . . . a fellow artist or a play (American). 2. Short for *pan*atrope, an electrically-controlled gramophone which, in some theaters, takes the place of an orchestra but is usually employed for sound effects. 3. a *pan*technicon, a lorry for carting scenery, furniture properties. Named from the Greek *pan*, all + *techne*, art.

pancake. Make-up used chiefly in the film industry and put on with a wet sponge. It resembles a very flat pancake, but the term may have been suggested by *panchromatic* make-up.

panorama cloth. See CYCLORAMA.

Pantaloon. Is a survival from the 16th-century Italian comedy— and is mainly associated with the harlequinade. He is rather a pathetic old man who is the butt of the clown's sallies, and generally provides the broad element in the pantomime frolic (cf. HARLEQUINADE). Wyld derives the name from the Italian *pantalone*, a Venetian character in a comedy, probably from the Venetian Saint *Pantaleone*.

panto. Short for *panto*mime.

panto comic. A pantomime comedian, a Dame, or one of the many other comic characters.

panto, fix. To *fix panto* is to have secured an engagement in a Xmas pantomime production.

panto, in. Appearing in a pantomime company.

pantomime. A composition of song, ballet, and "hearty" humour. It is a development from the folklore and masque entertainments into a Christmas season frolic, which reached its height in spectacular pantomimes, with transformation scenes, etc., in the Victorian days. The present version is a kind of topical revue written round a very tenuous nursery story, with stock characters like *Dick Whittington and his Cat, Cinderella, Prince Charming, The Demon King, Widow Twankey,* the *Ugly Sisters,* and others associated with "fairy stories." The pantomime is still very popular, if less spectacular than formerly. The Greek *pan,* all + *mimos,* a mimic (*pantomimos*).

paper = Complimentary tickets.

paper dicky. A waiter's paper shirt front sometimes used by vaudeville actors in arts that are "hard" on dress shirts. These "dickies" look very well on the stage, particularly when worn with cuffs of the same material. Three, or even four, of these articles are worn in one performance in a knock-about farce which would be death to evening dress shirts. Actors in straight plays wear these substitutes when a quick-change does not allow for a complete change of linen.

paper house. One largely composed of complimentary ticket holders. A FREE-LIST audience.

paper the house. To distribute complimentary tickets for a performance to compensate for the poor bookings, and so make it easier for the artists to perform. It is also policy to paper a flagging play, for it often gives it a new lease of life. The free ticket holders recommending the play.

parabasis. The addressing of the audience by the chorus in ancient Greek comedy. From *para*, beyond + *baino*, go, hence to go in front of the stage to speak. The *parabasis* has been used in modern plays with great effect.

parachronism. The introduction into a scene, or dialogue, of that which had ceased to be before the period in which the action of the play takes place. The Greek *para*, beside + *chronos*, time. Cf. ANACHRONISM, and PROCHRONISM.

paradise. The gallery. Cf. GODS.

paragammacist. A player who has difficulty in pronouncing the letters *K* or *G*. From the Greek *para*, beside + *gamma*, the letter G.

parlyaree (occasionally **parlaree**). Little is known about this language which has neither accidence nor syntax, but is built on a base of Italian phrases whereon cant terms and illiteracies are piled. The "language" has been ignored by the greater dictionaries and even Joseph Wright ignores it in his vast and famous dictionary of *English Dialects* (6 volumes from the Clarendon Press, Oxford). Eric Partridge, however, introduced this "bastard" language in his *Here, There, and Everywhere* (Hamish Hamilton, 1950). It crept into theatrical speech with the strolling players at fairground entertainments and portable theaters and, like regional dialect it acquired "squatter's rights." A number of Parlyaree terms will be found through this glossary. The name derives from the Italian *parlare*, to speak.

parquet stage-cloth. One painted to resemble a parquet floor.

part. A role; character acted in a play, or musical comedy. 2. The typewritten lines from which an artist learns a part. Cf. BOOK, and SIDE.

part is already cast, the. The stock reply to any unsuitable applicant (manager's and theatrical agent's). Cf. WE'LL WRITE TO YOU. In U. S., *Don't call us. We'll call you.*

parterre. The ground floor of a theater. 2. The lowest tier of boxes at the Metropolitan Opera House, New York. From the French *par terre*, on the ground.

pas. A step in ballet of which there are many and various. E.g. *pas de chat*, the cat-step; *pas de deux*, a dance for two; *pas de cheval*, a horse step; *pas de bource*, the progression on the points by a sequence of very small, even steps, one of the most beautiful effects in ballet, as in, e.g. *The Dying Swan*, which is largely composed of this step. The many steps are treated in *Alphabet of Ballet* by Lincoln Kirstein, Director of the New York City Ballet, and *The Complete Book of Ballet*, and *A Dictionary of French and English Ballet Terms*, both by C. W. Beaumont, the London ballet critic and authority.

pash it. To simulate passionate love (on the stage) to the leading lady. To make a love scene convincing to a hard-boiled audience (American in origin, and adopted in the English theater through the film studios).

pass door. The iron door through which one *passes* from the stage to the front of the house. There is a very strict rule about its use, the General Manager, Stage Director and his staff, and those engaged in essential work are permitted to make use of this door. Others, whether artists or staff, wishing to go through must ask permission of one of the above officials. Guests of the management, invited to meet artists, may be conducted through the pass door by their host, or hostess.

pass out check. A ticket given by the USHER to permit a patron to re-enter the auditorium.

Passion Play. A religious drama portraying the scenes of Christ's passion. The most famous is that presented at Oberammergau in Bavaria every ten years. It dates from the year 1633 when, after the plague, the peasants resolved to present the play as an act of devotion.

pasteboard. A theater ticket.

patent theater. (Brit.) The old type of theater, which was established by letters of patent and not licensed by the Lord Chamberlain.

patter. Quick speeches between their songs of music hall comedians. The glib sales talk (*pitch*) of a hawker or barker. The running gags or commentary of a performer, e.g. a magician.

pay-box. The small *guichet* through which pit and gallery patrons pay for admission.

peep hole. A small eyelet in the false proscenium, or advertising curtain, for use of the Stage Director—and more often than not the entire company—through which the house can be seen, without the peeper being seen. To frustrate this practice on the part of inquisitive players, the hole is sometimes a glass dummy.

pencilled date. An unconfirmed booking in a tour list. It is pencilled until confirmation of the contract has been received by the touring manager.

penny gaff. (Brit.) A fairground, or portable, theater which used to charge a penny as the price of admission. See entry at GAFF.

perches. (Brit.) Platforms on which the electrician and his assistants work at the switchboards. 2. Spotlights or floods stationed on the perches, and directed onto the stage through cuts in the TORMENTORS. "Are you using the perches in this scene?" "No, they are DEAD until the last act." In the days when limelights were used perches were called *lime-perches*. In U. S., *booms* or *boomerangs*. Spots affixed to vertical battens to provide light from the wings.

performance. The play itself or an individual piece of acting.

period play. Usually a "costume" piece. E.g. Sheridan's *School for Scandal*, Jane Austin's *Pride and Prejudice*, or any play performed "in costume."

permanent setting = STANDING SET.

personal props. Small properties such as handkerchiefs, cigarettes, money, etc., that are carried onto the stage by the artist, and are their *personal* property. Cf. HAND PROPS.

phonetics. The science of the voice, and analysis of sounds and the laws governing them. A highly difficult science.

phonies. Hangers-on in the theatrical profession, the "monied amateurs" as they used to be known in the Victorian era. Their meager talent prevents their attaining distinction. Phoney (i.e. *sham*) artists.

photo call. A *call* to which all artists summoned must attend under contract, for the purpose of being photographed in incidents from the play. The photographs appearing later in frames in front of the theater, or in the Press. Such *calls* are always given by artists without payment.

photogenic. Is applied to artists who photograph well; those suitable for motion picture work. "He's not photogenic."

pick up cues. To take one's cues without hesitation. "Let's go over that scene again and, please everybody, pick up your cues smartly, the scene is dragging."

picture. A tableau. A situation in a play where people are grouped round the central figure to form a striking pose. It is *held* for a dramatic curtain, and the *call* which follows.

picture, hold the. Keep positions for the curtain call.

picture batten = PICTURE RAIL.

picture rail. (On a flat) A wooden rail fixed between the rails at the back of a flat into which an eye is screwed to hold pictures.

piece. The Victorian term for play. "This new piece of Henry Arthur Jones is doing well at the Haymarket!" 2. Generic for any *piece* of scenery, e.g. *door piece, window piece, profile piece*, etc. 3. One's part, "Come along Joan, dear, it's your turn to say your little piece."

piece, bobtail. A *bobtail piece* is a domestic drama in a local setting. Such plays may still be performed in the Irish FIT-UP dates, and the term, now obsolete, originated in Ireland. One dealing with the *rag tag and bobtail,* or the common herd.

pill. A large and difficult part to SWALLOW.

pinch a call. (Of stage managers) To ring up the curtain for another ovation when the audience has virtualy ceased to "ovate." It is hoped that the raising of the curtain may revive the flagging house. Timid assistant stage managers are guilty of this offense when afraid of the wrath of the leading lady or leading man, who look toward the Prompt Corner (usually stage left) to indicate that there is "just another one." Cf. DEAD.

pinch a curtain = PINCH A CALL.

pin point. To narrow the beam of light from a "spot" by the use of an iris diaphragm. 2. To use such a light on an artist, or part of the setting. "Electrics! I want you to pin point the entrance through the double doors, just where I am going to stand, so will you please stand by." The Electrician then trains his spotlight on the face of the director, so that in that position the light will be full on the face of the leading artist making the entrance.

pin rail = fly rail, the *pins* being the cleats thereon for making fast the ropes.

pin-spot. The narrow beam of a spotlight.

pin up. Adjectivally applied to beautiful show-girls whose photographs appear in the "leg papers," or fashionable journals. Their pictures are cut out and *pinned up* on the walls of their fans, especially in the mess decks and barracks rooms of the naval and military services.

pirate. To LIFT the plot of an author's play, alter the dialogue and present it under a fresh title.

pirouette. To spin round on the toes (ballet). French for spinning.

pit. (Brit.) The part of the auditorium on the ground floor, behind the stalls and immediately below the dress circle. So called because originally the back of Drury Lane Theatre, London, was built on the site of a cock*pit*.

pit-door keeper. (Brit.) The attendant in charge of the door leading to the pit. He checks the admission tickets.

pit public. (Brit.) Playgoers who patronize the pit seats.

pit stalls. (Brit.) Seats midway between the stalls and the pit. The first two, or three rows of the pit itself.

pitites. (Brit.) The pit patrons.

pitch. The height or depth of the voice, the raising or lowering of the voice according to the size and acoustics of a theater. Aitkin, quoted by Egerton Lowe, says "Pitch is regulated by the tightness with which the vocal chords are stretched. In men they are about $7/12$ths of an inch in length, and the vibrations range in a bass voice from 75 to 354 per second; in a tenor from 133 to 562. In women and boys the length is about $5/12$ths of an inch; the range of a contralto is from 167 to 795 vibrations per second, and of a soprano from 239 to 1417."

places please! The Stage Manager's request to the beginners who open an act to take up the positions in which they are discovered when the curtain rises.

plank-downer. One who has paid for his seat as opposed to one on the free list. He *planks down* his money at the box office.

plant a gag. To interpolate a fresh gag into the book, usually with a local application. A reference to a favorite public house, a local character, or disreputable locality. It is a favorite habit with touring comedians in revue. They find out from the local stage staff what is likely to raise a laugh. Wilfred Pickles, the radio comedian has done this to perfection in his tours of the English towns and villages with the feature, *Have a Go*. 2. An actor who plays his part in an act from a seat in the auditorium or in the orchestra pit, and goes on the stage from there. There is much cross talk between the actor in front and the comedian on the stage. The actor is *planted* in the stalls, or orchestra pit, and very often the audience takes him for one of themselves.

play as cast. In advertisements for repertory artists the phrase means what it says. The management requires a player who is competent and versatile enough to portray any part assigned to him.

play down to the troops. The method of communicating an intelligent play to the alleged unintelligent minds of a service audience (E.N.S.A. in the Second World War). This impertinent and insulting technique defeated its own object, for the troops walked out and repaired to the N.A.A.F.I. canteen. But this is not to say that every performance given to the Forces was so rendered. Indeed, many first class plays were admirably acted in the worst of conditions for actors. Moreover, they faced some extremely critical audiences.

play for a laugh. To accentuate a line or broaden a piece of comedy business for the sake of a laugh.

play for a round. The deliberate stressing of "gallery" lines or "heroic" business to earn applause. STAGE HOGS cannot resist this.

play to capacity. To have a full house. Cf. PLAY TO COPPERS.

play to coppers. (Brit.) To have an empty house, the cheapest seats for which *coppers* (e.g. the fourpenny gallery) were paid. "What a date! we played to coppers on Saturday night" (obsolete).

play under canvas. To act in a large tent at, say, a fair ground where crude melodrama was still performed in the English provinces at the beginning of the present century.

play West End. (Brit.) To use the restrained method of naturalistic acting characteristic of that in London's West End theaters. The opposite of playing BROAD.

playbill. A poster advertisement. They have existed since the

16th century. Eliezer Edwards quotes (*Dictionary of Words, Facts & Phrases*) an entry in *The Register of the Stationer's Company,* dated October 30th, 1587; the quaintly worded: "*John Charlewood. Lycenced to him by the whole consent of thassistantes (the assistants) the onelye ympryntinge of all manner of Billes for players, iis, vid.*" This was the first entry of any exclusive right to print playbills, though they must have appeared before this time.

playdom. The world of plays and players, the theater world of New York. The variant *playerdom* is anywhere where stage artists congregate.

playgoer, earnest. A serious-minded stage "fan." The *earnest playgoer* is a cornucopia of knowledge appertaining to plays and players, possesses an elastic memory, and is quick to show pleasure or disapproval. Touring artists might remember this, for the local *E.P.* seldom misses a performance.

playgoers. Legitimate theater patrons, as distinct from vaudeville-goers.

playhouse = theater.

playitis. The *cacoethes scribendi* of the drama, the ambition to write plays. How small a percentage of good plays come out of the enormous output of these aspirants is evidenced by the number of REVIVALS that are presented in a year.

playwright. An author of plays; a dramatist. On the analogy of shipwright, or wheelwright. The *wright* element comes from the Anglo Saxon infinitive, to engrave, draw, write, work, fashion. Ultimately from *wyrhta,* a maker, worker, or builder.

plot. The main story of the drama. It is contended by Georges Polti that there are only 36 plots, of which all others are variants. French scholars are recommended in his admirable survey: *Les Trente-Six Situations Dramatiques.* 2. The list of furniture, lights, properties, etc., in a production. Hence *furniture plot, light plot,* etc.

plot, sub. The *sub*sidiary *plot* of a play.

plough the provinces. Tour with a company in the English provinces, especially the smaller dates. The term is a survival of the rustic theater when actors played to "turnips" (rustics). In U. S., *Tour the tanks; hit the sticks.*

plug. (Of a line) To stress it so as to ensure its efficacy—or to gain response from a dim-witted audience. Cf. PUT IT ON WITH A TROWEL.

Plush family. Empty seats. From the *plush* material with which seats are covered. A jocular analogy of WOOD FAMILY, "What's the house like, tonight?" "The Plush family, as usual, this tour is disastrous!" (Touring actors').

pocket. A stage light DIP.

poetic drama. The generic term for all plays written in verse. E.g. T. S. Eliot's *The Cocktail Party* or Christopher Fry's *The Lady's Not For Burning*.

points. The key lines, or words in one's part. A player who is not capable of "making his points" (i.e. stressing his lines properly) will never get over. 2. The tips of a dancer's toes. Cf. LES POINTES.

police lights. Non-electric lights in various parts of the house which, by the law of the land, must be kept alight during a performance. E.g. exit lights, which are known as "panic lights" because they prevent "panic" in the case of an electric light failure.

pom-pom dress. The conventional Pierrot costume of white pantaloons, white jacket decked with black pom-pom buttons or any other good combination of colors: mauve with gold pom-poms; black with orange; grey with pink. The costume is topped by a black silk head-scarf, surmounted by a coned hat of the same color as the dress and decorated with contrasting pom-poms. In the seaside Pierrot shows the hat was passed to collect the coppers from those outside the enclosure.

pong. To substitute words for those in the part when an artist fluffs. A resourceful player can obviate a too-obvious stick by intelligent *ponging*. Contrast, however, CUE BOUND, and CUE STRUCK.

portable. Short for PORTABLE THEATER, *infra*.

portable board. A six circuit switchboard, complete with dimmers, used for particular productions to supplement the stage switchboard.

portable-theater. A FIT-UP theater with scenery, properties, etc., which moves from village to village by rail or road. It can be a prefabricated theater, or a large marquee (tent). Cf. FIT-UP, and BOOTH.

positions. Those taken on the stage by artists for the opening of an act.

positions for curtain. The grouping of the cast for the curtain call at the end of an act, or the end of the performance, to receive the applause of the house. These positions are determined at the dress rehearsal.

positions please! = PLACES PLEASE.

pounce bag. "A muslin or lightly woven bag containing ground color for knocking against a stencil, thereby impressing the design for the final painting of a repetitive scenic piece" (A. O. Gibbons).

pounce wheel. "A sharp toothed wheel mounted in a handle for perforating the stencil, making possible the use of a pounce bag" (A. O. Gibbons).

poverty corner. (Brit.) The area around the London Hippodrome and Leicester Square, and the lower part of Charing Cross Road from Wyndham's Theatre to the Garrick Theatre. Here congregate the bonhommous "Thespian throng" to exchange the gossip of the day. Confidences are exchanged regarding projected plays or musicals. Old friends meet after several weeks or months "on the road," for it is usually the out of work *Pros* who foregather on Poverty corner, and "What do you know?" is the stock greeting. A successful musical play, and film, *Charing Cross Road,* was written around this region which is also known as *heartbreak corner.* Cf. WHAT DO YOU KNOW? and THEATRE ROYAL, OUT.

powder, face. Is used to *set* grease paint make-up, and for other purposes such as whitening the hair, etc. Its uses are outlined in any good book on stage make-up.

powder-off. To tone down a facial make-up; to *set* a make-up by powdering.

practical. Anything that *works* on the stage. Door handles that turn; windows that open; light switches that are connected with the main switchboard and can be turned on by the actor; a telephone bell that rings; in fact, anything not purely ornamental in

PRACTICALS *150*

a stage setting. It serves a *practical* purpose rather than an ornamental one.

practicals. Stage fittings that can be operated by artists on the stage. See PRACTICAL, *supra*.

Prada. The initial-formed name for *Pre R.A.D.A.*, a *pre*paratory department of the Royal Academy of Dramatic Art (pronounced *Pra*hda). Cf. RADA.

prairie comedian. A "corny" artist in an American touring show. A touring comic.

première. A first performance of a new play in London or New York, though it is applicable to any first night, anywhere.

pre-set board. One allowing of the pre-selection of circuits so that, at cue, several circuits can be dimmed out by a single master switch, and another pre-selection brought on by closing another master switch. These switches are known to electricians as *scene masters*.

press representative = PUBLICITY AGENT. One working in liaison with newspaper and journal publicity departments.

prima ballerina. The principal (female) dancer in a *corps de ballet*.

prima donna. Literally the first lady in (Italian) opera, though the term embraces all opera.

prime. To treat new scenic canvas with a solution of size and pigment. The preparation of the canvas for painting.

Prime Minister of Mirth. (Brit.) George Robey, the English comedian. Mr. Robey, still happily hale and hearty, has been the best loved figure on the music hall stage, and many of the songs he made famous are still heard at sing-songs and Service Reunions. During the First World War George Robey starred with Violet Lorraine in *The Bing Boys*, which was followed by *The Bing Boys on Broadway*. The lilting sentimental duet *If You Were the Only Girl in the World* was one of the biggest "hits" of *The Bing Boys*, and is a favorite number in the *Songs of the Great War* medley. His "it's naughty, but it's nice" style of humor is in a class by itself, cleverly inoffensive, robust, and altogether delightful. A man of culture and versatility, George Robey has written several humorous books and piquant short stories.

principal boy is, paradoxically, the principal *girl* who plays the Prince Charming in a Christmas pantomime.

principalitis. Small part singers or actors who consider themselves capable and worthy of the principal parts (or the jocular analogy of appendicitis).

principals. Players of the *principal* characters in plays or musical productions. The leading players. Cf. TAIL, THE.

prior to London production. The intimation on playbills that the play is being given a short run before its metropolitan première. Cf. TRY-OUT TOUR.

probation part. A role assigned to a young artist on the understanding that if he, or she, doesn't succeed in it, the part will be withdrawn and given to another player.

problem play. One that treats of a psychological or sociological problem.

procellous. As in "a very striking procellous effect." A storm scene, from the literal sense of the Latin *procella*, a storm (a pedantic adjective common with Victorian critics).

prochronism. The pre-dating of an event, or the use of up-to-date colloquialisms in a play whose action takes place long before such expressions became fashionable.

producer. (Brit.) This misnomer for Stage Director is so firmly planted in the theater soil that it is likely to prove as perennial as *female impersonator* and similar misapplications. He directs the actors in the rehearsal of a play, arranges the décor, lighting, etc., according to the period and atmosphere.

producer's play. One reflecting credit on the producer (director) rather than its intrinsic merits *as a play*. It provides scope for the producer's ideas, and allows him to thoroughly enjoy himself.

production. The entire set-up of a modern play, opera, musical comedy, revue, or cabaret show. Scenery, lighting, properties, publicity, even the artists themselves are included in this all-embracing term.

production account. The Stage Director's account of all properties bought: expenses for the hire of furniture, lighting equipment; wages to all stage hands employed during the course of rehearsals; the cost of lighting consumed at any other theater in which the play was rehearsed; the hire of rehearsal-rooms, and all incidental expenses incurred in the way of entertainment by the Stage Director and his staff, to say nothing of "palm-greasing" (as tipping is called in the theater). In fact, *all* expenses incurred up to the rise of the curtain on the first night.

Profession, the. The theatrical profession. Also known as THE BUSINESS.

professional jealousy. Though far less prevalent than it was during the last century, this form of cold warfare can be extremely dangerous and has caused much trouble "backstage." Professional jealousy is manifested in many subtle ways, by innuendo, gossip or, in blatant cases, by overt acts upon the stage. Masking the object of jealousy by deliberately standing in the line of sight; speaking, or moving, during lines and so distracting the audience's attention. Much of this jealousy is unwittingly created by the Press, which may give prominence to one artist at the expense of another equally entitled to "news space." Incredible are the shifts to which a professionally jealousy person would go in the days when this habit was more general.

profile. A *fret-piece* cut out of three-ply wood and painted in perspective where it would be impossible or unnecessary to build three-dimensionally.

program. A brochure describing the events in an entertainment. Specifically, the names of the actors in the cast.

projector. A spotlight, or lime, used specifically for the projection of light directionally, as opposed to the flooding or diffusion of light.

prologue. A speech or poem recited to the audience as introductory to a play. It was originally part of a Greek drama, preceding the first chorus. Cf. EPILOGUE.

proletarian opera. One dealing with the working class. Cf. LOUNGE-SUIT OPERA.

prompt book. The fair copy of the typescript of the play. It is kept in the Prompt Corner (usually stage left) and held by one of the stage managers. Cf. PROMPT COPY, *infra*.

prompt copy. The Stage Manager's marked 'script which contains the director's final instructions, the business, lighting, cues, effects, calls, etc. Prompts are given from this copy only, for it is to the play what a *definitive* edition is to a book, the director's last word. It is kept in the Prompt Corner during the running of the play, and in the Stage Manager's possession at other times, except during the rehearing of understudies.

prompt entrance. (Brit.) The way onto the stage from the Prompt Corner, which is for the use of the Stage Management. The cast may use this entrance if it helps them, but otherwise permission must be asked from the stage director.

Prompt proper. The customary (*proper*) position of the Prompt Corner in most English theaters is on the player's left hand when facing the audience. (In U. S., stage left.) Occasionally, however, the Corner is on the opposite side (stage right), which then makes the left-hand corner the O.P. side. Cf. REVERSED THEATER and entries at PROMPT SIDE and O.P. SIDE.

Prompt side. The side of the stage from which an artist takes a prompt. Cf. O.P.

prompt, take a. See TAKE A PROMPT.

prompt table. One used on the stage at rehearsals. The prompt book is placed thereon and the stage manager follows the text and *prompts* when an artist needs help. Also the stationary table in the Prompt Corner used by the person "on the book" during the performance.

Pro digs. (Brit.) Theatrical apartments. *Pro*fessional *diggings*.

Pro-donna. (Brit.) A theatrical landlady. A jocular analogy of the operatic *prima-donna*. Cf. MA.

Pro landlady. (Brit.) A *pro*fessional landlady, or boarding house keeper. Those kindly and understanding folk who have helped many *Pros* during their struggles "on the road," and whom most artists remember with affection when "looking back" from London eminence.

prop basket. Short for:

property basket. A large hamper containing stage or personal properties. It is the traditional boast of an old actor that he was born in a *prop basket* in the prompt corner. Cf. SKIP.

prop gag. Is short for *prop*erty *gag*. A trick effect. E.g. an expanding fish used by a comedian when retailing mendacious angling stories. Any fun-making instrument used in SLAPSTICK comedy, or pantomime.

prop room. Short for *property room,* the abode of the theater Property Master. It is a workshop-cum-store where this craftsman makes the properties used in a production when he lacks the articles in his *standard props.*

props, stage. Those used on the *stage* as distinct from HAND-PROPS or PERSONAL PROPS. E.g. flower vases, candle sticks, clocks, telephone apparatus, waste-paper basket, etc. In U. S., *set props.*

propaganda play. One having a message for a particular sect, or type of audience.

props, travel on one's. See TRAVEL ON ONE'S PROPS.

Pros. *Pro*fessional artist*s.* "The matinee was a wow, the house was stiff with Pros." It is on matinée days that fellow *profes*sional*s* attend performances of their friends' plays when such matinées fall on other days than their own. See MIDNIGHT MATINÉE.

pros (pronounced *pross*). The *pros*cenium.

pros batten. Short for *pros*cenium *batten* or Number One light batten.

pros border. Short for PROSCENIUM BORDER.

pros box. The stage box, adjoining the proscenium arch.

pros wing. See RETURNS.

proscenium. Part of the stage between the curtain and the orchestra. It contains the proscenium arch through which the audience views the play.

proscenium border. The permanent border in front of the curtain.

pross. This Victorian slang verb for cadge (i.e. drinks, cigarettes, etc.) has fallen into desuetude since the end of the Great War (1914–1918). A secondary sense of the verb is to coach, school, train (stage beginners), and in this sense it may derive from the Romany meaning of *pross,* to ridicule. 2. As a substantive in slang, is one who can be prevailed upon to stand a less fortunate artist a drink, or loan. Also a *cadged* drink.

pross, on the. Sponging for drinks on a stage beginner. The novice is expected to stand a round in appreciation of the tuition received from the mentor. This is more the sense 2 of *pross*, the verb.

prosser. (Brit.) A cadger. One of the HALF CROWN BRIGADE.

Prosser's Avenue. (Brit.) The old Gaiety Bar, so christened by the music hall singer, Ted Hughes.

protagonist. The chief character in a play. The leading actor. The Greek prōtos, first; agōnistēs, actor.

Protean act. See entry *infra*.

Protean entertainer. A lightning change artist. An impersonator in the manner of Brandsby Williams. From *Proteus*, the sea god, who had the power to change his form at will.

provinces. (Brit.) The English provincial towns. Cf. PLOUGH THE PROVINCES.

provincial actor. (Brit.) See the entry *infra*.:

provincial player. (Brit.) An actor, or actress, whose career is spent in the provincial theaters.

provincial theater. (Brit.) The stage outside London.

public. Is generic for audiences. An artist's FANS are known as a public. "My public will hate me in this part" (actress's lament when offered an UNSYMPATHETIC PART.)

public dress rehearsal. Sometimes follows a private dress rehearsal of an opera, or play. At the Glyndebourne Opera House, Sussex, it is customary to admit the public to the final dress rehearsal at a reduced price of admission.

publicity. Advertising generally. Bill boards, newspaper notices, shop, and hotel display cards, hand bills, throw-aways, and the rest.

publicity agent. The official in charge of advertising matter. Cf. ADVANCE MANAGER.

publicity chaser. An artist thirsting for any form of publicity.

publicity hog = *publicity hound* = *publicity chaser*. Cf. LIMELIGHT HOG.

pull-in. A leading player with power to attract (pull in) audiences to the theater. "Du Maurier was a good *pull-in*, whatever part he had." Cf. BOX OFFICE DRAW.

punks. Country audiences, rustics. Hence, *playing to the punks* is the American version of *playing to the turnips*. *Punk* is touchwood, worthless stuff, and is applied slangily to anything of poor (in this case, critical) quality.

pusher. A scenery *pusher*. A stagehand who runs the flats.

put a stool down. (Brit.) To hire a stool for the pit, or gallery queue.

put it on with a trowel. To overact the sentimental or comedy element, as a builder uses cement, slapping it on with his trowel. A variant of *Lay it on with a trowel*.

put on. Produce (a play or musical). "That new show of Tom Arnold's is beautifully put on." 2. (Of expression) Assumed. "He put on a pretty grim look when he heard the agent's terms."

Q

quarrel scene. A fight, or "high words" in a drama. Quarrel scenes and stage fights have to be very carefully rehearsed, especially in the old dramas when swords are used.

quarter, the. (Brit.) The *quarter*-of-an-hour before the OVERTURE is played. The call boy's "Quarter-of-an-hour, please!" "Have you heard the quarter yet?" "Yes, it went some time ago, he'll be calling the *five minutes*, anytime."

quartette. A group of four actors, or singers in an act or scene. From the musical sense.

queen it. (Of a leading lady) To give herself airs, and generally to become obnoxious to the rest of the cast. To seek the center of the stage and act the great lady.

quick change. A rapid change of raiment during a performance. Just sufficient time to leave the stage, change clothing, and be back in time for an entrance cue.

quick-change artist. A variety artist specializing in PROTEAN acts.

quick-change room. This can be a dressing room near the stage or a number of flats cleated together at the side of the stage. In musical shows having many changes of scenery and dresses, it is often necessary for an artist to change "at the side," especially in twice-nightly versions.

queue for stools. (Brit.) The queue which forms in the forenoon, to wait for the theater attendant to issue the stools for the pit (orchetra) and gallery queues. The stools are placed with the patrons' names on them and save the long wait—sometimes for hours—for the doors to open. Before the inception of queue stools, district messengers were sometimes employed to stand in the queue.

quius kius. Silence! cease! be quiet! (especially when waiting at the side of the stage for entrance cues). This obsolete catchphrase is recorded in Eric Partridge's *A Dictionary of Slang* *and Unconventional English,* Third Edition, 1950 (Addenda), and was current from 1880–1910. The *kius* reduplicates *quius*, from the Latin *quietus*.

quoth the raven. The quotation from Edgar Allan Poe's poem, the full line being, "quoth the raven, never more!" is often written in a theatrical landlady's visitor's book. It warns other lodgers that the DIGS are not good.

R

rachel. Face-powder of a lightish fawn tint. "It was devised in honor of Elisa Félix, stage-named Mademoiselle Rachel (1820–58); she achieved a fame second only, among French actresses, to that of Sarah Bernhardt. She excelled in tragic roles and was a creature of fire and quicksilver". (Eric Partridge, in *Name into Word*, 1949).

rack. The key rack in the stage doorkeeper's office. Actors "draw" their dressing room keys from him when they arrive at the theater, and surrender them to him when they leave after the performance. See entry at STAGE DOORKEEPER.

Rada. (Brit.) The *R*oyal *A*cademy of *D*ramatic *A*rt, Gower Street, London, presided over by Sir Kenneth Barnes, where students of the drama are trained in stagecraft, deportment, elocution, etc. *Rada* is the forcing ground of talent and many present-day leading players graduated here (pronounced *Rah*da).

radio show. An entertainment that, through its popularity as a radio feature, tours the country in a stage version. Cf. SOAP OPERA.

rag. The stage curtain. Cr. FRENCH TABS; ROLLER; TABS; TRAILER and VELVETS. "What time does the rag go up next week?"

rail. The horizontal wooden member at the back of a flat. Cf. STILE, and FLY-RAIL.

rain box. An oblong box about four feet by six inches, containing dried peas, or lead shot. By moving the box up and down an excellent rain effect is produced. Cf. RAIN DRUM, and RAIN PIPES, *infra*.

rain drum. A circular trough with a parchment base in which grape shot, or dried peas are rotated to give a tropical rain sound. Cf. RAIN BOX, *supra*.

rain pipes. Water pipes especially constructed with small holes in the undersides for visible rain effects. The pipe is connected

RAKE

to hydrants and arranged where necessary over doors and windows.

rake. A stage is raked (inclined) at half an inch rise per foot of stage depth. Modern stages, however, have no rake, though very often the auditoriums are slightly raked to give better visibility to the audience.

raking piece. A triangular piece of scenery painted to resemble a garden, road, or grass bank, which masks a ramp. 2. A length of wood tapered for placing under a scenic piece so that it will look level on a raked stage.

rally. (Brit.) Increased tempo in a scene, or at the end of an act in farce, or at a dramatic climax in a drama. "You were all rather slow at the rally last night, please quicken the scene, tonight."

ramp. The inclined side of a plank which takes the place of steps that lead up to a rostrum. 2. The slope from the dock-doors of a theater to the trucks, or floats. Do not confuse with *rake*.

rant. To act noisily, be bombastic in the manner of the barnstormers. To mouth and over-gesticulate. Cf. TEAR A PASSION TO TATTERS.

ranter. An actor who employs a flamboyant, clamorous, dramatic technique to GET OVER. This style of actor is rare today.

raspberry. A "rude noise" of disapproval from the gallery. Short for an indelicate rhyming on raspberry tart.

rave. To rant in the manner of the "hammish" melodrama actors. 2. To enthuse over a performance. "The Press raved over the show."

read. To read a part at rehearsal, or to do so at a performance when sudden illness causes a player to be "off," and no understudy is available. The part is usually read by the stage manager or small part player. It is never a satisfactory arrangement, and seldom resorted to except in desperation.

reading of a part, the. Its interpretation and portrayal.

realism. The presentation of plays according to "real life." Cf. NATURALISTIC ACTING.

recitative. An operatic "narrative," sung in the speaking style without a defined melody. It is neatly defined by Jeffrey Pulver as "the prose of vocal music." Cf. CALYPSO.

red, and blue boxes. (Brit.) The boxes on the right and left side of the auditorium at the Glyndebourne Opera House. See RED, AND BLUE SIDES, *infra*.

red side and blue side. Respectively, the right and left sides of the auditorium at the Glyndebourne Festival Opera House, Sussex, where there is no center aisle. The seat tickets are either red or blue, according to which side of the house the numbers are situated. People holding *red* tickets enter the auditorium through the *red-painted* corridor in the Covered Way, and *blue* ticket holders enter through the *blue-painted* corridor on the Tudor garden side of the theater. In row C, for example, there are 22 seats, numbers 1 to 11 have red tickets, numbers 12 to 22 have blue tickets, and this division of colors obtains through the house: boxes, balcony, and stalls. Prospective patrons (see GUESTS) might remember this color ruling which would save time in case of a last-minute arrival. The entrances to the boxes and balcony are in the COVERED WAY, the right-hand door being for *red* ticket holders, the left hand for *blue*.

red-nosed comic. (Brit.) A variant of Lancashire comic. He wears grotesque clothes and reddens his nose in the manner of the traditional clown.

Ref, the. (Brit.) The defunct *Sunday Referee*, a favorite newspaper read by thousands of *Pros* on Sunday train journeys from the 1880s to the 1920s when the paper died. The "Sunday Ref" contained notices of plays, variety gossip, as well as the famous "Mustard and Cress" column which was started by the late George R. Sims. The "Ref" was to actors what the *Sunday Times* and *Observer* are to literary men.

register, high/low. (Of the singing or speaking voice) "Take it at a lower register, Miss Gay."

rehearsal pay. That given to artists who rehearse over the prescribed number of "free" calls. Since the advent of Equity a more reasonable scheme of payment has been agreed upon by managements. In U. S., forty dollars per week expense money during usual rehearsal period of three to four weeks.

rehearsal-rooms. Hired rooms used for rehearsing plays when no stage is available.

remote control board. A lighting switchboard that operates independently from the main board.

Rep. Short for *rep*ertory.

Rep, in. Appearing in a Repertory Company. "What are you doing these days?" "Well, I'm in 'Rep' at the moment, but I am going out with *Mr. Roberts* next month."

Rep producer. One specializing in Repertory theater work.

repartee. Quick, witty replies. "Snappy come-backs" in cross talk comedy on the music-halls. The *answers* in stage conversation. French *repartie*, "an answering blow, or thrust (in fencing, etc.) and thence, a return of, or answer in speech" (Ernest Weekley quoting Cotgrave).

Repertory Players. (Brit.) The leading Sunday Society which has produced plays in London for over thirty years. Its members include leading managers and artists, and only original plays are staged, revivals being prohibited by the rules of the Society. The Committee, composed of leading lights in the West End theater, are extremely conservative, and such plays as are selected for production are of high merit and are frequently bought for the London theater and become successful. An average of eight new plays a year are presented by the Repertory Players.

Repertory performance. This is a disparaging description of a poor version of a town success. An under-rehearsed performance in the style of the hurried production methods of weekly repertory in which there is little time to concentrate on finesse.

repertoire. The program of plays in a weekly repertory company or a play-per-night touring company, as e.g. A Shakespearean Company, or the Macdona Players who did one Shaw play a night. The company's stock of plays.

répétition générale. A midnight performance following the ordinary evening show. 2. A dress rehearsal to which the public is invited.

repose. Ease upon the stage, ability to keep still without appearing awkward, stiff, or self-conscious.

resident manager. The manager of the theater as distinct from the company manager of a visiting company. In U. S., *house* *manager*. He handles all the local business. Cf. RESIDENT STAGE MANAGER.

resident staff. The permanent staff of a theater. They live locally and are known as *"the boys."* Cf. TOURING STAFF. In U. S., *House Crew*.

resident stage manager. (Brit.) The title by which the permanent *carpenter* of a theater likes to be known. In a provincial theater he works with the carpenter of the visiting company. The R.S.M. is an important functionary in any theater and is worthy of the greatest respect for, under his control, work the RESIDENT STAFF.

resin box. A shallow box containing resin. One is kept at each side of the stage for dancers to step into and cover the soles of their shoes with resin, which prevents their slipping on the stage.

resistance. See DIMMER.

responsible player. (Brit.) One that can be relied upon to give a competent performance in character as well as straight parts.

responsibles. (Brit.) Responsible parts assigned to touring, or repertory artists. 2. The players of such parts. "We have fixed a joint engagement as responsibles in Rep." "Wanted, sound actor for responsibles and Stage Management" (newspaper advertisement).

rest lights. To reduce lighting to the bare essentials at rehearsals or during the act waits (intermissions). A working light, or *T-piece*, is sufficient when "walking" scenes without books. In U. S., *work light*.

Restoration comedies. Those produced during the Restoration period of English history, from the time of King Charles' return to the throne in 1660 to about 1730. It was an age of witty and distinguished writing. The best known and most representative of Restoration dramatists are: Sir William Congreve (1670–1729), who was perhaps the greatest of them all, and whose brilliant *The Way of the World* (1700) has been frequently revived in recent years; William Wycherley (1640–1716), who adapted *The Plain Dealer* from *Le Misanthrope* of Molière, and whose *The Country Wife* is still a popular revival. Thomas Otway, somewhat embittered by his association with the actress

Elizabeth Barry, produced in 1682 that great play, *Venice Preserved,* and translated Racine and Molière. He learned his stagecraft as an actor. One of the biggest successes of the Restoration period was John Gay's *The Beggar's Opera.* Other dramatists whose plays have been "restored from time to time" are Sir John Vanbrugh (1664–1726), an original, witty and "grossly indecent" writer. George Farquhar (1678–1707), another ex-actor who will be remembered by his delightful *The Beaux' Stratagem.* The age was one of adventure, intrigue, and healthy, if coarse, humor, and the very spirit of the period is reflected in the comedies.

resting. Euphemistic for out of work. In the Theatrical Card column in stage newspapers one finds *resting* to be the state of quite a number of artists in this very overcrowded profession. Cf. AT LIBERTY.

return date. A further booking at the same theater as a result of a very successful and profitable week (touring companies).

returns. Pieces of scenery placed at right-angles to the up and down stage flats. 2. The ticket counterfoils that are checked on the morning after the performance by the business manager. 3. Unused theater tickets, *returned* before the performance for resale. In U. S., name often used for TORMENTORS, q.v.

Reunion Theater. (Brit.) Whose motto might well be "Should old acquaintance be forgot," is an organization acting as liaison between the returned Service artists and the commercial theater. With the Services Sunday Society, Reunion Theater—which was formed at the end of the Second World War—has done much to help bridge the gap between 1939 and the postwar years. Two outstanding London successes, *The Noose* and *The Man from the Ministry,* were first produced by this organization, whose aim is to produce eight new plays a year.

reveal. The "thickness" of a wall between the stage setting (flats) and the door.

reversed theater. One having the Prompt-side on the O.P. side. In England the usual side for the Prompt Corner is on the artist's left, but occasionally the position is *reversed* and the prompter works from the right-hand corner of the stage. In American theaters the Prompt Corner is generally on the right, and the terms *right* and *left* (from the stage) are in common usage.

revival. The production of an old success as a stop-gap pending a new production at a metropolitan theater. Revivals are usually put on for a limited RUN or SEASON.

revolve. A *revolv*ing stage. A turning section of the "acting area" on which a scene is set. When a set is being performed upon, other sets are ready on the reverse sides of the "revolve" which, as required, are brought forward. At the end of an act or scene the set is revolved and the next one faces the audience. It is of great value in plays with multiple scenes, demanding quick changes. The revolving stage was invented by Karl Kautenschlager and first used in Munich in 1896.

revolving batten. A light batten supporting a four-sided magazine compartment containing color media, frosts, reflectors, etc. It is wired in circuits so that the lighting can be set for the production, and appropriate lighting brought forward according to the plot. These units can be electrically or manually operated.

rice. Is sometimes used by the Property Master for rain effects.

right. In stage directions the right-hand side of the stage *facing* the audience. The actor's right. In most British theaters the O.P. SIDE.

rig lights. To place spotlights, floods, lighting towers, lengths, etc., in their correct positions on the plot. The term *rig* must not be confused with *set*, which means to light (i.e. switch on) the scene. See SET LIGHTS.

Ring, the. The *Ring des Nibelungen* of Richard Wagner which comprises the four operas: *The Rhinegold, The Valkyrie, Siegfried* and *Götterdämmerung*. 2. The West End "ring" of Theatrical managers (Brit.).

ring the band. The stage manager does this from the Prompt Corner a few minutes before the Overture, or at the end of each act when the band is required to play the entr'acte music. He also rings the band when he wants them to end on a coda, to shorten an act wait (intermission) when the play is running over the usual time.

ring up/down. In many theaters there is a light warning signal from the Prompt Corner to the fly-platform. A *green* or *red* light (according to the colors decided upon for this) warns the flymen that the rise (or fall) of the curtain is imminent, and the men "stand by" for the other light (see entry at WARNING AND GO) which tells them to haul the ropes. At one time, and in some theaters still, a bell was the curtain warning, and the term *ring up* or *ring down* has remained in the stage managerial vocabulary. Thus "We'll be ringing down five minutes earlier tonight, it's a poor house." In U. S., frequently *light on* is warning signal; *light off* signal to *go*. Since the stage manager usually *works* the show from *stage right*, he can often give a physical sign or verbal command to the curtain operator.

role. Is obsolescent for part, or character. See TITLE ROLE.

roller curtain. The old-fashioned DROP CURTAIN, now rarely found except in very old theaters. Rollers were very dangerous, for they came down at speed and were very heavy. The compiler of this glossary remembers—and always with a shudder—a narrow escape from such a curtain which came down within six inches of his head when lying on the stage after being "shot" by the crook in *The Fourth Wall*. After that incident the "corpse" preferred to be killed further up stage.

rolling stage. A platform, or two sections of a platform, set on rollers to facilitate quick changes of scenery. One scene is set behind another and rolled down stage when the other is struck.

Romantic opera. Is written round a legendary figure or theme. E.g. *The Nibelungen Ring* of Wagner, *Prince Igor* of Borodin, and some of the works of Monteverde and Gluck.

rooms. The "superior" artists' term for PRO DIGS.

roost. The top of the gallery.

Roscius. Is descriptive of any brilliant young actor, usually *infant Roscius*. After Quintus Roscius, the Roman actor who died in 62 B.C., aged about fifty. A friend of Cicero, who defended him in a law suit (Pro Q. Quintus Roscius Comoedo), he was regarded as the greatest actor of his time, especially in comedy. Eric Partridge in *Name into Word* cites William Betty, who retired in 1824, at the age of thirty-three, as *"The Young Roscius."* The name *Roscius* has become generic for an outstandingly brilliant actor.

rostrum. A portable platform built upon a folding frame, used for Shakespearean and Classical plays.

rotten apple. An American variant of RASPBERRY. To guy a performance, or individual performer.

rouge. A red cosmetic; a polishing powder used for facial make-up (French for red).

rough out. (A scene) To erect a set on the stage in order that the positions of windows, doors, fireplaces, etc., can be determined. 2. To engage in preliminary *blocking* of a scene, i.e. rudimentary staging, actors' movements.

round. Short for *round* of applause. Cf. HANDS.

round, entrance/exit. One given to a favorite artist on his first appearance on the stage, and one on his departure. An exit round, however, can be accorded to any artist whose exit follows a good line.

round of parts. Those portrayed by an actor in nightly repertory.

round, play for a. To overact in order to evoke applause. Playing to the gallery.

round, go. See GO ROUND.

rounds, do the. To call upon the round of theatrical agents in London. To call from one to the other after the manner of the milkman on his delivery *rounds.*

roundels. Footlights so shaped. They are rather uncommon and not very popular.

row. Is short for GROUND ROW.

Royal, the. The Theatre Royal, anywhere. "I hear you are playing Sheffield next week; where are you, the *Royal* or the Lyceum?" Cf. KINGS, THE.

Royal Family of Broadway. The famous Barrymore family; Florence, Ethel, John and Lionel; the aristocrats of the New York stage. They have reigned long and successfully on Broadway and were the subjects of a play by Edna Ferber and George S. Kaufman, entitled *The Royal Family* (1927).

rube show. A drama with a rustic setting. From *Reuben,* a country bumpkin. Cf. HICK.

run. (verb) To finance a production or individual player. "Who is running the show?"

run, the. The length of a production's *run* at a theater or on tour. Theatrical contracts are made for "the run of the play." 2. The duration of a play's acting time, e.g. "How long does this scene run?" Cf. RUNNING TIME.

run a flat. To move a flat by gripping with both hands the leading stile. The left—or right, according to the direction the flat is to be run—hand grasps the toggle on the first rail, the right hand holds the stile about three feet higher than the toggle. Held thus the flat can be balanced and moved about the stage with ease.

run over. (Lines) To rehearse a part merely for the *words*, no expression or intonations being put into them. Just an assurance that one knows one's lines.

runner. A length of cocoa-nut matting placed behind the stage and at the sides, to deaden the footsteps of actor's walking "to and fro" to take up positions for entrance cues. 2. A curtain track.

running account. The Stage Manager's weekly account of all expenditure on properties bought for use regularly on the stage, such as tea, milk, sugar and consumable goods generally. The hire and repair of furniture, stage staff salaries for the week, in fact, all expenses connected with the backstage department incurred during the running of the show.

running time. The actual time the play takes in performance, act by act, excluding intervals and final curtain calls, which are logged separately. See TIME BOOK and TIME THE ACTS.

runway. Also known as the gangway. It ran from the stage into the auditorium, and was used in burlesque when the girls paraded before the audience. Now used occasionally by a director during rehearsals, as it saves him making frequent use of the pass door. U. S. *legitimate* houses do not have runways. Occasionally a primitive crossover may be erected for the convenience of the director.

Ruritania. This imaginary country is the locale of Musical Comedy and romantic drama. The name was invented by Anthony Hope (1863–1933) in his best-selling novel and successful play, *The Prisoner of Zenda.* On the analogy of *Aquitania, Mauritania.*

rustic drama. Any play set in the country and dealing with country people. E.g. Eden Philpott's *The Farmer's Wife*, which gave Sir Cedric Hardwicke—in *Churdles Ash*—the finest character part of the century, and how superbly he played it.

rustic comic. A comedian specializing in "comic farmer" parts in melodrama. Now seldom seen, except in burlesques or revue sketches.

S

S.A. Short for *sex appeal*.

Sadler's Wells dip. (Brit.) An "Old Pro's" term for chalk with which a dark smudge can be obliterated from a white garment, or evening dress shirt front. The *modus operandi* being an application of white chalk followed by a dash of powder. The Sadler's Wells theater was named after the man who, when digging in his garden at Clerkenwell, found an ancient *holy well* that had not been open since the Reformation. He founded a Spa and "Musick House" which afterwards became a theater. The present-day Sadler's Wells is the home of Opera and Ballet, at popular prices.

salad parade. A parade of ballet dancers.

Salzburg. The rallying point of international opera lovers in early autumn. A festival of Mozart and classical operas lasts for a number of weeks, and some of the world's finest singers and conductors are engaged to present the operas to perfection. The Salzburg Festival has been revived after its cessation during the war years.

Sammy French's. The firm of Samuel French, Limited, publishers of acting editions of popular plays. See FRENCH EDITION. In U. S., Samuel French, Inc., N. Y. and Hollywood.

sand cloth. A painted stage cloth representing a road or lane, used for exterior scenes.

sandwich batten. Two flat pieces of wood screwed together with the top edge of a cloth *sandwiched* between them.

satire. A sarcastic commentary on current affairs, or a particular way of life. The plays of Noel Coward and Frederick Lonsdale produced during the 1920s were perfect examples of this form of comedy, notably Coward's *The Vortex* and many of his mordant sketches in revue, and Lonsdale's *Our Betters, On Approval* and *Canaries Sometimes Sing*. In the Greek theater this form of play was performed with a fantastic background of satyrs.

save your lights! The same as "rest your lights!" the order to switch off all unnecessary lighting during an act wait or at rehearsals.

Savoyards. Original members of the famous D'Oyly Carte Opera Company, which presented the popular Gilbert and Sullivan operas at the Savoy Theatre, London. These operas have remained firm favorites with the theater publics in England and America; and the greatest honor paid to this wonderful partnership of Sir W. S. Gilbert and Sir Arthur Sullivan was the American exhibition of manuscripts, engraved and printed matter, at the Pierpont Morgan Library. This exhibition was owed to the generosity and industry of two American gentlemen, Reginald Allen and the late Carrol A. Wilson. Mr. Allen's collection was "on deposit" in the library and, on the day the exhibition opened, Mrs. Wilson presented her late husband's material to the library. Rarities from the Harvard theater collection and other contributions were lent to this magnificent assembly, which was surely the finest tribute ever paid to Gilbert and Sullivan's art, which is as keenly appreciated in the United States as in Great Britain, and has been increasingly popular with American audiences from 1875 when the operas were first presented. 2. Gilbert and Sullivan enthusiasts.

say one's piece. To speak the lines of one's part. 2. To make a curtain speech.

scarlet flush. (Brit.) A heavy loss through the failure of the production. The scarlet (red) side of the ledger indicating debt. In U. S., *in the red.*

scarper. (Brit.) To decamp, leave lodgings without settling the landlady's account. From the Italian *scappare*, to run away. There is an old story of the theatrical landlady who, asked by a neighbor where her "lets" were going the following week, answered: "They say they are going to *Scarper*, but I can't find it on the map." The term is a Parlyaree survival, mainly used by touring artists.

scenario. A term borrowed from the film industry. It means a

SCENE

synopsis, the plot, characters and details of the play. From the Italian.

scene. The setting, the painted canvas of the flats, backings, etc. The general "set up" of an act in a production. From the Greek *skene*, a tent (i.e. booth) or stage.

scene change. The striking of one scene and the erection of another.

scene dock. Usually shortened to *dock*. A storage space at the back or side of the stage where scenery, furniture, "rostrums" and the like are stacked.

scene master. A *master* switch on a PRE-SET BOARD.

scene painter. The out-moded term for a SCENIC ARTIST.

scene plot. The diagrammatic *blueprint* of a production.

scene shifter. A stagehand employed to move (*shift*) scenery and run flats. Cf. DECK-HAND, GRIP-HAND, STAGEHAND, etc.

scenic artist. The modern title of the SCENE PAINTER and, modern décor being what it is, he has to be more skilful and more artistic than his predecessor of the Victorian era.

scenic effect. The general appearance of the décor, lighting, costumes, etc., of the production. If approved by the director stands for the run of the production.

scissors cross. An awkward movement made by a beginner when crossing the stage. He starts on the wrong foot, his legs crossing after the manner of a pair of scissors.

scissors stage. A stage superimposed on castors, used to expedite changes of scenery. Two stages of equal length to the proscenium opening, and varying depths (depending upon the amount of off-stage room) are pivoted at the down-stage corners. While one stage is in use, the other can be struck and reset with a different scene. Sometimes a third stage is used and moved on castors from back stage in between the open scissors. This type of stage is a substitute for the more convenient revolving stage. Cf. BOAT TRUCK and ROLLING STAGE. In U. *wagon stage*.

scoring line. Where the flats meet each other when cleated together.

scorpions. Restless children in an audience—usually at matinée. Their *stinging* remarks are "distracting," to put it mildly, to artists. Those who have appeared at children's matinee performances of Shakespeare will appreciate this. The term, originally American, is very, very apt.

Scotch comic. A Scottish comedian in the traditional manner of the great Sir Harry Lauder (1871–1950).

scrim. A gauze cloth that looks transparent when lit from behind. Literally, *scrim* is a kind of lining cloth. 2. Loose cords of rope or canvas.

'script. Short for manu*script* or type*script.*

sea row. A *ground row* representing a seascape.

seasonal shop. (Brit.) An engagement for the summer season in, say, a concert party or in a touring company that visits theaters which open only in the summer months. Also a pantomime engagement during the Xmas season which lasts until mid-March at some theaters. Cf. SUMMER SHOP.

second picture. The second curtain call whilst the PICTURE at the first curtain is held.

secondary lighting. That which supports the dominant lighting. 2. Emergency power used in case of a breakdown in the primary supply system.

secondary plot. See SUB PLOT.

sections. The circuits in a row of footlights or light battens. "Check your blue section, Electrics!" Cf. CIRCUIT.

see and be seen. The slogan of the fashionable opera goers at, say, the Metropolitan Opera House, New York, or one of the European Festivals. These functions are as much a fashion parade as an operatic feast.

send out (into the country). To send a company on tour with a metropolitan play, which has to be a "Chinese copy" of the original production, with mannerisms, intonations, business, etc., faithfully copied by the touring cast.

sentimental comedy. A mawkish play marked by stilted dialogue and inept characterization. This type of play originated in the *comédie larmoyante*, the "sob drama," in a middle class setting.

sepia chanteuse. Miss Josephine Baker, the vaudeville singer, so described in a Broadway billing.

sepia show. A revue performed by colored artists, e.g. the famous *Black Crows*, or *The Christy Minstrels.*

Services Sunday Society. (Brit.) Was formed at the end of the 1939–45 war to help actors and actresses, demobilized from the British Forces, to re-establish themselves in their profession by re-introducing their names and work to managements that had forgotten them during the war years. A re-educational service is operated in U. S. by the American Theater Wing's Professional Training Program.

set. Short for stage *setting*, or scenery.

set, standing. See STANDING SET.

set back to the wall. To erect a scene as near as possible to the back wall of the stage. This has to be done in a small theater with a shallow stage. In such a theater a large set takes up the entire stage depth from the setting line to the back wall, giving no room behind the back-cloth for artists to pass across the stage. This usually means that one must *cross over* under the stage in theaters where this is possible.

set lights. The electrician and his assistants light the scenes according to the plot at the lighting rehearsal. To *set* means to switch on the stage lighting at any time, whether at the performance, or at rehearsal. The order "Set your lights" is given by the Stage Manager a few minutes before the curtain rises, and the opening combination is switched on. Footlights (floats), spot, and flood lights, backing lengths, etc., are all set as soon as the overture commences.

set piece. A small setting within a setting, e.g. the gable of a house, entrance gates, a balcony, an outhouse. Generally used to heighten perspective.

set up. To erect scenery and furnish a setting.

setting. The scene when built upon the stage. Decor, furniture, etc.

setting line. A fixed line down stage near the apron, below which scenery cannot be set up.

settle. To obtain an engagement. "I have just settled for the new show at the Palace" (touring, and vaudeville artists').

seven movements in ballet. 1. *plier*, to bend; 2. *étendre*, to stretch; 3. *relever*, to raise; 4. *glisser*, to glide; 5. *sauter*, to jump; 6. *élancer*, to dart; 7. *tourner*, to turn.

seven unknown languages of the stage. A reference to the odd essays at dialect in regional plays. Cf. MUMMERSETSHIRE.

sexational. A punning adjective descriptive of a sen*sational sex* play (a journalistic coinage).

Shakespearience. Experience in Shakespearean repertory. Most actors in the front rank today owe much to this kind of acting in their stage apprenticeship under the tutelage of such managers as the late Sir Frank R. Benson, the late Henry Baynton, Charles Doran and, in recent years, Donald Wolfit, who has carried on the tradition. These companies regularly toured the English provinces and filled the theaters. A visit of F. R. Benson was an event of the utmost importance, and his pupil, Henry Baynton, was equally popular during the 1920s. Of fine presence and delivery, Baynton was earmarked for a great career, but he retired from management in his thirties and lapsed into obscurity. He made sporadic appearances in minor roles in London, his last important part being in the musical comedy, *The Vagabond King*, during the war years of 1939–45. He died in the winter of 1950. Artists who had their *Shakespearience* under these important managements owe them much. See entries at BAY and PA.

shamateurs. A conflation of sham-amateurs. Unsuccessful ex-professional artists who, having failed to make a living on the "stage proper," act in amateur dramatic societies.

shatter prices. To reduce the prices of seats when a production is not doing well. See entry at TWOFERS.

Shavian. The epigrammatic, hyperbolical style associated with the dialogue in the plays of George Bernard Shaw.

sheet. The box-office seating plans. In the plural, posters, playbills, etc. A *six-sheet* is six times the size of a double crown poster, equivalent to six sheets.

shoe. A toggle. 2. An electrical plug board which allows several units to be fed from one service. Cf. WAY-BOARD.

shop. (Brit.) A theatrical engagement. The past participle of the verb means that one has fixed an engagement. "So and So has just got himself shopped for panto" (obsolete and mainly used by old-timers in the profession). 2. Professional conversation.

shop, seasonal. See SEASONAL SHOP.

short. A short circuit (electricians').

show. A colloquial term for a play or, indeed, any production. When first introduced into theater speech it was frowned upon by conservative people, but the term is now accepted as standard English.

show-box. The theater. A provincial actor's term dating from the days of the peep-*show* (*box*). The Sunday evening routine of the old touring actors was to discover the whereabouts of the *show-box*, the general post office, and the actor's pub.

show business. Meaning the entire theater industry, dates from 1887 and is American in origin. A song of that title was featured in the successful musical *Annie Get Your Gun*.

showmanship. The flair for producing spectacular musicals or pageantry generally. 2. The parading of an outstanding (theatrical) personality.

show must go on, the. The traditional slogan of the TROUPERS. Whatever tragedy may enter the life of a player, or however ill he may feel, it is a point of honor not to let the other players down by deserting them when no understudy is available. Cf. DISCIPLINE and WE NEVER CLOSED.

show people. Generic for theatricals; the American version of the English PROS.

showy (part). One providing opportunities for fine delivery, and the display of acting ability. Cf. MEATY.

shrieking ostrich. (Brit.) An elaboration of the BIRD. "The show got a shrieking ostrich at Blackpool."

shutter dance. One performed on a slatted platform which emphasizes the tapped-out rhythm.

shutters. Reduce the area of the light beams in spots and floodlights.

sides. The pages of an actor's part typed on one side only.

sidewalk artists. Those ambitious and frequently out of work players who gossip on the pavements of New York.

siffleur. A whistling artist in vaudeville (French).

silent cue. One given by means of stage business, or a time lapse. Not a *spoken* cue. The stage direction may be: "As Nora moves up stage R, after tearing up the letter, George enters through door L." As the player who is to make the entrance may not be able to see this "silent cue" he usually takes the signal from the assistant stage manager, who will observe Nora's movement through a spy hole in the flat or, say, the fire-place opening. In U. S., also a *sight cue*.

sill. A flat iron bar, with the top rounded to prevent people from tripping, connecting the base of the opening of door pieces or French windows. One inch wide by a quarter of an inch thick, sill irons are screwed to the back of these pieces and counter-sunk into the base rail.

silly ass part. See DUDE.

Simon Legree. The American term for a Stage Manager. From the slave-driving, sadistic slave-owner of that name in Mrs. H. B. Stowe's *Uncle Tom's Cabin*.

sinks. Stage traps, or any portion of the stage capable of being lowered (*sunk*) into the cellar.

Sing us a song! A call from the gallery when an artist is disapproved of. This exhortation is euphemistic for something grosser. Ask any old Pro.

singer's farewell. The oft-repeated farewell performance of famous "Prima donnas" and tenors. Unlike the *soldier's farewell*, there is little finality about it.

singing ensemble. The full chorus of a musical comedy.

singing ladies and gentlemen. A fanciful replacement of the more expressive word chorus.

single act. A solo performance in vaudeville. E.g. a ballad singer, a juggler, impersonator or *raconteur*. Cf. DOUBLE ACT.

sister act. A vaudeville act performed by sisters. E.g. the famous Dolly sisters, the singing Andrews sisters, of radio.

situation. The position in which players find themselves in relation to the plot at any time during the action of the play. The dramatic situation.

size. A thin glue, or gelatine solution, used by scenic-artists and stage carpenters for glazing and stiffening canvas flats. The word comes from the Italian *sisa*, diminutive of *assisa*, painter's glue, and ultimately from the verb *assidere*, to make to lie, or sit down, from the Latin *assidere*. The smell of this solution, though extremely pungent, is as nostalgic as that of grease paint to the stage artist.

sizzle for. Cf. PASH IT.

skate. Part of a setting that can be slid (*skated*) into position for cleating.

sketch. A playlet in a revue, or as a music hall turn.

skin. An animal skin, e.g. of a cat, monkey, goose, used by animal artists in pantomime.

skin of the part. When an actor thoroughly knows his lines and is WELL FIRMED he is said to have *got into the skin of the part*. The phrase has its origin in pantomime animal artist's donning the skin of the cat in *Dick Whittington*. An excellent metaphor, it was adopted into standard English.

skip. (Brit.) A hamper, PROPERTY BASKET. A variant of *skep*, a basket. The word comes either from Old Norse *skeppa*, or the German, *scheffel*, meaning a bushel. Hence a basket to hold that measure. 2. To dance, hence: *skippers*, stage dancers.

skipper. A stage dancer (American).

skit. A short farcical or satirical sketch in revue. A burlesque, parody. Etymological history obscure.

slap. Make up materials, grease-paint, powder, rouge, removal creams, etc. One *slaps* it on. In U. S., also *muck, smear, war paint*.

slap-stick. Broad, knock-about comedy. From the harlequin's wand. See PANTOMIME.

slapstickery. Slap-stick comedy business, broad farce, or stage fooling generally.

slate. (Brit.) To criticize severely, to condemn a play on the grounds of "inadequacy" or ineptitude. "In spite of the *slating* in the Press, the play ran for six months." The conservative etymologist Skeat derives *slate* from the Anglo-Saxon *slaetan*, to bait, get the dogs on (an animal); causal verb from *sliton*, to slit, tear, rend. H. C. Wyld—an admirable scholar—considers, however, the connection with *slaetan* improbable, and Ernest Weekley suggests a relationship with the old Irish practice of "bonneting," ramming an opponent's "slate" over his eyes. *Slate* being a variant of "tile," the slang for hat.

slay (an audience). A musical hall "comic" is said to slay his audience when he reduces them to helpless laughter. (Past tense: slayed.)

slick ham. A well turned out and "polished" provincial actor.

slinger. A prompter who *slings* the lines across the stage from the Prompt Corner, to one who has dried up.

slip a program. To place a printed *slip* inside a program when there is a change in the cast. If a star, or one of the principals, falls ill the slip will read "Owing to the indisposition of So and So, the part of Charles will be played at this performance by WALTER PLINGE."

slip connector. A male and female plug with a pliable cable for connecting when using auxiliary lighting, such as remote control cue signals and the like.

sloat. (Brit.) An apparatus, generally of wood, consisting of two or more parallel rails erected perpendicularly, or at an angle wherein a set of bearers may be raised by means of a winch, or weights, carrying a scenic piece, platform, person, etc. It is used with stage traps, special effects. The *sloat* is also known as a boot (Strand Electric Company Glossary).

slow clapping. Is indicative of disapproval, as is the rhythmic stamping of feet.

small part man/woman. One who always plays the subsidiary parts in London or New York productions. One who specializes in the creation of minor, though often very important, roles.

smalls. The small towns. Cf. the American sticks, tanks, and contrast FIT UP, and ONE NIGHT STAND.

smash hit. A huge success. A long running play, or musical comedy, that *breaks* all records.

snow box. A pierced sack stretched over a wooden frame (*box*) and filled with finely clipped paper. Suspended from a set of lines and masked by a border, the box is swayed slowly, the paper falling from the holes in the sack and producing the desired snow effect. The *snow box* was in frequent use in melodrama when, in the "strong" scene, the erring daughter returned to the old home bearing the wages of sin in her arms. She collapsed on the snow covered doorstep and the flakes fell heavily on her dejected and penitent figure.

snow brown. To substitute another article for a missing property on the stage. When the man working the *snow box* ran out of white paper he used brown. Cf. VAMP.

soap, drop. To drop a piece of soap in a dressing room is considered unlucky. Also to leave one's soap behind on Saturday night on tour. This is an old theatrical superstition whose origin is lost.

soap opera. A serialized radio drama, usually of domestic life.

soap over. All mirrors or light reflecting surfaces on stage are smeared with soap to prevent the reflection of foot, or overhead lights being seen from the front.

sob stuff. Sentimental or WEEPY drama popular with Victorian audiences. E.g. *East Lynne, A Woman's Love,* and similar fare

social, comedy. One dealing with "Society" life; DRAWING ROOM COMEDY.

sock and buskin. The drama. A reference to the half shoe (Latin *soccus*) worn by actors in Classical comedy, and the high shoe made of buckskin (Greek *bursa*, hide; Latin *borsa*, Italian *borzachino*) worn by the tragic actors. The buskin had a platform sole to give height to the player.

social comedy. A drawing room comedy. One dealing with "Social" life.

Society drama. One dealing with life in "high society." Cf. SOCIAL COMEDY.

soffit. The lower part of an arch or balcony architrave. It gives depth.

sold out. Every seat in the theater occupied, including standing room. Cf. HOUSE FULL and TURN AWAY MONEY.

solid. Describes a competent, though not brilliant, actor. One who never forgets a line or piece of stage business, and is a tower of strength to the cast. An all round TROUPER.

soliloquize. To speak alone on the stage as in e.g. Hamlet's soliloquies. The Greek *solus*, alone and *loqui*, to speak.

soliloquy. A lone speech.

solus. To perform alone on the stage.

sonant. As opposed to SURD. Sounding, a voiced letter or sound. In phonetics, the sounds in *a, l, n, b, z, v.* Latin, *sonare*, to sound

soprano. The highest register in women or boys. "From middle to the A an octave and a sixth above. The *mezzo-soprano* has compass lying about a third below that of a soprano, but tone is fuller, richer and softer!" (Jeffrey Pulver).

sorry performer. A mediocre artist (Pros' colloquial).

sottie. A broad farcical comedy peculiar to the French theater during the 15th and 16th century.

soubrette. The "singing chambermaid" or juvenile girl of melodrama.

soundboard. A board at the back of the gallery which helps to absorb and distribute the sound from the stage, and obviates echo.

souvenir. An illustrated booklet of a popular play, sold to the audience in addition to the *give away* program.

Spanish guitar. A cigar. Rhyming slang of the music halls (Brit.).

sparge pipe = drencher pipe. From the Latin *spargere*, to sprinkle.

Sparks. The nickname for one of the Electrician's staff. The usual term, however, is ELECTRICS (Brit.). In U. S., *Alec, juice hand, lamp man*.

spec. Short for *spec*tacle, or *spec*ulation (American originally, but now general in England). "Putting on that leg show was a good *spec*."

speciality artist. A vaudeville artist who specializes in impersonations, juggling, or an instrument. E.g. Larry Adler, the "virtuoso on the harmonica."

spectacle. Any impressive display or scene, e.g. the finale of a pantomime. The Lyceum Theatre, London, in the Victorian era used to specialize in "spectacular drama."

speech. More than half a dozen lines in stage dialogue is considered a *speech*.

speech, broken. An interjection, e.g. "Yes, I know but. . . ." It cuts into another's speech. To be effective a broken speech must be taken up quickly, otherwise it falls flat and the speaker looks foolish.

spill. The spread of a spotlight beam. Stray light which *spills* on the scenery and can usually be controlled with cut-offs: funnels, high hats, flippers, etc.

spit black = EYE BLACK = WATER BLACK.

split week. A week of performances of a touring company divided between two theaters.

Spokeshave. Jocular for Shakespeare (Shakespearean actors).

sponge bags. Trousers made of black and white check, worn with a black morning coat, a style very much *de rigueur* in the early 1920s, and the mark of the successful actor. The jacket was short, and white spats were worn with the trousers, over black patent leather shoes. The pattern of the material of which the trousers were made resembled that used for sponge bags popular at that time.

Spoonerism. An accidental transposition of letters. E.g. The *Sw*een has *qu*ooned, for the Queen has swooned. The term commemorates the late Rev. W. A. Spooner, Oxonian, who had a tendency to commit such linguistic lapses.

spot. An engagement. A part in a play. The American variant of the English SHOP.

spot bar. The tumbler batten on which the spotlight lanterns, and floods, are fixed. Cf. TUMBLER BATTEN.

spot batten. See spot bar, *supra*.

spot broker. An American booking agent for plays, or artists. Cf. SPOT, and FLESH PEDDLER.

spot frost. A frosted gelatine, with a hole in the center, to give greater light transmission from the center.

spotlight chaser. One whose egotistic tendencies make him seek the center of the stage. A LIMELIGHT HOG. Cf. FOOTLIGHT FANNY.

spot line. Is a line from the grid to the flies, used for supporting chandeliers and similar objects.

spotting attachment. A lens attached to a spot-lantern to intensify the beam.

spread. To enlarge the diameter of a spotlight beam. As a substantive, the stray light from a *spot*, caused by the diffusing medium.

spread a part. To play it on broader lines than was originally produced. One *spreads* comedy in towns where audiences like such technique, and where subtlety would be wasted.

Spring tour. Runs from January to June. Cf. SUMMER TOUR and AUTUMN TOUR.

sprinkler. Nozzles in the stage ceiling, close to the grid, which are operated by the hydraulic system, or fusible link, on the outbreak of fire. Cf. DRENCHER PIPE.

spirit gum. An adhesive solution for fixing crepe hair beards.

spirit gum part. One that requires the wearing of a beard which is made from crepe hair and stuck on with spirit gum.

spy drama. Any play that has espionage as the theme.

squared paper. Drawing paper ruled in inches and twelfths, used for sketching ground plans of scenes. The standard scale for stage design is half an inch to a foot. A large square on the paper would equal one foot, and a small one two inches.

S.R.O. Standing *r*oom *o*nly.

S'roswald. (Brit.) A nickname-slurring of the late *Sir Oswald* Stoll, who built the London Coliseum and popularized the music halls in the provinces. Sir Oswald was a severe stickler for propriety, and allowed nothing that was tinted with the palest shade of "blue" in the program at his theaters, and peccant performers were given very short shrift. This censorious attitude may have been due to his being entirely without a sense of humor. Sir Oswald was formidably respectable, and greatly respected, and a theater bearing his name stands in Kingsway, London. W. Macqueen Pope, in his delightful *An Indiscrete Guide to Theatreland* (Muse Arts, Ltd.) gives an admirable "profile" of S'roswald.

stag mag. Short for *stage ma*nager; by reduplication. Also, as a verb, to stage manage.

stage board. The *stage* switch*board*, as distinct from a remote control switchboard.

Stage Censorship. Before a play can be produced in London, or in the provinces, it must be passed by the Lord Chamberlain and properly licenced, to prove that it is free from salaciousness or lines that might offend. Though this censorship is admirable up to a point, opinions differ as to what constitutes the "censorable," and many playwrights have, in the past, been penalized for what today would pass without giving offence. There is a freedom of words allowed in print that may not be permitted in the spoken word, though in recent years censors have been more inclined to pass words that have hitherto been taboo. But what would be innocuous on the London stage may often offend in provincial towns where a Watch Committee is appointed to attend first nights of touring versions of London plays. There has been some agitation on the part of Equity and other movements for the abolition of Stage Censorship following a debate in the House of Commons, but so far the censorship remains.

stage cloth. A cloth (often an old sail) that covers the setting area over which carpets are laid. The stage cloth covers the bare boards of the stage. In U. S., ground cloth.

stage clothes. Clothes worn *on the stage* only. Dresses, or suits, worn in the part. In West End or "straight" plays or musical comedies these clothes are often provided by the management, but there is no general rule about this, and artists usually have to provide their own wardrobes. Cf. STREET CLOTHES. In U. S., management may require an actor to furnish modern wardrobe only.

stage curate. See STAGE PARSON.

stage death. A dying upon the stage—that calls for a most delicate and "subdued" acting if it is not to create bathos by the over playing. It is a most difficult technique and few actors are good at *stage deaths*. One actor named Hicks was, however, so convincing in death scenes that he earned the sobriquet "Die again Hicks."

stage depth. The depth of the stage measured from the setting line near the footlights to the back wall, when the stage is empty.

stage dip. Is a plug set in a square trap some five inches under the stage floor into which a lead from a spot or floodlight can be fixed. Dips can be operated on resistance (dimmers) from the main switchboard, and their main advantage is that they help to reduce the amount of *scrim* (long leads, etc.) on the stage.

S.D. Short for:

Stage Director. (Brit.) Until recent years he was known as the Stage Manager, and is still so addressed by conservative people. He is the producer's right-hand man and next in authority during rehearsals of a production, and is in sole charge of the stage once the play is running. His duties are manifold, the main ones being the supervision of scenery, the arrangement of lighting and property plots, the engagement of the stage staff, etc.

He is assisted in these duties by a Stage Manager (formerly known as the *assistant* stage manager), and maybe an A.S.M. (q.v.) to whom he delegates such work as the checking of lights and plots, prompting and the several traditional jobs carried out by assistant stage managers. The desiderata of a Stage Director are efficiency, patience, tact, and a sense of humor. In U. S., designation is still that of Stage Manager and Assistant.

stagedoor. That through which all artists and backstage staff enter the theater. Cf. PASS DOOR.

stagedoor Johnny. The Victorian buck (man-about-town) who haunted the stage door of the Gaiety Theatre, London, during the heyday of the George Edwards's régime when some of the most beautiful women of the day were members of the chorus, and many of whom married into the peerage.

stagedoor keeper. It is said to be as difficult to pass a stagedoor keeper as to enter Buckingham Palace. Certainly they are an uncompromising class of men. Indeed, they have to be, for the number of besiegers at any stagedoor after the first night of a play starring a public favorite is amazing. Stagedoor keepers are credited with knowing the secrets of everybody and divulging none. Be that as it may, they are as one in withholding the private addresses of artists and refusing admittance backstage to anyone not producing the necessary credentials. The stagedoor keeper is also the custodian of the keys of all dressing rooms when they are not in use. He is also the deliverer of the company's mail.

stagedoor lounger. One who hangs around the stagedoor of a revue theater in the hope of "getting off" with one of the chorus girls when they leave the theater. The term is also applied to an autograph hunter.

stage duchess. An actress whose deportment is so *grand* as to be untrue. Like the stage Irishman, the type is seldom met in real life. Such characters are comparable to those in the "Society" novels that were popular in the '90s.

stage etiquette. Is most strictly observed, and severely censured are those who violate its canons. Seniority counts almost as much in the theater as in the Royal Navy, and the Stage Manager's Prompt Corner is sacrosanct; no artist from the leading player to the small part actor would dream of entering it, or pass through onto the stage, without asking the formal permission of the S.M. Permission is also asked of the Stage Manager to have guests on the stage, for he is in sole charge of the stage and responsible for anything that happens thereon. Artists are usually punctilious in thanking the call boy when he calls the acts or themselves individually; there is then no excuse if the artists are late for entrances. The boy has been thanked, and that constitutes a check, but the Stage Manager always makes sure that that boy calls a second time if there is danger of an artist being OFF. The dressing rooms are allocated "in order of seniority," and the people with quick changes of clothing are given rooms conveniently near the stage, even when this violates the privilege of the stars. Such allocation is never, or seldom, questioned by good troupers. The heads of departments: Master Carpenter, Master Electrician, and the Property Master run their own staff and, as long as the work is efficiently carried out by those departments, they are not interfered with. The *front of the house* staff is the province of the Business Manager, and the Stage Manager has no jurisdiction over them. As a rule theaters are run very pleasantly and smoothly, thanks to this traditional etiquette that has promoted a wonderful team spirit.

stage flex. Double or treble cored cable heavily insulated with a braid covering. It is chiefly used between large wattage portable equipment and the stage dip boxes.

Stage Golfing Society. (Brit.) The address of this society is: 90 St. Martin's Lane, London, W.C. 2.

stage gossip. The *chit chat* and scandal (usually the denigration of players more fortunate than the gossipers) of the dressing rooms, and in "theater street" generally. At one time it was known as GREEN ROOM GOSSIP.

stagehand. A scene shifter, or one assisting the Property Master. Cf. DECK HAND, GRIP HAND. Adopted from the nautical *hand*, a sailor on the lowerdeck, who has one hand for the King and one for himself.

stage, hold the. To "grip" an audience. To have complete control of oneself and one's fellow players. A well disciplined performance respected by artists and audience alike. "The audience was held from start to finish, a remarkably fine performance" (Press review).

stage Irishman. An exaggerated "Paddy." Like the stage parson this caricature was a convention of the Victorian stage.

Stage Letterbox. (Brit.) Under this heading a list of names is given each week in *The Stage* newspaper of people to whom letters have been addressed care of the Editor. The addressees may either call at the Stage Office or send for their correspondence. This courtesy on the part of the proprietors is much appreciated by artists who are often able to get in touch with those whose addresses they have misplaced, and very often a manager wishing to have a certain artist in a new production may make contact with him through the Stage Letterbox.

stage lighting. Cannot be adequately treated in a dictionary, although several important terms are listed. For a conspectus of the subject the reader is recommended to consult the standard text books. *The Technique of Stage Lighting* by Gillespie Williams, T.I.E.S., published in London by Sir Isaac Pitman, Limited, is especially recommended.

stage make-up. The term used by artists to differentiate between the make-up used on the stage itself, and the much lighter make-up used outside the theater. Cf. STREET MAKE-UP.

Stage Manager. One of the hardest worked men in the theater. The "buffer" between the director and the heads of departments. For the first few weeks of a "run" he, in addition to "working the corner," holds the prompt book of which he has been in charge since the beginning of rehearsals, marking the business and noting such suggestions as are made by the director. When artists have settled into their parts, the S.M. (as he is known) may hand over the book to his assistant, though he himself will remain in charge of the Prompt Corner. During the act changes the setting, furniture, and properties are checked by the Stage Manager, who will ring up the curtain on the next act when he is sure that all is ready and the artists have taken their positions on the stage. More stage managerial duties are referred to throughout this work.

stage parson. Is often a caricature of the genuine article. A prototype of all stage parsons being *Spalding* ("a bath bun and a glass of milk") in the old farce *The Private Secretary*.

stage plugs. See DIPS.

stage policeman. Like the stage Irishman he is a "figure of fun," except in thrillers when he conforms to the conventional theatrical type of *straight* P.C. with slow, deliberate movements and, of course, the note book and pencil.

stage screw. A large hand screw for securing braces or the fixing of scenery to the stage floor.

stage-struck. The desire to "go on the stage," the itch to act, encouraged by anything to do with the theater, playgoing, reading stage literature, etc. Also known as *stage fever*.

Stage, The. (Brit.) The theatrical newspaper, published at 19 Tavistock Street, London, W.C. 2. It is the voice of the profession and contains all information concerning productions in London or the provinces. It covers theater events in America and the Colonies. Published weekly, *The Stage* gives a list of the companies on tour, and several columns of advertisements, including "Artists Wanted," "Engagements Wanted," and "Artists' Cards," also the very useful Stage Letterbox. *The Stage* has superseded the defunct *Era* as the *actor's bible*. In U. S., *Variety* is the theater's leading weekly trade journal.

stage trap. The traditional pantomime trap on the stage through which the *Demon King* springs into view. 2. It is also used as a *grave trap* in Hamlet.

stage voice. That used by stage artists. It is pitched stronger than off stage to ensure its being audible in every part of the house. Cf. PITCH and DELIVERY.

stage wait. A hold up in the performance due to an artist's missing an entrance cue. The stage *waits* for the artist to appear, and often there is a complete DRY-UP because the next lines depend upon the absentee.

stage whisper. A *sotto voce* aside, or remark that can be heard in every part of the house, although the words are spoken in an (apparent) whisper.

stage width. Is measured from side wall to side wall on an empty stage.

stagey. Theatrical in manner or dress. Cf. THEATRICAL.

stall pot. (Brit.) A very "big pot" (i.e. important person) occupying a seat in the stalls. More often used in the plural, and is exclusively a music hall term.

stalls. (Brit.) Short for *orchestra stalls*, the seats between the orchestra and the pit. In U. S., corresponds to the front rows of the orchestra (lower floor), the pit being the remainder.

stalls circle bar. (Brit.) The refreshment rooms for the stalls and circle patrons, very often used for rehearsals, on non-matinee days.

stance. The position in which one stands on the stage. The posture for delivery of a speech, particularly a soliloquy.

standard. A flood lantern mounted on a telescopic stand. Used for lighting cloths (drops) and backings.

Stand by! A warning from the Stage Manager to artists that the curtain is going up, or to the stage staff concerned with an ACT CHANGE or other BUSINESS. "Stand by, Joan, you are on in a minute." Cf. PLACES PLEASE!

standers. Patrons who have paid for standing room only. Cf. S.R.O.

standing set. A scene that *stands* throughout a play and is not struck when the curtain falls. It is built for the run of the play. A Stage Manager's dream. Cf. PERMANENT SET.

star. An actor or actress in public favor. In advertising English they are *starred* for quality. 2. As a verb, to feature in a play or film; play the leading (*star*) part.

star bill. One advertising the *artist* in large letters. The title of the play appears in much smaller letters and the author's name in even smaller.

star dressing room. The best dressing room in the theater; the one nearest the stage, which is allotted to the leading lady or leading man.

star gaze. (Of the public) To stand outside a theater at a Premier performance watching the galaxy of stage or film stars, who are usually present on these "see and be seen" occasions.

star in a night. An artist who achieves fame by an outstandingly brilliant performance on the first night of a Town production. In one night she establishes her STARDOM. As was recently remarked by a leading player: It takes some years to become *a star in a night.* Several years work in provincial theaters or in repertory, usually precedes that star in a night achievement.

star letters. The large letters in the name of the star on a playbill. Cf. STAR BILL.

star part. One given to, and not infrequently written for, a player with a name.

star queller. A clumsy actor whose slow movements and bad acting worry the leading player.

star role = STAR PART = STELLAR ROLE.

star system. That by which plays are written round the personalities of an actor or actress, so that such a part is a typical *So and So* part. A review of a play featuring George Arliss read: "Mr. George Arliss was very good as George Arliss in a typical George Arliss part." Cf. TYPE CAST.

star trap. The stage *trap*-doors on the left- and right-hand sides of the stage near the footlight trough. The lids are built in sections to open in the shape of a star. They are used in pantomime.

star turn. A popular music hall act by a favorite comedian. Also said of any comic situation off-stage. "It was a real star turn, believe me!"

starlet. A child star in a play or film.

State Theater. One run by the State, as opposed to a private theater. Most European opera houses (e.g. The Berlin State Opera House) are State controlled.

stationery. Free tickets. A synonym of PAPER.

stays. Wooden wedges that keep flats firmly in position after they have been erected and cleated.

steal the spot. To occupy the center of the stage and so usurp the privilege of the leading players. Cf. LIMELIGHT HOG and SPOTLIGHT CHASER.

steal the thunder. To out-act the star and filch his applause. The phrase originated from one John Dennis (1657–1734), who invented thunder for a play of his which was a failure and damned by all the critics. A few months afterwards Dennis saw a play at Drury Lane in which there was a storm scene and his own thunder invention was utilized. He complained that though his own play was not allowed to run, they might have asked *him* before stealing his thunder.

stellardom = STARDOM.

stellar role. A fanciful variant of STAR ROLE.

step on the laughs. To speak on top of a laugh line, thus killing its efficacy. Cf. KILL A LAUGH.

stick. To dry-up; to BALLOON, MAKE AN ASCENSION (American). To forget one's lines and suffer from complete aphasia. Literally *stuck* for the words, and incapable of PONCING (*ad-libbing*).

stick on lines. An elaboration of the preceding.

sticks, in the. Playing the American provinces. Cf. LONG GRASS, SMALLS, etc.

stiff. The reverse of repose. Stage beginners hold themselves stiffly and look ill at ease until their self-consciousness wears off with experience. The arms are tensed instead of being held naturally and easily, movements are awkward, and the chin is apt to fall instead of being held level with the dress circle. Dramatic schools have done much to lessen this stiffness in beginners. But before the advent of these institutions novices came to the stage "green" and took several weeks to overcome their audience-shyness.

still. A photograph depicting a scene in a play. "The stills look good, let's go in and see the show." From film jargon. The *still*, not the motion picture.

stock company. A touring or resident company carrying a *stock* of the standard dramas.

stock gag. A time-worn wisecrack.

stock line. A cliché line in drama or revue. E.g. "You may break your mother's heart; but you won't break mine" (the stage sergeant major).

stooge = FEED.

Stoops. (Brit.) Short for *She Stoops to Conquer*, by Oliver Goldsmith (repertory artists').

stop gap. A revival of an old play put on at a theater as a *stop gap* between the end of one production and the beginning of another. It helps to pay the rent and running costs.

stop the show. A comedian is said to *stop the show* when his gags cause "prolonged laughter," and the show cannot proceed until the laughter dies down. "That gag of Danny Kaye's stopped the show."

straight actor. One who performs a STRAIGHT PART, q.v.

straight part. A misnomer for other than character (eccentric) roles, frequently used in this day of *type casting*.

straight play. A drama, comedy or farce. A non-musical production.

stranded. Destitute in a town in consequence of a company's inability to pay salaries, or to settle the local theater expenses. Deserted by a bogus management. Cf. DRY-UP COMPANY.

Stratford-on-Avon. The birthplace of William Shakespeare and the home of the Memorial Theatre, where a yearly festival of Shakespeare's plays takes place.

street clothes. A player's private wardrobe, as distinct from the clothing he wears on the stage. Cf. DRESS WELL ON AND OFF and GOOD MODERN WARDROBE.

street make-up. An actress' term for the lighter make-up she wears off the stage. Cf. STAGE MAKE-UP.

strike. To dismantle a setting at the end of an act (or scene). To clear it off the stage into the scene dock (if DEAD) or stack it at the sides of the stage for its use at a later period in the play. There is sometimes a very short interval in which to strike one set and erect another. "Hurry up, boys, this is a three-minute strike." 2. "To light an arc projector by closing and then opening the electrode" (*The Circle*, November issue, 1950).

strip. To place a *strip* of canvas across the back of a flat that is wearing thin and so prevent the possibility of any light showing through.

strip tease. A vaudeville act in which a female dancer divests herself of successive articles of clothing.

stroller. A strolling player (obsolete). 2. *The Stroller*. The pen-name of the writer of a theatrical causerie in a London newspaper.

strong actor. A drama man accustomed to broad technique and the old style of delivery. An ACTOR LADDY.

strong play. A heavy domestic drama or controversial sex play. E.g. *Desire under the Elms*; *No Room at the Inn*, or the old-fashioned sob-drama with a Surrey-side flavor: *The Silver King, The Manxman, The Worst Woman in London,* and the like.

strong scene. Any highly dramatic or sentimental scene that appeals to the gallery.

strut. A wooden supporting brace for scenery.

study, good/bad. A player with a retentive memory who learns a part quickly and thoroughly, or one who has a poor memory and holds up the rest of the company at rehearsals. See SWALLOW.

sub. (Brit.) An advance of salary (*sub*sistence money). The classic "chestnut" is told of an indigent actor who asked his manager for a small sub to enable him to have a shave. When asked what part he was to play that evening, the man replied *Hamlet.* "Then you will play Othello" ordered the manager. Another *fit-up* actor who had the temerity to ask the manager for the sub of a sovereign was told that "If I had a sovereign, Laddy, I'd have another company on the road."

subordinates. The subordinate roles in a play. Cf. TAIL and SUPPORTING CAST.

suburbs, playing working. Touring the outlying districts of London or the big cities. Legitimate companies *play* theaters; vaudeville and musical comedy shows *work* them.

sub plot. The *sub*sidiary plot of a drama, or play.

succès d'estime. (Of a play) An artistic success acclaimed by the Press but having little monetary advantage to the author. An enthusiastic success marked by extravagant applause and first night furor.

succès de scandale. A success due to the scandalous nature of the plot.

sugar daddy. An elderly business man who takes out chorus girls. Sugar = money in American slang. Hence *big sugar* means monetary success in the theater.

suitcase drama. A touring play presented with the barest of scenery. The décor and wardrobe can be carried in suitcases from village to village.

suite de dances. Several dances connected by mood and music but not by theme, e.g. *Le Sylphides.*

Summer Theater. That which is regarded as a "holiday date" and usually closes at the end of September, or mid-October at the latest. The seaside theaters which book SPLIT WEEK companies. In U. S., summer theater usually *winds up* in August.

summer tour. (Brit.) One running from May or June to late September or October. On these tours the company is booked by the seaside or inland Spa theaters, and the smaller towns. Such theaters either close for the winter or run a repertory season. In U. S., there is virtually no professional *road* activity during the summer months.

Sunday Opera Club. (Brit.) Is run in connection with the Glyndebourne Opera. Its members subscribe for the Mozart cycle of operas which are performed on Sunday evenings during the season. By law the Sunday audiences must consist only of members of the Club and their guests.

Sunday Societies. (Brit.) Play producing societies of professional artists who present plays at West End theaters on Sunday evenings, as a *shop window*. There are several well known organizations (see entry at Repertory Players), *The Fellowship of Players; Services Sunday Society;* the *Player's Guild; The Green Room Society;* the *Under Thirty Group,* and others, who all have the common aim of placing before London managers, producers, dramatic agents, "talent scouts," casting directors, and other influential bodies, the worth of a new play, and the individual merits of the performers. In an overcrowded profession it is only in such societies as these that artists' talent can reveal itself in the West End. Many members have engagements in London productions but, in a long run, individual actors are apt to become "stale" in the monotony of one part, and Sunday Societies provide the opportunity of fresh work in a number of parts. Productions are on the highest West End level and there are four weeks rehearsal for each performance.

supers. Supernumeraries. "Walking ladies and gentlemen." Walk-ons. Cf. CROWD.

super master. He who has charge of the supernumeraries in a big production. He is also known as *the head of the supers.* On the analogy of Chorus Master.

superstitions. In the theater these are legion, and in defiance of logic, reason and example they are still regarded as sacred. Too numerous to list here, I have cited only the commonest, and without the origins which are mostly lost in the mists of theatrical history. Real flowers are barred, artificial ones only are used for stage decoration, the reason most likely being that fallen petals or leaves are sometimes apt to cause an actor to slip on the stage, as happened to a leading man in Shakespeare when real leaves were strewn about the stage in *As You Like It*. To leave soap behind when on tour is considered an ill omen, as it is to whistle in a dressing room, the belief being that the one nearest the door will be "whistled out" (i.e. sacked). A make-up box should never be tidied, but left "anyhow." Powder, if dropped, should be danced upon (chorus girls' superstition) to bring luck. A hare's foot is considered lucky as a personal mascot, and presented to an artist ensures success. How this superstition arose is not certain but Hindus regard the hare as sacred to the moon because, they say, there is the silhouette of a hare in the full moon. To fall on the stage augurs a long engagement for the faller, and this was proved to the compiler's knowledge for, on the first night of Bram Stoker's vampire play, *Dracula*, a player tripped over the doorsill and fell heavily on the stage. The play ran for over two years in London and had a New York run. Knitting on the stage by actresses is taboo, but to find a piece of cotton which will wind around a finger without breaking indicates a contract with a management bearing the initial suggested by the number of times the cotton went round the finger. Thus three times would be letter C, which would suggest an engagement with a Noel Coward show or the late Sir Charles B. Cochran. Certain tunes are considered unlucky, especially the Barcarole from *The Tales of Hoffman*, and the nursery rhyme *Three Blind Mice*, but stage superstitions need a chapter to themselves in a history of the theater.

supporting cast. The artists following the leads and seconds. Cf. TAIL.

surd. A sound made without the vibration of the vocal chords. A sharp sound, e.g. f, k, s, t, p. From the Latin *surdus*, deaf. Hence *surdation*, the slipping of a sonant into a *surd* sound.

surf. An artist, musician, or stage worker who combines night work with a day job in another sphere of utility. Unless from *serf*, the origin of the term is a mystery.

surnames. Connote fame in the theater. When Walter is dropped from Plinge, Plinge is said to have "arrived" and will henceforth be a name.

surprise pink. The blush-like color of No. 36 gelatine supplied by the Strand Electric & Engineering Company. When first used this tint was a *surprise*. Now it is known as lavender.

suspense. The breath-holding period of anticipation and uncertainty felt by the audience during a drama.

suspension barrel. See SPOT AND FLOOD BATTEN.

Swaff. (Brit.) The nickname of Mr. Hannen Swaffer, the London journalist and critic (born November 1879), whose provocative notices did much to keep alive the interest in good acting. *Swaffer*, as he is more generally known, is an uncompromising writer, and his theatrical column was always stimulating if not always palatable to the criticized.

swag. To loop-up draperies or curtains which, thus treated, are technically *swagged*. As a noun, a *swag* is a looped-up curtain. The term comes from the Scandinavian *swag*, to sway: Norwegian *svagga*, and Icelandic *sveggja*, to cause to sway. Skeat quotes Palsgrave, "I swagge, as a fatte persons belly swaggeth as he goth." Shakespeare (*Othello*, Act II, scene III) has "swag-bellied."

swallow. (Brit.) The ability to assimilate a long part. To be a good study. "Give the part to Robinson, he has a pretty good swallow." One swallows and digests the part. A repertory term that has survived the days of stock companies.

swallow and sigh. (Brit.) A theatrical rhyming slang for collar and tie. A tight-fitting collar occasionally causes one to do this. There is nothing more uncomfortable than an ill-fitting collar.

Swan of Avon. William Shakespeare, whose home was at Stratford-on-Avon where is the Memorial Theater. The sobriquet was coined by his friend Ben Jonson. Pythagoras held that, on their decease, poets turned into swans. Cf. NATURE'S DARLING.

swan song. An artist's last performance, or a writer's last play. A swan is said to sing when about to die.

Swedish nightingale. Jenny Lind (1820–1887), the Swedish singer whose first appearance in England was in Meyerbeer's *Robert le diable* in 1847. She lived in the United States from 1850–52 and returned to England, where she settled until her death.

swifter. (Brit.) A steel line along which scenery, properties or electrical gear, etc., are carried *swiftly* into position when setting a scene during a very short interval.

syl-slinger. (Brit.) An actor with a tendency to "elocute" or mouth his lines to the embarrassment of the audience. Short for *syl*lable-slinger.

T

tab. See TABS.

tab hook. A spring hook that suspends running *tab*leau curtains.

tab show. A musical show (usually a concert party) played in a setting of velvets or *tab*leau curtains.

table part. One played from the waist upwards, the artist being seated at a table or desk. The late Oscar Asche became so corpulent that he had to play the leading part in *Big Business* thus seated.

tabs. Short for *tab*leau curtain*s*. They part in the center and open outwards. Cf. ACT DROP, BLIND, RAG, ROLLER, etc.

tag. The *tag* line, the last line in a play, to speak which at rehearsals is said to be unlucky. The theater historian W. Macqueen Pope records that one of the finest English actors, Matheson Lang, always substituted as a tag line "The Colleen Bawn," which was the title of an old drama. Every stage beginner is warned against speaking this dreaded line at rehearsals, or at any time before the opening night (Scandinavian for *end, point*).

tail. The supporting cast, the players of the subsidiary parts. The names of the artists at the bottom (tail) of a variety program (cf. WINES AND SPIRITS). In the plural, any loose pieces of canvas, electrical cables hanging from the battens, rope ends from the flies (cf. SCRIM). 2. Full fig evening dress, as opposed to a tuxedo.

take a call. To receive the applause of the audience when the curtain is raised for that purpose at the end of an act. These calls are taken according to the etiquette of the stage, precedence being taken by the leading artists in the first call, the second leads in the second call, and an ensemble at the final one. See POSITIONS FOR CURTAIN.

take a prompt. To receive the correct line from the Prompter in such a way that the *dry up* is not apparent to the audience.

take the corner. (Brit.) To move toward the Prompt, or O.P. Corner during the action of a scene. "When John comes on through the French window, you take the corner and let him have the stage." 2. To take over the Prompt book, or to "run the corner" in the absence of the Stage Director.

take the nap. (Brit.) The art of receiving a blow on the open palm of the hand with the object of deceiving the audience into the belief that the blow was struck on the face, the sound of the blow being much the same. The technique was perfected by knock-about comedians in the music halls. A variant of *take the rap*, it is dialectal in origin and common in Devon and the West of England.

takings. The amount of money *taken* at the box office for any performance.

talent scout. An agent who travels round the country on the look out for potential stars. There are as many good artists today as there ever were, but many remain in obscurity unless "luck," or the talent scout, discovers their worth.

tat. A piece of tawdry scenery or clothing. Hence the adjective *tatty*, applied to anything shoddy in the way of stage décor or wardrobe. *Tat*tered, from the Anglo-Saxon *taetteca*, rag.

T.B.O. *T*otal *B*lack *O*ut (electricians').

tear a passion to tatters. (From Hamlet's speech to the players) To rant; give an embarrassingly flamboyant portrayal of an emotional or tragic role. This method of HAM acting is seldom employed today, and was largely a dramatic technique popular south of the Thames in the Victorian era.

teaser. See GRAND DRAPERY.

technique. The tricks of the actor's trade. Deportment, diction, modulation of the voice, the ability to move an audience at will. The mastery of his art.

telegrams. It seems to be a convention in the theatrical profession that letters should never be sent if telegrams can go instead. It is customary to send telegrams of good wishes to artist friends on the first night of their productions. It is also considered unlucky to preserve such telegrams which are religiously destroyed after the performance.

telegraph. To indicate to the audience an intention of putting over a line or gag. Very crude technique associated with melodrama and very cheap vaudeville acts.

ten percenters. Theatrical agents who charge ten per cent of the artist's salary in return for obtaining the engagement, and/or negotiating contracts.

tenderloin. The theater district so named in New York City. From the most succulent part of the loin of lamb. The reference may be to the juicy performances at some Broadway theaters.

tenor. The highest natural voice in the male. The average compass is from C in the second space of the base staff to the A an octave and a sixth above. Exceptional voices reach higher notes —sometimes the second octave of the low C or even higher (Jeffrey Pulver).

ten shilling squat. (Brit.) A seat in the stalls or dress circle which cost that price when this obsolete term was coined.

terms. The remuneration according to the *terms* of a theatrical contract. "What are your terms for the part?" (Managers and theatrical agents').

terp. A stage dancer. Short for *Terp*sichorean.

Terpsichorines. Stage dancers, particularly in a troupe. *Terpsichore*, one of the nine muses of Greek legend, represented the dawn and song. The Greek *terpein*, to delight, and *choros*, to dance in chorus.

thank you both! Like "God bless you both!" this is a traditional stage aside when the applause is weak. Cf. IT MUST BE THE LANDLADY!

thanks for having me. A catch-phrase uttered by a boarder departing from his rooms after an unsatisfactory week. The emphasis is on the participle. The bill was too large.

that's out! Said of any gag or piece of business that falls flat when tried out during a rehearsal, or one that, introduced in a performance, had no response. Cf. KEEP THAT IN . . . AND AT THE MATINEE.

that takes me off! A catch-phrase expressive of defeat (as in argument) or incredulity. "That took me off (the stage), I couldn't argue any longer." A reference to an exit line.

theater. The name derives from the Greek *theatron*, an arena for seeing shows. From the verb *theaomai* to view, gaze at, behold.

theater-goers. The generic term for patrons of the theatrical art, from the legitimate drama to vaudeville. Cf. VAUDEVILLE-GOER.

theater good/bad. (Of a play, or acting) Containing the elements of art, drama and entertainment. A play is good or bad according to the judgment of a competent critic and the reaction of an intelligent audience. "I liked that scene between Sylvia and Michael in Act II, it was such brilliant theater"; "That scene ought to be re-written, it is bad theater."

theater Knight. (Brit.) An actor who has achieved a Knighthood in recognition of his service to the theater.

Theaterland. The theater district in London, New York, or any big city. Cf. PLAYDOM.

Theater Royal Out. (Brit.) The jocular reply to the question "Where are you playing next week?" It means that the week is vacant and the company will be *out* of work. See NO PAY; NO PLAY.

theater ship. (Brit.) Any converted merchantman that functions as a theater. A notable example was the old *Gourka*, the Royal Fleet Theatre ship anchored at Scapa Flow in the 1914-18 war. These ships are fitted like any theater ashore and can seat quite a large audience.

theatrical. The adjective applied to anyone possessed of the worst traits of the lesser Pro, loud in dress and manner, affected, showy and meretricious. A type that is gradually dying out.

theatrical card. An artist's card giving his address, telephone number and line of business. It is handed to an agent's receptionist when seeking work, or to the management of a theater when applying for complimentary tickets.

theatrical maid. An actress's dresser (American theater).

theatricals. Professional actors and actresses. "Mrs. Harris has some *theatricals* boarding with her this week." 2. Short for amateur *theatricals*, a variant of private theatricals.

theatrical stores. Warehouses in which managements keep scenery and properties when a production ends its run in Town, or returns from a tour.

theme song. In musical comedy the recurring melody that is associated with the two leading characters. Cf. LEIT MOTIV.

Thespian. Generic for theatrical. Thespis was a semi-legendary figure, a strolling player cum poet, who lived in the latter half of the 6th century B.C. He is credited with being the first to introduce a player to whom the chorus leader responded, thus starting dialogue in the theater. Eric Partridge adduces Pickard-Cambridge's proposal that the origin of *Thespis* is in Homer's *Odyssey,* Bk. I. 328–29, where *thespis aoiden* means "inspired songstress."

Thespian rage. Simulated anger. After Thespis, the supposed founder of the Greek drama. Lower-cased *thespian* is an adjective for any theatrical behavior, especially in an actor.

thud and blunder. A humorous inversion of *blood and thunder,* the crude, noisy technique of melodrama acting.

they sat on their hands. Said of a dull audience which refused to applaud.

thinker. One who "plays" a *walking part.* A stage super who has no lines to speak but makes up for this by adopting a pose similar to Rodin's celebrated work, *The Thinker.* Cf. THINKING PART, infra.

thinking part. A walk-on part. The artist stands, or sits, on the stage and looks wise.

this is an orchestra, not an elastic band! The classic observation by an exasperated Musical Director after trying in vain to keep pace with the woman vocalist, who was hopelessly out of tune and time.

thriller. The stage version of the *shocker* novel. A detective play containing at least one murder.

throw. The effective area of light provided by a spotlight lantern. Cf. SPILL.

throw a cleat. To join one flat to another by throwing a sash-line over the cleat and making fast to the tie-off screw. Cf. THROW A LINE, *infra.*

throw a line. Is the same as the preceding. The sash-line, which is about eighteen feet long and attached to the top of one flat is.

with an outward flick of the wrist thrown over a wooden cleat of the same height on the other flat. It is then laced behind the screws in the stiles of both flats alternately, the line being then made fast with two half hitches at the base of its own flat.

throw a temperament. (Brit.) To make a scene at rehearsal, or after an act in a play. Such conduct on the part of (usually) mediocre players is ascribed to the "artistic temperament," and far more indulgence is shown than would be the case in a less "free and easy" profession. Competent artists seldom throw temperaments.

throw away. To under stress lines in order to lend emphasis to one that needs pointing later in a speech. 2. A brochure of a play. A handbill.

thunder drum. A slackened bass drum, beaten with a padded stick, can be used as a substitute for a THUNDER SHEET.

thunder roller. An obsolete method of creating a storm effect. Iron balls were rolled down troughs and a rumble of thunder was produced, but the result was not as convincing as the modern method of creating the effect.

thunder sheet. A piece of sheet metal about six feet by two feet, suspended by a line from the stage grid. It is hung at a convenient height for the effects man to shake the handle at the foot of the sheet, and create a most realistic thunder effect. It is very necessary that this sheet be hung well clear of the stage wall or scenery.

thunder tank. A galvanized iron tank suspended by line in the same way as the thunder sheet. When struck with a padded drumstick the same effect as the thunder sheet is produced, though the sheet makes a more realistic "crack" and reverberation. But thunder effects can now be recorded on the panatrope (radio-phonograph).

Thursday off for study. It is the custom in some weekly repertory companies to have a rehearsal-free day on Thursday, which allows actors to study their lines thoroughly in time for the week-end dress rehearsal of the following week's play.

tie off. To make a line fast when a flat has been cleated to another, or when a batten was been "deaded" and is *tied off* on the flyrail.

tie off screw. A screw on the stile of a flat, around which a line is made fast.

ties. Pieces of cloth, or canvas strips, used for tying rolled cloths onto the battens, or otherwise securing cloths (drops) for traveling on lorries or for storage.

tiers. An obsolete name for the Grand or Dress circle, particularly in theaters where they have more than one circle. Cf. DIAMOND HORSESHOE.

tights. Tight fitting costumes usually for the lower part of the body, worn by ballet dancers or actors in Elizabethan plays.

timber. The distinctive quality of a voice apart from intensity or pitch. French *timbre*, a small bell.

time book. The book in the Stage Manager's corner, in which he times the length of the acts at each performance as well as the overall running time.

time the acts. The Stage Manager notes in the time book the exact minute the curtain rises on an act and the time the curtain descends. At the final curtain the exact running time is calculated exclusive of the intervals which are timed separately.

timing. The pace of a production or any fragment thereof. A highly important technical skill in the playing of comedy.

tin beard. A crepe hair beard that has not had its edges painted in. Such a beard has a hard line which gives the impression that it is likely to fall off at any moment.

tin pan alley. Any district where song publishers congregate, the "grave of the song writer's hopes" (Eric Partridge in *A Dictionary of Slang and Unconventional English*).

toe dance. To dance on the POINTS, as in ballet.

toesmiths. Stage dancers. On the analogy of blacksmith, silversmith, etc.

toe terpery. Tap-dancing. A jocular formation from *toe* dance and *terp*sich*ore*.

toga play. A Classical drama in which the male characters wear togas.

toggle. A cross bar on a flat. The term came to the theater from nautical speech, possibly via an ex-seaman stagehand.

tonsil test. An audition for a stage or screen part. A voice test.

Tony Lumkin part. A yokel or any country character in comedy that has a rustic flavor. From the character in Goldsmith's *She Stoops to Conquer*.

top lighting. The light battens, spot and flood lighting, acting area lanterns, etc., in the upper region of the light plot.

top-liner. A leading vaudeville artist whose name is on the *top line* of the program or playbill. A *headliner*. Cf. TOP OF THE BILL.

top of the bill. See top liner, *supra*.

torch warbler. A feminine song stylist. A torch singer with a repertoire of songs of unrequited love. Singer of *blues*.

tormentors. The two permanent flaps just inside the proscenium arch which meet the corners of the setting and thus prevent the audience from seeing behind the set. From the Latin *tortus*, past participle of *torquere*, to twist.

torso-tosser. A lightly clad stage dancer. A *hip dancer* of the burlesque houses.

touch the part, he or she can't. It is beyond the competence of the person who has been cast for it. "It was a wonderful part, but she couldn't touch it."

toucher. One of the HALF CROWN BRIGADE.

toupee. A wig, or false hair, covering a semi-bald head. The French *toupet*, the top knot of a periwig. In U. S., *divot, scalp doily, door mat*.

tour en l'air. A turn of the body made in the air by a ballet dancer.

tour list. The list of dates (the towns and names of the theaters at which the company will play) given to artists contracting for engagement.

touring cast. The cast of a touring version of a Town show.

touring production. A replica of a metropolitan success (or otherwise) and TYPE-CAST as near as possible. The voices, intonation, business and mannerisms must be faithfully copied, "Chinese fashion," so that the production is a true version to present to out-of-town audiences.

touring rights. The rights to tour a version of a Town show. 2. (jocular) If anyone makes a good joke or tells an original story, the hearer might say, "I like that, it's good, may I have the touring rights?" Cf. BAND PARTS.

touring show. A play, musical comedy, revue, or vaudeville act that tours the provincial dates. Less formal than TOURING PRODUCTION.

touring staff. The front of the house and stage staff carried by a touring company. Cf. RESIDENT STAFF.

track. The rail for runner curtains or tabs.

tragédie lyrique. A tragedy set to music but with no spoken dialogue. French for grand opera.

tragedy. "Is primarily a conflict or collision leading to catastrophe. Aristotle noted that the catastrophe commonly follows guilt or error, leading to the view, developed by later writers, that the tragic motive is a working out of poetic justice" (Webster's *New International Dictionary*). The word derives from the Greek *tragodia*, which is compounded of *tragos*, a goat, and *aeidein*. In the early Greek tragedies the players were dressed as goats, satyrs or fauns (half men; half goats).

tragedy queen. A leading actress in tragic drama. A weeper and wailer in the grand tradition.

tragi-comedy. A play containing both elements, the balance being such as to produce no catastrophic ending.

trailer curtain. See FRENCH CURTAIN.

tramplin. A table framework, the top of which is made of intersecting elastic or spring webbing upon which a person may fall from a height without injury. Sometimes used to assist a ballet dancer's leap from off-stage. A slurring of trampolin, variant of *trampoline*, the word comes from the Italian *trampoli*, a pair of stilts, hence a *trampolin act*, a turn on stilts. Trampoline is also a kind of spring mattress.

transparency. A cloth painted on lines of scrim so that it becomes transparent when lit from behind. Cf. GAUZE CLOTH.

travel in one's trunks. A variant of TRAVEL ON ONE'S PROPS.

travel on one's props. (Brit.) To leave luggage with the railway company as security against the traveling facilities granted, money being lacking for the fares and freight of the company.

traveler. A traverse or draw curtain operating from a track. It is divided in the center and is drawn apart to reveal the stage.

travesty. A burlesque of a serious play. 2. v. to ridicule, make a grotesque and unkind imitation. From the Latin *trans,* across, and *vestire,* to clothe.

Treasury. (Brit.) The conventional term for payment in the theater. "What time's treasury tomorrow?"

Treasury call. (Brit.) The time at which salaries are paid. In some theaters there is no formal payment, the manager taking the envelopes to the dressing rooms. When there is a stated time for the payment of artists, the notice goes on the Call Board on the eve of payment. At the time given the artists go to the manager's office to collect their packets. Cf. GHOST.

trick line. A length of cordage with a block (pulley) used for swinging or lifting gear, scenery, etc. A kind of theatrical "handy billy." 2. Very strong twine used to pull things off the stage in sight of the audience, or to pull down hinged parts of a flat in a quick change of scenery.

trip = CLEW.

tripe. Electric cables hanging from overhead equipment. Cf. TAILS.

trough. The old-fashioned type of footlight container. It was superseded some years ago by the almost universal magazine compartments.

troupe. A theatrical company of any sort, a concert party revue, dancing *troupe,* touring pantomime, etc.

trouper. A member of the above. The term is used in a laudatory sense. "He, or she, is a jolly good trouper." A loyal, reliable "never-let-the-side-down" colleague.

trunk hose. Breeches worn over the tights by Shakespearean actors. They reach from the waist to the middle of the thigh, and were fashionable during the 16th and 17th centuries. Cf. TRUNKS.

trunks. The theatrical shortening of *trunk* hose.

trunnion. The U-shaped bracket supporting the housing of a spot or floodlight lantern, by which the lamp can be tilted and secured at any angle. Also known as the *fork.*

try back. A rehearsal direction for the repetition of a scene, or part of a scene, to ensure that the actor has fully understood a change that has been made in the dialogue or business. In U. S., *go back.*

try it on the dog. To give a new production several weeks run out-of-town. This enables the company to settle into their parts and to make any improvements, or adjustments, before the metropolitan opening. Cf. OPEN COLD.

try out theater. One used for the presentation of new plays prior to Town production.

try out tour. A short tour of out-of-town theaters which allows the cast to get used to the reactions of several kinds of audience.

tumble. In a theater not high enough to take a flown cloth (drop) out of sight of the audience, it can be "taken away" on lines, one on top, another at the bottom, and a *tumbler* batten placed in the fold of the cloth to prevent creasing.

tumbler. An acrobat.

tumbler batten. A round batten used for rolling cloths when they are placed in a scene store. It is also used to ballast an empty set of lines, in place of sand bags.

turkey show. One played to country audiences. In reference to turkeys (rustics).

turn. An *act* on the vaudeville stage, usually a single performance. "I liked the juggling turn."

turn away money. To display *house full* boards outside the theater. Every seat is sold and no more money can be taken. The disappointed people—and their money—are turned away.

turn out. An old term for an interval. The patrons *turned out* of the theater for a breath of air, or a drink "at the pub opposite." "There doesn't seem to be much of a house at the Royal, it was a poor *turn out* after the first act."

tushery. Archaic expressions and exclamations used in romantic costume plays. "Tish! tush!" etc. The word tushery is said to have been coined by R. L. Stevenson.

tutu. A skirt of tarlatan material worn by dancers in classical ballet. Lincoln Kirstein, General Director of the New York City Ballet, says that there are two styles of this ballet skirt. One the long "romantic," bell-shaped skirt which originated *circa* 1832 with Taglioni, and a short "classic" skirt originating with Zucchi in 1887, who cut short the length of tarlatan in the old-style skirt to create the new. Kirstein adds that *tutu*, a term adopted from the French, usually refers to the later style. Cf. FROU FROU.

tuxedo. A dinner jacket named after the Club at Tuxedo Park, N. Y., where it was first introduced.

twenty pound actor. A baby born into the theatrical profession. Cf. BORN IN A PROPERTY BASKET.

twice nightly cuts. (Brit.) Those judicious deletions made in the text to reduce the running time of a play that has to be performed twice in one evening. The once-nightly version usually runs from 2½ to 2¾ hours, whereas the short version has to be performed in two hours. The cutting of the 'script has to be done with skill and delicacy, as leading players are apt to be touchy over what they consider their best lines. In fact, every line is a best one when it is in danger of being cut out of the part. Usually, however, time is saved by increasing the tempo of the play and shortening the act waits.

twofers. Tickets admitting *two* people *for* the price of one. When a play was in danger of *flopping* this "twofer" expedient was adopted in some of the London theaters as a means of reviving interest. Those seeing the play talked about it and, tempted by the scheme of payment, other people began to fill the houses and the management thus recouped their loss.

two lines and a spit. A very small part. A relic of the days of melodrama. See BIT PART, and cf. THINKING PART.

two/three/four-handed scene. Describes a scene in a show where two, three, or four artists take part.

type. Short for TYPE CAST.

type cast. To assign parts to actors who most nearly approximate the types drawn in the play. 2. (Of touring managements) To engage a cast that most resembles that in the Town production.

U

Uglies. The ugly sisters in *Cinderella*, the Xmas pantomime, are always referred to as *the Uglies*. "Who are playing the Uglies this year?"

ultra violet. Lighting using the maximum output of any source emitting ultra violet rays. The output from the source is filtered of the greatest possible percentage of visible light, and the residual rays are used for luminous or trick effects. Cf. BLACK LIGHT.

ululation. The *howl* of disapproval from the cheaper seats when a play disappointed that section of a Victorian audience. A journalistic term now obsolete, modern audiences being far better behaved. But the term was common in newspaper reports of first nights. (Latin *ululare*, to howl.)

under dress. In order to facilitate a quick change, it is advisable to don as much of one's "following clothing" as can be worn with comfort. Thus a bathing suit under pyjamas, and both under a lounge suit or evening dress. Thus one has only to take off instead of put on garments, and much time is saved thereby.

underpart. To give a part to an artist that is unworthy of his reputation and talent. "It was a very good production but Robinson was disgracefully underparted, he should have had the lead."

under rehearse. Producers of weekly repertory have necessarily to give inadequate attention to plays and players, but there is no excuse for this if a production is several weeks in rehearsal. Nevertheless, one has to sit through performances of plays that are all too frequently under rehearsed. Cf. OVER-REHEARSE.

understudy. One who studies a role and rehearses it during the run of a play, in case the original artist falls ill or is otherwise prevented from appearing.

understudy call = UNDERSTUDY REHEARSAL.

understudy's chance. The time when he, or she, plays the part understudied. A *chance* to make a success (especially in Town) and attract the attention of managements, agents, and the critics.

understudy rehearsal. The call for all, or individual understudies who perform the play in its entirety, or in part, under the direction of the Stage Manager. Such rehearsals *should* take place weekly if the understudies are to be efficient and able to "go on" at short notice.

Under Thirty Group. (Brit.) A London Sunday Society of young artists founded in the 1940s by two ex-students of R.A.D.A., Oscar Quittak and Karris Mond, who felt that too many young players of talent were being forced out of the profession through non-recognition. To qualify for membership, a player must be under thirty years of age and have had six months experience on the professional stage.

undressary. An under-dressed revue, A LEG SHOW.

unity. In drama, means unity in time, place and action on the lines of the traditions of Classical drama.

unsympathetic part. One likely to make the artist unpopular with an audience. It puts them out of sympathy with the player. "I've been given a wretched part next week, the audience will hate me" (young actress' lament in repertory).

up in a part. Having thoroughly learned it, and DEAD LETTER PERFECT. Cf. WELL FIRMED.

up in the Park. (Brit.) Playing in Shakespeare up in Regent's Park Open Air Theater, London. "What are you doing these days?" "I'm up in the Park this summer."

upper circle. The tier of seats immediately above the dress circle.

uproar. Grand Opera. The pun being suggested by the noise in, say, Wagner's works.

up-stage. As a stage direction this means that the player walks away from the footlights toward the back of the setting. One moved *up* because most early theaters had raked stages. 2. Used somatically: thus, up-stage hand, down-stage foot, etc. When standing sideways, facing center stage, an artist's up-stage arm or foot is the one farthest from the audience. 3. A slang term for anyone prone to conceit. "So and So has become rather *up-stage* lately."

up-stage and county. (Brit.) To be "high and mighty." Accustomed to being up-stage of one's fellow artists and aloof (off-stage). The manner, supposed to be that of the best county people, connotes extreme gentility.

upstairs. The seating accommodation above the ground floor. The boxes, dress and upper circles, balcony, and gallery. Cf. THE FLOOR.

use of play titles by theatrical landladies. Is the common practice, thus: "I have *Hay Fever* in the house this week." This struck the caller as a poor excuse for not taking him in, until he realized that *Hay Fever* was the title of the Noel Coward play at the opposition theater.

use the stage. The advice to an artist by a director when he wants him to make more of a scene he is playing, without giving him precise moves to bring him center stage. "You are effacing yourself at the back; take more of the stage." In U. S., *take stage*.

usher. One who shows patrons to their seats, hands them programs and generally dances attendance. From the Middle English *uschere*; Old French *ussier*; ultimately Latin *ostiarium*, the accusative of *ostiarius*, a doorkeeper.

usherette. A female USHER.

util. Short for *util*ity (actor).

utility, or **general utility.** Is a person whose sphere of usefulness embraces scene shifting, scene painting, or rather the touching-up of scenery, and the portrayal of very small parts that are unimportant.

U.V. Short for ULTRA VIOLET.

V

V.A.F. (Brit.) The Variety Artists Federation, London.

valence. A pleated border.

vamp. To improvise; make shift. To make anything that resembles the genuine article. E.g. to cover padded ginger-beer boxes with tapestry or chintz to give the appearance of a divan or settee. The derivation is from Middle English *vampay* (*vaumpe*) and Old French *avanpie*, the front part of a shoe. Hence to *vamp* was to re-patch or repair shoes. The general acceptation today is to improvise. For instance, one *vamps* tunes on a piano. 2. Short for *vamp*ire, a female "siren" who battens on men, a gold-digger. Hence a *vamp part*. 3. A *vamp*ire trap. Cf. SNOW BROWN.

vamps. Doors cut in a flat and fitted with rubber springs for an actor to go through. Its main use is in pantomime.

variety. Music hall entertainment comprising songs, "comic turns," sketches, impersonations, acrobatics, juggling displays, "stunts" (e.g. the famous "sawing through a woman" act), one-act skits on current events. In fact, any piece of original entertainment worth putting on. In recent years variety theaters have extended their scope to include revue and musical comedy. Cf. VAUDEVILLE.

variety, the father of. (Brit.) The late William Morton, who founded the first London music hall, The Canterbury, in Westminster Bridge Road, *circa* 1848. He later managed the London Palace of Varieties.

variety public. Music hall addicts, as opposed to play-goers.

variety stage. The music hall side of the theater world. Cf. LEGITIMATE STAGE.

vaudeville. Is synonymous with variety. It originates in (Chansons de) *val de Vire*, the songs of the Normandy valley where Olivier Basselin, the 15th century ballad writer, lived and so named his

213

songs. They were light, satirical pieces in a style similar to the numbers in present-day Revue, though, of course, far less sophisticated.

vaudeville black out. A music hall sketch played on quick lines and ending in a black out. Cf. BLACK OUT CURTAIN.

vaudeville-goer. Patron of the variety theater.

vaudeville house. A variety theater; music hall; burlesque house.

vaudeville, in. Appearing on the variety stage.

vaudevillian. One who burlesques a melodrama villain in a vaudeville sketch. A jocular pun of the music halls.

velarian. An unbattened ceiling cloth used as a canopy, or other effect. Literally, an awning.

velvets. Velvet curtains or borders, used for sketch settings in Revue.

vennette. To cut an irregular circle out of a piece of gelatine (medium) which, when slotted into a spotlight frame, will throw a whitish patch of light in the center of the color projected, the irregular circle preventing a hard line from appearing around the center of the spot. From *venet*, an obsolete, rare form of *vignette* (ultimately from the Latin *venetus*). As in the photographic sense of vignette, to *venet* is to shade off and soften the edges, leaving only the central position. The color of *venet* is a bluish-gray; "water," as it was anciently known.

vent. Short for *vent*riloquist.

ventilator. A poor play, or any show, that empties the theater. One doing such bad business that there is no danger of the auditorium becoming overheated.

ventriloquist's guy. The doll he works with, his FEED.

Vera Lynn. (Brit.) A drink of gin. Rhyming slang of the music halls. See FORCES' SWEETHEART.

vertical line of sight. That from the gallery onto the stage. From this coign the spectator should be able to see the whole of the setting and every movement made by the cast. The Stage Manager, however, must be very careful to check the border when there are steps or a rostrum at the back of the setting. If the border is "deaded" too low, the gallery patrons will not be able to see above the actors' shoulders. See the entry at MASK.

vet. To patch up a bad play; to doctor the BOOK. To make it more palatable to the taste of a provincial, or otherwise "awkward" audience. Often metropolitan successes with risqué lines, or suggestive business, have to be toned down for the provinces where the local Watch Committees are somewhat narrow-minded. Not that many provincial audiences are pleased with the Watch Committee's interference on their behalf and, in these enlightened times, there is far less arbitrariness in the matter of local censorship than there was during Queen Victoria's reign.

Vic/Wells ballet. (Brit.) The Old Vic and Sadler's Wells Ballet Company.

village blacksmith. An actor who seldom keeps an engagement longer than a few weeks. Euphemistic for a failure. From Longfellow's famous lines: "Week in, week out, from noon till night, you can hear his bellows roar" (Cited by J. Redding Ware in *Passing English*).

villain of the piece. The "dirty dog" of melodrama. The would-be seducer and rogue who is invariably frustrated in his nefarious plans by Juvenile John, the hero. Probably the effectual prototype of all stage villains was Iago.

Victoria the Great. (Brit.) The title given to Anna Neagle, the British stage and film star who gave a magnificent and memorable portrayal of Queen Victoria in the film *Victoria the Great*.

v.i.r. Short for *v*ulcanized *i*ndia *r*ubber cable of one or more strands of wire with v.i.r. insulation protected by a braid, usually of red or black. This type of cable is run in metal conduit and is chiefly used for permanent wiring. The use of a number of them, in fire-proofed canvas hose, can be substituted for MULTICORE.

vis comica. Strong comedy. Latin *vis*, force plus *comica*.

vision. A portion of a cloth covered with gauze, which renders a figure visible to the audience when illuminated from behind, thus creating the effect of a *vision*. Used for ghost scenes and transformation scenes.

vision cloth. That used for vision effects. See the preceding entry and cf. TRANSPARENCY.

visiting company. A touring company which *visits* a theater during its itinerary.

visitor's book. Is kept by a theatrical landlady and, as the guests leave, they are requested to "write something in the book." As a rule it is a pleasure to pay a compliment to a landlady who has done her best to make one's stay comfortable, or whose cooking has justified the *cordon bleu*. Sometimes, however, the book is left unsigned or "Quoth the raven" written across the page, in reference to Edgar A. Poe's lines, "Quoth the raven, nevermore!"

voice, in good/bad. (Of opera singers) Singing well, or ill. "I heard So and So in *Manon* and thought her excellent, but I was told afterwards that she wasn't in very *good voice* that night."

Voice, the. (Brit.) That of the late Henry Ainley, who had the finest speaking voice on the English stage during the early twentieth century. Illness cut short his stage career at its peak.

vomedy. A merging of v(audeville c)omedy. An American coinage which has been adopted by the English theater.

W

waffle. To dither, fluff lines, or generally prove awkward in a scene.

Wagnerite. An ardent admirer of Richard Wagner's operas. From George Bernard Shaw's book, *The Perfect Wagnerite*, published in the Victorian era.

wagon-stage = platform stage = rolling stage, all of which run on casters.

wait. The interval between the acts of a play or musical comedy, variety or concert entertainment. Cf. STAGE WAIT.

waiter's dress front. Is sometimes worn by an actor who has a very quick change into evening dress and has no time to change his shirt. A paper front is placed over the day shirt, and collar and tie fixed; thus are the minutes saved in the change and, with evening clothes donned, there is no difference from the genuine article dress shirt.

walk a scene. To carry out the movements and speak the lines mechanically. At rehearsals, *walking a scene* enables the director to check the effectiveness of his direction. Cf. ACT IT and MECHANICS.

walk hands. When a flat is lifted from the stage it is *footed*, and the stage hand who lifts the top of the flat uses his hands in the manner of feet walking, which enables him to bring the flat to an upright position. Cf. FOOT A FLAT.

walk it. To walk a scene as distinct from *acting* it. "Walk the scene, please, I want to get the picture."

walk on. To have a lineless part. The artist merely helps to *dress* the stage. Cf. WALKING GENTLEMAN; WALKING LADY; THINKING PART, and SUPER.

walk the stage. To move with ease and grace upon the boards of the stage. This art is difficult to acquire; some, indeed, never acquire it. Carriage, balance, gesture and the correct method of turning, come within the meaning of "walking the stage." One should walk on the ball of the foot, for this ensures perfect balance when turning up or down stage. The arms should be held loosely and naturally by the sides, neither tensed nor swinging. Gestures should be few, and when made they should be quite bold. Costume comedy and Shakespearean repertory gave excellent training in the art of walking the stage.

walk the ties. To walk along the railroad tracks from one date to another, through not being able to pay the railway fare. "If this rotten business persists we'll have to walk the ties this weekend."

walk through. To walk through a scene at rehearsals for *movements*, little attention being paid to words. Cf. WALK IT.

walking gentleman. (Brit.) A male supernumerary. One of a stage crowd (euphemistic).

walking lady. (Brit.) A female supernumerary. She walks elegantly on the stage showing off her dress.

wall, the. The side or back wall of the stage.

wall as background. Where no cyclorama is fitted, the permanently whitened back wall is often used for lighting effects.

Walter Plinge. The program name, corresponding to A.N. Other on the football field. It hides the identity of the player who substitutes, or DOUBLES for another. There are several versions of the origin of this name, but the one most in favor is that Plinge was the proprietor of a public house near Drury Lane Theatre, London, and was once called in to play a small part when no actor was available. Some say that the part was created for him. Sir St. Vincent Troubridge has communicated the following: "There is no doubt that Walter Plinge is of Bensonian coinage. The version I have heard most often, and seen in print, is that Plinge was the name of the landlord of the public house opposite the stage door of the Lyceum (not Drury Lane), who was in high favor with the company through allowing its young impecunious actors to run up modest scores for drink 'on the slate.' His immortalization was in the nature of a joke between Henry Jalland, the Acting Manager (and, as such, responsible for the program matter) and the men of the company, for some ambitious youngster protested his subordinate capacity being emphasized by his doubling being indicated on the program. Jalland laughingly substituted *Walter Plinge."* In U. S., George Spelvin, q.v.

wardrobe. Private or property clothing worn by the cast. Cf. STAGE CLOTHES and STREET CLOTHES. 2. The domain of the wardrobe mistress and her assistants. Where they make and repair dresses, costumes, etc., worn in the production.

wardrobe mistress. The woman in charge of the theater wardrobe. She is responsible for the upkeep and good repair.

warm. (Of an audience) Generous-hearted, quick to appreciate good lines and to applaud at the right time.

warn. A direction in the Prompt Copy of the script which applies to all *calls*, light or effects cues, etc. See WARNING, AND GO.

warning, and go. The signal system from the Prompt Corner to the flies, electrician's perches, or to any part of the stage where effects are to be carried out. The *warning* is a red light, and the *go* is green. In some theaters the colors are reversed, or one light is used as a warning and the *go* is the light switched off. The warning tells the hand who works the effect to *stand by*. In spectacular productions where there are many effects there is a large cue board with lights wired in series, but it is always safe to work on the two-light system. Bells are also used, but they are better for remote control effects, for they are too noisy for near-stage warnings.

war paint. Stage MAKE-UP.

water black. Mascara, a cosmetic for eyelashes. Water must be applied to the substance before the black can be produced, hence the term. It is vulgarly known in the dressing rooms as *spit black*.

wax. To make a gramaphone record of scenes in a play. E.g. an act in opera. "We are waxing Act II tomorrow night."

way board. A board with plugs for feeding electrical equipment. It can feed several units from one source. Cf. SHOE.

ways. The number of circuits on a switchboard, MULTICORE cables, etc.

weapons. Make-up. Under this heading come sticks of grease paint, liners, orange-sticks, powder boxes, and all the appurtenances of the art.

we don't like that sort of thing 'ere! An expression of censure from a stagehand in a provincial theater. It is applied to a play with risqué lines or near-the-bone acting. The local staff know to a hair what type of play will "go" in their town.

week out. A week during a tour when no theater has been found to take the show and a *week out* of work results. "We do six weeks, then a week out, then four more weeks before coming to Town."

weekly rep. A one play per week repertory company.

weepie. A sentimental play, a sob drama, tear-jerker. 2. An emotional part.

weights. Are used, in several sizes, to reinforce braces. They are also placed on the stands of floodlights to ensure stability.

well firmed. (Brit.) Having a *firm* knowledge of one's part, perfect in the words and business. Dead letter perfect: "Don't worry about Smythe, he is *well firmed* in the part." It was an old Stock actor's phrase, and seldom heard today.

well put on. A lavishly produced musical comedy or straight play that has impressive décor and a well-dressed cast.

we'll write to you! The stock promise to an *un*promising actor or actress after an audition. It has become a theatrical catchphrase, and is often directed at anyone singing out of tune in the dressing room. In U. S., "Don't call us; we'll call you."

we never closed. (Brit.) The proud slogan of the Windmill Theatre, London, which kept open through the fiercest blitzes on the capital and during the flying bomb attacks. A film was made of the company and presented under that title.

West End technique. (Brit.) Polished acting in the manner of London's West End stage. "Play it West End this week, they are pretty conservative in this town." Cf. BROAD.

wet white. Liquid cream for whitening the hands. It is applied wet, and very quickly dries.

we've done a deal! (Brit.) A phrase meaning that the libraries have thought the show good enough to block-book a number of seats for a certain length of time. The bookings are at a cut rate and guaranteed.

what do you know? The stock question asked of a friend on POV-

ERTY CORNER, London. It is ironical, for seldom is anything known about new productions.

wheel. A circuit of theaters owned by a syndicate. Cf. CIRCLE and RING.

wheeze. (Brit.) An old term for a music hall gag. It originated in the traveling circus and was applied to the clown's patter, which used to be given in a *wheezy* enunciation. The term is general slang for a trick, a plan. "That's a good *wheeze*, let's try it."

when I was with Irving. The sarcastic rejoiner to a boastful actor who is always referring to the stars with whom he has shared dressing rooms during his lengthy stage career. In the old days the ACTOR LADDIES used to boast that they were in the same cast as Sir Henry Irving at the Lyceum. The stock comment was "Walking on, I suppose."

when the gaffs burst. (Brit.) The time the people come out of the theaters (gaffs) at the end of a performance. A London taxi-drivers' phrase. Cf. GAFF STREET.

whiskey seats. The end seats in the stalls or dress circle, from which it is easy to slip into the adjacent bar for a whiskey and soda or gin and lime when bored with the show. The movement occasions no inconvenience to the other patrons in the row.

whispering baritone. The late Jack Smith whose husky, whispered songs were immensely popular in the 1920s when he was the rage of London. He returned to the United States after a tour of the English provinces, and died in 1950.

whistle in the dressing room, to. Is said to portend a dismissal from the company, the one nearest the door being the unlucky one.

whistle out. The one who whistles in the dressing room *whistles out* (of the company) a fellow player.

white elephant. An unlucky theater, or unsuccessful play. When the Kings of Siam wanted to ruin a courtier, they presented him with a white elephant, whose sacred nature made the keep and the attendants so expensive that the owner was reduced to poverty.

white-haired boy. Corresponds to blue-eyed boy, one in public favor. "With two shows on Broadway, Christopher Fry has be-

come the white-haired boy of the American theater too . . ."
(C. V. R. Thompson in a *Daily Express* article). Fry's brilliant *The Lady's Not For Burning* and *Venus Observed* were two of the biggest London successes of 1949–50.

White Hart varnish. (Brit.) A solution often substituted for spirit gum. It is cheap and very efficient. Very popular with impecunious actors in their apprentice days of SHAKESPEARIENCE.

whodunit. A murder drama, or any mystery play. *Who done it* is the illiterate shape of *who did it* (the murder, or crime). "Have you seen the new *whodunit* at the Playhouse?"

whooperup. (Brit.) A raucous, noisy music hall singer of the Victorian era. Cf. the very apt American variant CALLITHUMPIAN.

wicket. (Brit.) The reception at the box office. "What's the wicket so far?" Acting Manager's from the game of cricket.

Widow, the. The ever popular operetta *The Merry Widow* by Franz Lehar (artists' abbreviation).

wind effect. This can be produced by a record on a panatrope (radio-phonograph), or by the electrical wind effect worked by a sliding dimmer which, moved up and down, can give the force of wind needed. See WIND MACHINE, *infra*:

wind machine. Generally wind effects are created by electricity in modern theaters, but older houses, lacking such refinements, have recourse to the old-fashioned *wind machine*. This is a slatted drum turned by hand on a spindle. A sheet of canvas is stretched over the drum, made fast at one end to the base of the drum carriage, and at the other to a wooden batten. This, in turn, is attached to a treadle and the operator can tauten or slacken the canvas which, rubbed against the slats, gives the desired wind force.

Wigan, that went better in. (Brit.) A music hall comedian's *sotto voce* remark when a gag fails to get over. Wigan is a music hall joke that has become a national one in England, though why this Lancashire town should be so treated is not known. It may be that Wigan is so typically Lancastrian that many regional jokes are tried out there, and if they go well it is safe to try them elsewhere.

Wilk, on one's. (Brit.) To obtain a complimentary ticket on one's *Wilky* Bard, rhyming slang for (theatrical) *card*. It is the traditional privilege of artists to gain free admission to theaters when business will allow the granting of complimentary seats. The late Wilky Bard was a favorite music hall star.

wines and spirits, among the. To be at the bottom of a music hall bill. The name of the artist is mixed up with the names of the Wines and Spirits Merchants, advertized on the program.

wing (a part). To play a part without knowing the text, relying upon the prompter *in the wings* to help one through.

wing floods. Light units mounted on telescopic stands placed in the wings to give additional lighting to a scene. Cf. BOOMS, BOOMERANG.

wing men. Stagehands who attend to the wing flats, or handle properties that are taken on and off the stage through the wings.

wings. The flats which mask the sides of a set, used mainly in exteriors: woodland scenes, courtyards and the like. Cf. PROFILES.

wire. The flexible steel cable in the counterweight system.

with books. The first rehearsals when players walk through their parts with typewritten scripts in their hands to mark positions given by the director. A certain number of rehearsals are allowed *with books*, after that time the artists "act" their parts without books.

without books. To rehearse without the written part in one's hand.

wood borders. Those used for pastoral scenes. E.g. Shakespeare's *As You Like It, A Midsummer Night's Dream,* or the pantomime *The Babes in the Wood.* A pattern of leaves and branches, perforated and backed with gauze, and well lit wood borders give a very realistic picture of woodlands.

Wood family. (Brit.) Empty seats. Cf. PLUSH FAMILY.

wooden. (Of a player, or audience) Dull and uninspired. Cf. FLAT.

wooden arm. (Brit.) A long pole with a large hand behind which is a hook. The "local talent," offering their wares in a talent spotting competition at the music hall, are gently removed from the stage by the wooden arm when their turns are too painful to be borne.

wooden O. The Elizabethan stage because it is so shaped.

wooden walls. The boardings in front of a booth theater on a fair ground or village green. Posters depict the high lights in the drama.

Woolworth circuit. Jocular for a tour of small dates. Woolworth connotes cheapness. This is no disparagement of the famous firm that runs the five and dime stores, but a comparison.

word, the. A prompt from the Corner. An artist who forgets lines often boldly—and sensibly—asks the prompter for the word: "Give me the word please!" Cf. LINE.

word perfect. A thoroughly assimilated part. DEAD LETTER PERFECT.

working light. A pilot light, or a single batten used for rehearsals.

working line. A length of cordage (rope) that is in constant use during the running of the production.

working 'script. A prompt copy of the play in which the movements, cues, and director's notes, etc., are made at rehearsal. From this working 'script the fair, or Prompt Copy, for use during the run of the play is made.

workshop flex. Small flex used for connecting semi-permanent spots and floods. It is not as large as STAGE FLEX.

worst night of the theatrical year. Thursday before Good Friday when people are preparing to leave London for the Easter recess, and theaters are empty in consequence.

wow. A tremendous success. Said of a production generally, or an individual performance. Echoic of the approbatory noise that greets such success.

write in. To apply to a theatrical management for employment, or to the manager of a theater for complimentary seats. "I should *write in* for seats, they are not doing too well at the moment" (actors').

X

X. As a stage direction in the typewritten part, means that an artist crosses the stage at that point.

Xmas show. A pantomime, or any of the evergreen revivals of that time: E.g. *Where the Rainbow Ends; Charley's Aunt; Toad of Toad Hall,* and the like.

xylophone act. Either a "straight" performance on the xylophone, or one in which a "feature" has been created, the instrument forming a background. Teddy Brown was an "outsize" feature on the xylophone, and perhaps its finest exponent. From the Greek *xulon,* wood and *phone,* sound.

Y

yell. A farce or comedy in which the "yells" of laughter are continuous. "The show was a *yell* from beginning to end." E.g. the wartime farcical comedy *Worm's Eye View* by R. L. Delderfield, which outran the famous record breaker *Chu Chin Chow*. The term is obsolescent, the current one being "a hoot."

Yorkshire comic. A North country comedian using Yorkshire dialect.

you could have heard a pin drop! An old catchphrase meaning that the audience was completely absorbed in the proceedings.

you're codding! (Brit.) A theatrical expression of incredulity. "You don't expect me to believe that yarn, do you? You're codding." See COD.

you're in full view! Said of an artist standing in the wings and visible to the audience in the front rows of the stalls.

Z

zarzueala. A short sketch, or a stage cameo, in the Spanish manner.
zingaresca. A Romany song, sometimes featured in vaudeville. *Zingari* is the Italian for gypsies.